SOUTHERN TITLED
TRAINS

D. W. WINKWORTH

SOUTHERN TITLED TRAINS

DAVID & CHARLES
Newton Abbot   London   North Pomfret[Vt]

To Sidney
For patience, guidance and appreciation

British Library Cataloguing in Publication Data

Winkworth, D. W. (Derek William) 1924–
 Southern titled trains.
 1. Southern England. Railway passenger transport. Services
 I. Title
 385′.37′09422

 ISBN 0–7153–9179–8

Typeset by Vine & Gorfin Ltd, Exmouth
Printed in Great Britain
by Butler & Tanner Ltd, Frome, Somerset
for David & Charles Publishers plc
Brunel House   Newton Abbot   Devon

Published in the United States of America
by David & Charles Inc
North Pomfret   Vermont 05053   USA

Contents

1 Perspective   7
2 Westward Ho!   21
3 Into Wessex   56
4 Outward Bound   80
5 To Sussex-By-The-Sea   90
6 Through the Garden of England   115
7 Via Chatham with the Kent Coasters   129
8 To Dover for Paris   163
9 Train Across the Channel   191
   Appendix – a note on SR coaching stock
        marshalling   214
   Sources, Further Reading and Acknowledgements   217
   Index   221

CHAPTER ONE

Perspective

Very early in the consideration of this volume various problems pressed themselves to be resolved and it may be useful for the reader to know of the considerations which have been taken into account in framing this definitive account of Southern titled trains. In more spacious days the book might have addressed its subject as *The Titled Passenger Trains of the Southern Group of Railways Being a Complete Account of Such Trains Timetabled and Operated by the Southern Railway, its Predecessors and Successor.* Even this extended definition is not entirely satisfactory as will soon be seen!

Analysing it step by step the first point is 'titled'; titled is by no means synonymous with named – John Brown is named but Sir John Brown is titled. Some pre-grouping companies, especially the South Eastern & Chatham, delighted at times to litter descriptive matter in the timetable columns on the lines of Excursion, Continental Express or Folkestone and Dover Fast Train and such indicative terms do not qualify, whereas the titles *Southern Belle* or *Royal Wessex* do. There are grey areas even here and the selection has been influenced by the use of heavy type or capitals in the timetable columns or by the addition of the definite article so that *The City Express* is selected while City Express is excluded. Admittedly this has not been without some hesitation in the case of some services in Kent in pre-grouping days but a decision of this nature became imperative.

Mention of the definite article brings another problem in its wake, namely, whether or not to include it every time with the titles throughout the volume. As even the railways themselves at times could not settle on a consistent policy, either in the timetables or on the trains, it has been decided – despite the remark about selection in the last paragraph – to accept it as read.

Titled is not generally taken to embrace nicknames, so Beeswing, Folkestone Flyer, Lancing Belle and similar do not qualify for inclusion.

Passenger as an adjective needs little elaboration, so goods trains which, in British Railways days, could be seen with titles such as *Medlanc* pasted on the sides of wagons cannot be noticed.

The term Southern covers all lines and routes forming the Southern Railway Company and, in turn, the Southern Region of British Railways.

Timetabled is taken to mean appearing in the company public timetables with the title. Most titled trains were introduced as a new service at the time of christening but some, such as *Atlantic Coast Express*, had a name bestowed upon them after a period of operation in which case brief, but not detailed, reference will be found to the service in pre-titling days and, in appropriate cases, in the period after a name was lost. So non-qualifiers include *Tourist*, *Regency Belle* and a host of one-off charter special trains (*Marchwood Volunteer*, etc) as well as regular private trains such as the *Venice Simplon-Orient Express*, although a note later in this chapter will glance at the more exotic of these. Notwithstanding, a large breach of this decision will be found in Chapter 4 because the Ocean Liner traffic was considered to be an exception that proved the rule.

Titled trains originating from other company or region areas are excluded and this affects two services which, at their southern end, did use Southern metals but initially were, in the one case, composed entirely of another company's stock and motive power or, in the other, of stock only. However, some mention is made in this chapter of both *Pines Express* and *Sunny South Express*.

So much for how the elite titled trains have been chosen. A word of explanation of why a geographical, rather than genealogical, approach to the subject has been made may be useful. It was considered that a strict historical record through the years from 1876 down to 1980 would not be very helpful to readers seeking information on one particular train or, perhaps, a selected route in having to deal with a welter of data scattered throughout the book. Nonetheless, an outline resume in chronological order shortly follows as an adjunct to the detailed record and to place such detail within a frame; as a visual aid a bar chart is included.

Throughout, the actual times used in the public – rather than working – timetables have been used, including the 24-hour notation introduced in June 1965. To avoid tedious references to very minor alterations in timings those of less than five minutes, in general, have been ignored. In quoting charges it has, as with the times, been the policy to give the amounts current at the particular date; no attempt at equating the amount to decimal currency where that could be done has been made. The conversion is not very difficult and to assist a brief selection of equivalents is: 2s 6d – 12½p; 3s – 15p; 4s 6d – 22½p; 5s – 25p; 7s 6d – 37½p; 10s – 50p. Such equivalents, of course, do not have much relation in value for the price of a daily newspaper (23p) in 1985 would have procured dinner in a Southern Railway restaurant car in 1929.

A glance at the chart (table 1) immediately indicates the number of titled trains operating at any given point in the 100 year period. The South Eastern

BRIGHTON AND NORTH WESTERN RAILWAYS.

(34 N.W.)

SUNNY SOUTH EXPRESS.

BRIGHTON
TO
RUGBY

[W. & BLtd.]

One of the labels produced by the London, Brighton & South Coast Railway for the so-called Sunny South Express. *Author's collection*

Railway after launching the first titled train in the country was quickly followed by the London, Chatham & Dover Railway with a competitive express from London to Ramsgate. These two expresses were joined, especially on the LCDR, by a few other titles and continued thus until joint working, at the end of the century, came into force with the South Eastern & Chatham Railway encompassing the two rivals. Then, in the summer of 1905, like a hot potato, all the titles were dropped.

Meanwhile the London, Brighton & South Coast Railway had launched its *Brighton Limited* which, towards the end of 1908, blossomed into what was to become a firm favourite with the public – the *Southern Belle*. In 1911–2 came a revival on the SECR with two trains on the erstwhile LCD route but no *Granville*. World War I then intervened.

Early in 1921, the LBSCR named the up morning business train from Brighton to London Bridge and its return in the evening *City Limited* and then, after the coal strike difficulties of that year had been resolved, came a cascade of SECR trains – some of them previously endowed – having titles bestowed upon them including a Sundays-only all-Pullman train which was an innovation for Kent. All during this period the London & South Western Railway remained aloof from such matters and never did succumb to the temptation before being grouped with the lesser companies to form the Southern Railway.

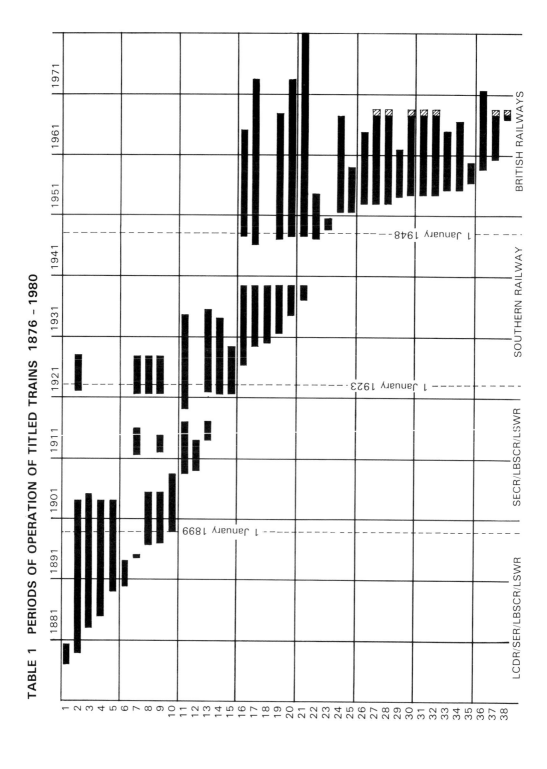

TABLE 1 PERIODS OF OPERATION OF TITLED TRAINS 1876 - 1980

At first the new company had its hands full with more pressing problems than considering titles of trains. In the summer of 1926, however, the Western Section – as the old LSWR had become – saw its first titled train, *Atlantic Coast Express*. This appeared to have caused a policy to be formulated for the Southern Railway which was put into effect progressively. With the exception of the *Thanet Pullman Limited*, all titles were abruptly discarded on the Kentish routes in summer of 1927. There followed a gradual expansion;

KEY TO TABLE 1

1 GRANVILLE SPECIAL EXPRESS (SER) 22 December 1876 – 31 May 1880
2 GRANVILLE AND WESTGATE-ON-SEA SPECIAL EXPRESS (and successors) (LCDR) 1 April 1878 – 30 June 1904; 11 July 1921 – 9 July 1927
3 KENT COAST EXPRESS (and successors) (LCDR) 1 June 1882 – 30 June 1905
4 GRANVILLE EXPRESS (and successors) (SER) 1 April 1884 – 30 June 1904
5 KENT COAST EXPRESS (and successors) (SER) 1 October 1888 – 30 June 1904
6 CLUB TRAIN (both LCDR and SER) 4 June 1889 – 30 September 1893
7 CLIFTONVILLE EXPRESS 2 July – 29 September 1894; 2 October 1911 – 30 November 1915; 11 July 1921 – 9 July 1927
8 CITY EXPRESS 1 July 1896 – 30 June 1905; 11 July 1921 – 9 July 1927
9 THANET EXPRESS 1 October 1896 – 30 June 1905; 3 May 1912 – 31 October 1914; 11 July 1921 – 9 July 1927
10 BRIGHTON LIMITED 1 January 1899 – 25 October 1908
11 SOUTHERN BELLE 1 November 1908 – 31 December 1916; 2 March 1919 – 28 June 1934
12 EASTBOURNE PULLMAN LIMITED 6 June 1909 – 25 May 1913
13 EASTBOURNE SUNDAY LIMITED 1 June 1913 – 31 December 1916; 4 December 1921 – 30 June 1935
14 CITY LIMITED 7 February 1921 – 6 July 1934
15 THANET PULLMAN LIMITED 10 July 1921 – 30 June 1929
16 ATLANTIC COAST EXPRESS 19 July 1926 – 9 September 1939; 6 October 1947 – 5 September 1964
17 GOLDEN ARROW 15 May 1929 – 3 September 1939; 15 April 1946 – 30 September 1972
18 BOURNEMOUTH LIMITED 8 July 1929 – 9 September 1939
19 BOURNEMOUTH BELLE 5 July 1931 – 9 September 1939; 7 October 1946 – 9 July 1967
20 BRIGHTON BELLE 29 June 1934 – 9 September 1939; 6 October 1947 – 30 April 1972
21 NIGHT FERRY 14 October 1936 – 25 August 1939; 15 December 1947 – 31 October 1980
22 DEVON BELLE 20 June 1947 – 19 September 1954
23 THANET BELLE 31 May 1948 – 24 September 1950
24 ROYAL WESSEX 3 May 1951 – 8 July 1967
25 KENTISH BELLE 2 July 1951 – 14 September 1958
26 NORMANDY EXPRESS 30 June 1952 – 10 May 1964
27 CUNARDER 2 July 1952 – Circa 1968 (1)
28 STATESMAN 8 July 1952 – Circa 1968 (2)
29 MAN OF KENT 8 June 1953 – 10 June 1961
30 UNION-CASTLE EXPRESS 16 July 1953 – Circa 1968 (3)
31 HOLLAND AMERICAN 15 July 1953 – Circa 1969 (4)
32 SOUTH AMERICAN 9 October 1953 – Circa 1968 (5)
33 BRITTANY EXPRESS 8 June 1954 – 27 September 1964
34 GREEK LINE Circa May 1954 – Circa October/November 1966 (6)
35 AROSA LINE Circa 1955 – Circa September 1958 (7)
36 SPRINGBOK 1957 – Circa Summer 1971 (3)
37 SITMAR LINE 1960 – Circa 1968 (8)
38 UNION-CASTLE SAFMARINE 2 February 1966 – Circa 1968 (3)
39 (Not indicated on table) CONQUEROR 11 May 1987 – 2 October 1987

The dates are first and last days of the services. In the cases of services which were seasonal (such as 15, 22, 23 etc) or irregular (such as 6, 26, 27 etc) details of operating days/periods will be found in the relevant chapter.

2 *Perspective*

FOOTNOTES TO KEY TO TABLE 1

(1) The Cunard Line gradually changed over from regular North Atlantic sailings to cruising and, for *QE2*, a mixture of each. The title probably lapsed in 1968. Certainly no title was used for the first sailing (14 August 1982) after the Falklands operation which was otherwise made a special occasion.
(2) The final sailing from Southampton was November 1969 but the title may not have lasted beyond 1968.
(3) The last Union-Castle arrival was in September 1977 and the final Safmarine arrival the following month but it is considered that the title was dropped before then. *Springbok* was still in use in July 1971 (but not in September 1971) while the others had disappeared earlier.
(4) Regular sailings ceased about 1970 (there were some cruises in 1973) but the title had been dropped by then.
(5) Final sailings were in February/March 1969 but the title may not have been used until the end. There was at least one Special Traffic Notice (and possibly more) in January 1961 which referred to *Royal Mail Lines* but headboards etc. do not appear to have been noticed.
(6) Regular trans Atlantic sailings ceased in 1959 but cruises continued for some years.
(7) The Arosa Line met financial difficulties in September 1958 but sailings did not entirely cease until December that year.
(8) The final sailing was on 24 June 1970 but it is thought that the title did not survive until the end.

Golden Arrow and *Bournemouth Limited* – summer 1929; *Bournemouth Belle* – summer 1931; *Southern Belle* to *Brighton Belle* – summer 1934 with culmination in the *Night Ferry* in October 1936. World War II put a stop to most of these services and all titles were suspended indefinitely.

A quick reinstatement of the majority of these trains was made by the Southern Railway after hostilities ceased and some new ones introduced, a trend which was continued in the early years of nationalisation. Eventually the decline set in, brought about by route downgrading, changing habits of the travelling public and regular interval services introduced at electrification so that, one by one, the *Devon Belle, Kentish Belle, Man of Kent, Atlantic Coast Express* disappeared from the timetables until there remained none but the *Night Ferry*. Even that piece of, by now tarnished, glamour faded away in an autumn morn of 1980 to bring to a close the fluctuating fortunes of the titled trains of the Southern.

Of the trains to which a sobriquet had become attached probably none was better known, or longer lived, than the special service that the Carriage Department of the LBSCR had to be responsible for when the new works at Lancing displaced the old establishment at Brighton. To transport its

LBSCR class B2 4-4-0 No 323 *William Cubitt* about to set off from Eastbourne in the summer of 1905 with the LNWR train which was termed the Sunny South Special. *Author's collection*

workmen from Brighton daily the Carriage Department had to provide rolling stock and guard for the purpose; the works at Lancing (which included a special platform for the train) seem to have been opened progressively over a period of several months, the special train first appearing in a working timetable supplement in October 1910 eventually – after some amendments – to be taken into the main body of the working timetable in June 1913. Calls were made at Hove and Portslade with a departure from Brighton at 5.30am returning about twelve hours later on weekdays, except on Saturdays when the return was at midday. Not surprisingly down the years the sets of stock assigned to this duty were of a vintage likely to excite the carriage historian and this, coupled with numbered compartments for allocated seats, gave an element of exclusiveness to the ensemble so that, with the *Southern Belle* operating locally, it was inevitable some wag would dub the train *Lancing Belle*.

As time passed working hours decreased enabling later departures to be made from Brighton and additional stops were included at Southwick and Shoreham-by-Sea. In its last three weeks the train was hauled by a diesel-electric locomotive but as this could not be accommodated at the works platform the works steam engine was used to head the train within the precincts of the carriage works. The last day of operation into the works was 6 July 1964. Until the total closure at the end of that year an ordinary electric multiple-unit ran between Brighton and Lancing but this, of course, had none of the vestiges of the *Lancing Belle* which had run for over half a century.

In order to serve Bournemouth the Somerset & Dorset Joint Railway had to traverse about eight miles of LSWR (later Southern Railway) metals from Broadstone to Bournemouth West. There had never been any problem here because the LSWR was an interested party in the SDJR and allowed – perhaps encouraged – the traffic, although playing no part in the operation so far as rolling stock and motive power was concerned. Likewise with the Southern Railway in grouping days when LMS stock appeared.

A daily Manchester – Bournemouth service by this route had been inaugurated, at the instigation jointly of the London & North Western and Midland Railways in October 1910, and it was the lineal successor of this train that from 26 September 1927, took the title of *Pines Express*. The train operated without title during the war period regaining it on 23 May 1949. By this time nationalisation had come and in its wake the shuttlecock allocation of responsibility for the route between London Midland, Southern and Western Regions. The coaching stock remained under LMR aegis and while within the Southern fold, Bath shed did have West Country class 4-6-2s to haul it but this by no means made it a Southern titled train. Nor, when diversion away from the SDJ line took place on 10 September 1962 to the Southampton-Basingstoke-Oxford route, did this substantially alter the position, even if Southern Region locomotives worked the train to and from Oxford. As from 4 October 1965 it was extended back to Poole and its demise came on 4 March 1967, by which date it was in the charge of diesel-electric power.

The other penetrating titled train on the Southern also connected Manchester with the South Coast. It had its origins in a through carriage express launched by the London & North Western Railway on 1 July 1904 between Liverpool and Eastbourne via Kensington (Addison Road) and Brighton. The public response was sufficiently good not only for the train to be continued without a break into 1905 – rather than ceasing at the close of 1904 as had been the intention – but also for the LNWR to up-grade it to seven corridor vehicles complete with dining car (in the Manchester portion) from 1 April 1905. This LNWR train the London, Brighton and South Coast Railway immediately dubbed in its timetables as *Sunny South Special*! The LNWR did not favour this appellation and throughout the years never elevated it to anything more than Eastbourne and Brighton Luncheon and Tea Car Express.

Southern Railway L12 class No 424 about to leave Willesden Junction on 30 May 1936 with the Brighton and Eastbourne portion of the LMS *Sunny South Express. K Nichols*

Although it was a totally LNWR train the LBSCR was keen to make it a success and even printed luggage labels headed Brighton and North Western Railways with Sunny South Express under in large capitals (despite calling it Special, rather than Express, elsewhere). Another curiosity was that, for a period, a guard from each company worked outwards each Monday and back and forth over the entire route to finish the week in home territory. Except for the through running in the autumn of 1909 of LNWR No 7 and LBSCR Nos 23 and 26 between Brighton and Rugby in proficiency tests, the train always exchanged engines at Willesden Junction, each company being responsible for haulage on its own metals.

Suspended in 1915 during World War I and reinstated from 2 October 1922, it went into grouping days still untitled by the LNWR or LMS even though Bradshaw and the Southern Railway had it simply as 'Sunny South', unable to make up their minds whether it should be an 'Express' or a 'Special'. The Southern apparently wearied of this game and in its timetable of 10 July 1927 dropped the reference whereas Bradshaw had plumbed for 'Special'.

Contrariwise the LMS, in its next winter timetable, gave it the title *Sunny South Express* and extended it to include a Kent as well as Sussex coast portion. So, from 27 September 1927, it became one of a brace of newly titled through LMS trains to the South Coast, the other, as has been noted, being the *Pines Express*.

Eventually carriage roof boards bearing the title were used and in 1929 the Southern Railway built some sets of coaches each complete with a restaurant car of which one rake was supposed to do duty on the service. For reasons never satisfactorily explained this set was not used; instead the SR provided a collection of ex LSW corridors as its contribution to the service but the northern company continued to supply the dining vehicle so that Mancunian stewards staffing these cars must have spent a good many nights and Sundays (it did not run that day) in Sussex.

The conflict of 1939–45 saw the *Sunny South Express* immediately stopped never to be resumed in its old form even if a few summer Saturday through trains after the war had some kinship. A faint echo today is the Manchester-Birmingham-East Croydon-Gatwick Airport-Brighton service which was resurrected in 1986.

In the mid-1920s period the Isle of Wight provided a microcosm of the process of railway unification taking place on the mainland and eventually the island lines became a system within a system maintaining an individuality with, amongst other things, a stud of named locomotives and a titled train not acknowledged by the timetable compilers at Waterloo. The precursor of this titled service was an East and West through train put on in the summer of 1932 between Shanklin and Freshwater; from 17 July 1933 this was extended to start from Ventnor at 9.55am calling at Wroxall, Shanklin, Sandown, Newport, Yarmouth and arriving at Freshwater at 11.16am. The return from Freshwater was 5.20pm and, with the same intermediate stops, arrival at Ventnor was timed for 6.48pm. Running every weekday it became known locally as *The Tourist*, each coach being equipped with appropriate nameboards. The popularity of the train, so far as holidaymakers were concerned, was demonstrated by 2700 passengers travelling during the course of one week.

Motive power for the six coach formation was an E1 class 0–6–0 tank locomotive between Ventnor and Newport and an O2 class 0–4–4 tank to and from Freshwater. The train at first consisted of four bogie coaches and a couple of four-wheelers but the latter gave way in 1934 to an old Central Section bogie saloon, converted at Lancing works to give an observation compartment and coupé for first class passengers and a large open compartment for third class travellers, and an old Isle of Wight Central Railway bogie rail motor coach over 25 years old converted at Ryde works to an open third class saloon with corridor and coupé compartment. Thus it continued each summer until September 1939, when war brought matters to a premature conclusion.

Isolated charter trains are far too numerous to mention. A prolific source of these has been the railway enthusiast society railtours, almost each of which had a title coined for the occasion. One or two trains of a recurring nature, however, may be mentioned. First of these, unique in respect of its rolling stock, is the *Venice Simplon-Orient Express*. Note we have the bonus of being able to write of it in the present tense. The *VSOE*, as it is known, owned by Cable & Wireless and leased to Seaco (the associate of Sea Containers), is a train of preserved European luxury rolling stock operating between London, Paris and Venice on certain dates with, because a train ferry is not used, the English part of the operation having an isolated formation of Pullman cars which maintains the London (Victoria) – Folkestone Harbour leg of the service. These are hauled by Southern Region electro-diesel locomotives. When not in use on the *VSOE* working the rake is available to undertake other trips to such venues as Hollingbourne and Chichester or to destinations off its host region. The inaugural *VSOE* run took place on 28 May 1982 and the first year's loss was about £6.3m, when start-up costs were written off, being reduced in the second year to £417,000; these figures, of course, are for the whole operation not just for the English part.

A service which, sadly, did not prosper was the *Regency Belle*. For seven guineas one could expect 'Champagne ad-lib, gorgeous girls in glamorous Regency costume (to) greet you . . . on the most exotic train in the World.' A nosegay for every lady, dinner and dancing at an hotel with breakfast – haddock and brown Sussex eggs were promised – on the train were all included in this night out at Brighton from London. The first run was on Saturday 28 March 1964 and thereafter it was to operate every Saturday and Sunday.

The 'most exotic train in the World' turned out to be none other than electric *Brighton Belle* five-car set 3052 – admittedly specially decorated for the occasion – which set out from platform 1 at Victoria (an unaccustomed departure point for a 5BEL set) at 7.15pm and returned from Brighton at 2.15am. The thought of being ejected at Victoria from this train in the chilly, dark, small hours of a Sunday morning must have been a daunting prospect for the clientele, however well fortified with champagne and brown Sussex eggs!

When the railway engineers indulged themselves with weekend night possession of the Brighton main line the return had to be via Steyning and the

Brighton-bound *Lancing Belle* leaving Shoreham-by-Sea in the charge of two E4 class 0-6-2 tanks, Nos 32468 and 32479, on 12 September 1962. *W. M. J. Jackson*

The northbound *Pines Express* draws into Blandford Forum on 18 August 1962 headed by BR class 9 2-10-0 No 92245 in the last year that the train ran via the Somerset & Dorset Joint route. *Author*

train became steam hauled and expanded to seven Pullmans – *Evadne, Lydia, Octavia, Phyllis* and cars 64, 84 and 334 – in the charge of rebuilt Battle of Britain class 4–6–2 No 34088. Unfortunately all this fun was halted abruptly during its fourth weekend, doubtless because of lack of patronage. About one hundred participants were required to cover the cost of the train charter apart from anything else.

Finally comes the *Bicycle Belle* which, like the *VSOE*, is another product of the 1980s. This is a 'Chartex' train run by a cycling organisation to convey its members, complete with their machines, from Central London to a suitable starting point for an exploration of the countryside awheel, thus avoiding long preliminary and return rides on heavily trafficked highways. Eridge, for example, from London Bridge has on occasion been a destination, in which case a diesel-electric locomotive heading nine vehicles in a 2 to 1 proportion of passenger coaches to vans has been the formation. So the *Belles* are neither silent nor dead yet!

CHAPTER TWO

Westward Ho!

Atlantic Coast Express

Alone of the three large pre-grouping companies forming the Southern Railway the London & South Western Railway did not bestow titles on any of its trains, so there was no inheritance of named trains nor, for that matter, of named express passenger engines which in much earlier days had graced the line. Thanks to the efforts of Mr J. B. Elliott, who had been engaged to project a better public image for the recently-formed company, the year 1925 did see named locomotives in the shape of the King Arthur class, both new construction and the older Urie 4–6–0s.

To capitalise on these pleasant names – especially those bestowed on the older engines such as *Joyous Gard, Maid of Astolat* or *Tintagel* – Mr Elliott prevailed upon the management to christen the 10am, 11am and 12 noon departures from Waterloo. The first of the trio, serving Bude and Padstow was to be dubbed *North Cornwall Express* and the mid-day departure for Exmouth, Sidmouth and Seaton was to carry the title *East Devon Express*. For the 11am departure *Devonian Express* did not gain hierarchical approval and in order to cast the net wide for suggestions the *Southern Railway Magazine*, in its July 1925 issue, announced a competition for a title for the train, entries to be submitted by 1 September.

There was a good response by the staff and eventually the name *Atlantic Coast Express* was adopted. Guard F. Rowland of Waterloo received the three guinea prize for his proposal with Messrs King (Nine Elms), Bray (Richmond) and Metcalfe (Waterloo) each receiving a King Arthur locomotive model paperweight for suggesting the same title but failing to be so quick in making their submissions.

It was no upstart train that was to carry the new title because as far back as 1890 the May timetable had a departure for the West of England leaving Waterloo at 11am, calling at Surbiton (to pick up), Basingstoke, Andover Junction and arriving at Salisbury at 1pm. There the front portion went forward at 1.5pm leaving the rear section to follow ten minutes later to serve most stations to Exeter and giving branch connections; after calling at

21

The up *Atlantic Coast Express* in its early days passing Yeovil Junction in the charge of King Arthur class No 457 *Sir Bedivere*. *F. R. Hebron collection*

Templecombe Junction no further halt was made by the front portion until Exeter Queen Street was reached at 3.12pm and with more divisions the times at the various destinations were Holsworthy 5.11pm, Launceston 5.29pm, Ilfracombe 5.25pm, Torrington 5.17pm and Devonport (via Marsh Mills) 5.22pm.

The 11 o'clock train had a history going back to the construction of lines in the far southwest. As the LSWR metals were extended in the west the 11 o'clock served more stations. By October 1892 Devonport was being reached by the direct route from Tavistock and the terminus became the Friary station at Plymouth while on the Launceston branch the track had got to Tresmeer where the service ended at 5.31pm. By the beginning of 1900 the winter service had been established with the stops all as previously with destinations in the west including Bude (5.28pm) and Padstow (6.40pm); in high season that year the 11am was the Ilfracombe and Torrington train there being a

10.50am for Plymouth and an 11.10am for North Cornwall. For the 1900/1 winter the 11 o'clock was supplemented by the 10.50am Plymouth and North Cornwall train. This pattern was then retained as a basis for departure times although the 11 o'clock in 1905 was the Plymouth and North Cornwall service, which even managed to avoid a halt at Exeter St Davids. This feature was perpetuated in the next decade when the winter train split at Exeter into three separate trains. After World War I the 11 o'clock service (in October 1920) proceeded in the same fashion: calls were made at Salisbury, Sidmouth Junction and Exeter Queen Street where the front part went to Plymouth (connections for Padstow and Bude at Okehampton) followed by the Ilfracombe and Torrington portion.

Despite the 1926 General Strike and the continued coal strike, the *Atlantic Coast Express* title was able to be applied for 19 July 1926. In the event the *North Cornwall* and *East Devon* proposals were dropped – due in some measure, no doubt, to the timetable having been altered – and the selected name appeared against the 11am Ilfracombe/Plymouth service and 11.10am Saturday excepted Bude/Padstow schedule. The main train to carry the title was the 11am which ran without stopping to Salisbury in ninety minutes. Engines were changed and within four minutes the train was off non-stop to Exeter Queen Street where it was due at 2.16pm. Nine minutes later the front portion, complete with its restaurant car, left for Ilfracombe calling at Exeter St Davids, at Portsmouth Arms by request of passengers who had joined at Waterloo or Salisbury, to arrive at Barnstaple Junction at 3.31pm. After this it called at all stations to Ilfracombe where it arrived at 4.24pm. A connection by the narrow-gauge train at Barnstaple Town enabled passengers to arrive at Lynton at 5.33pm while Torrington passengers finished their journey at 4.12pm, all stations from Barnstaple Junction except Fremington being served on that section.

Meanwhile the Plymouth portion had departed from Exeter Queen Street at 2.33pm and called, in addition to the compulsory halt at St Davids demanded by the Great Western Railway of all Southern trains, at Okehampton, Tavistock, Devonport, Plymouth North Road (4.16pm) and Mutley to complete its journey at 4.29pm at Friary station.

The second portion left Waterloo at 11.10am, called at Surbiton, Salisbury, Yeovil Junction and arrived at Exeter Queen Street at 2.43pm where the restaurant car was detached. After making its stop at St Davids it arrived at Halwill Junction at 3.56pm, called at Launceston at 4.20pm, Otterham at 4.48pm, Camelford at 4.58pm and all stations except St Kew Highway to complete its course at Padstow at 5.41pm. The Bude portion came off at Halwill Junction and had a 38 minute all stations journey before the terminus

RAILWAYS IN THE WEST COUNTRY, 1959
(Showing pre-nationalisation ownership)

Great Western	
Southern	
Somerset & Dorset Jt	
Lines dismantled	

0   5   10   20 miles

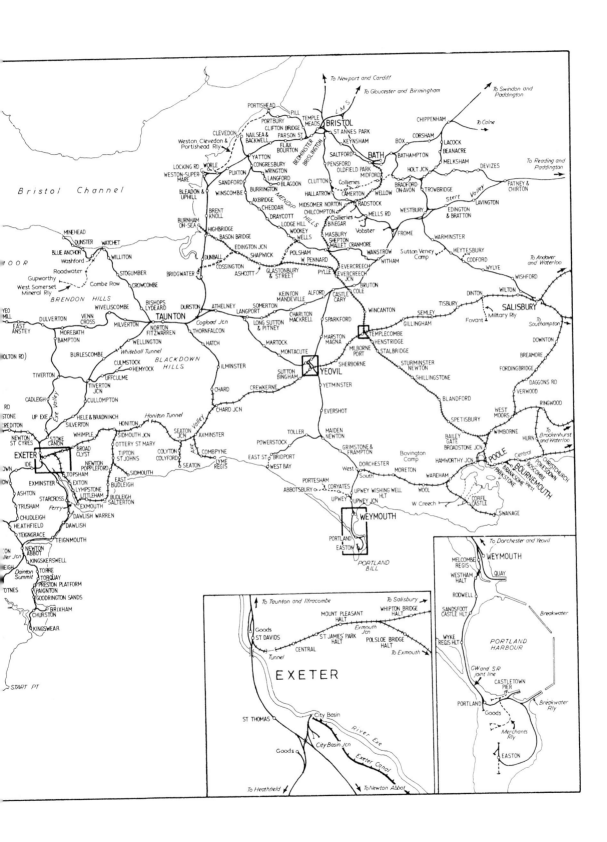

was reached at 4.42pm. The East Devon section was detached at Yeovil Junction and proceeded at 1.48pm to give arrivals at Sidmouth at 3.24pm (fast from Sidmouth Junction) and Exmouth at 4pm (all stations except Newton Poppleford from Sidmouth Junction).

Saturdays saw the train run in four parts of which only two were designated *Atlantic Coast Express* in the Southern Railway timetable. These were the 11am, which operated as on weekdays, except that the Plymouth portion ran about eleven minutes later west of Exeter, and the 10.25am from Waterloo which called at Salisbury, Exeter, Halwill Junction where the Padstow and Bude sections divided giving arrivals respectively at 4.35pm and 3.37pm, the latter including the restaurant car. There was a 10.45am restaurant car train to Ilfracombe (arrive 4pm) and the 11.10am ran as weekdays from Waterloo to Yeovil Junction, where it picked up the weekday 1.48pm departure timing to Exmouth taking its restaurant car right through to that destination but neither carried the title.

The inaugural 11am *Atlantic Coast Express* was headed out of Waterloo by No E779 *Sir Colgrevance* and was followed ten minutes later by No E776 *Sir Galagars* on the second part of the train, King Arthur class engines being the normal power east of Exeter in both directions with changeovers at Salisbury. As these locomotives were not permitted west of Exeter smaller – and usually older – engines officiated into North and South Devon and North Cornwall. On 12 October 1926 the then recently-built *Lord Nelson* locomotive first operated the train each way between London and Salisbury but it was to be some years yet before this class was to have a regular duty on the *ACE*.

The up services chosen to carry the title were the 12.4pm and 12.32pm trains from Exeter Queen Street. The 12.4pm was made up of portions departing from Padstow at 8.35am and Bude at 9.35am which, after calling at all stations, left Okehampton at 11.12am and stopped at Yeoford and Exeter St Davids, attached a restaurant car at Exeter Queen Street and then halted at Yeovil Junction (for the East Devon section to be attached), Salisbury and Surbiton and arrived in the capital at 3.39pm.

From Ilfracombe the restaurant car portion of the main train left at 10.22am and called at every station to Barnstaple Junction. Passengers from Lynton had to leave there at 9am and the narrow-gauge train was due to deposit them at Barnstaple Town at the precise moment of departure of the *Atlantic Coast Express* from Ilfracombe. The Torrington departure time was 10.25am with all stations, again with the exception of Fremington, being served to Barnstaple Junction. The combined train, including a through carriage from Ilfracombe to Brighton, then left the Junction at 11.9am and, depending whether or not a call was required at Portsmouth Arms to pick up Salisbury or London passengers,

The unique large-boilered member of the Lord Nelson class – No 857 *Lord Howe* – heading the up *Atlantic Coast Express* near Oakley in June 1937. *Dr Ian C. Allen*

was fast to Yeoford and after a four-minute call at Exeter St Davids appeared at Queen Street at 12.23pm. The Plymouth portion was due to have arrived at 12.12pm having left Friary at 10.15am and made calls at Mutley, North Road, Devonport, Bere Alston, Tavistock, Okehampton, Yeoford and, of course, St Davids. There then followed a 96 minute non-stop run to Salisbury, where the through Brighton coach was detached, for the last stage to Waterloo to be run in 92 minutes for a 3.44pm arrival.

On Saturdays the Ilfracombe/Torrington/Plymouth arrival at Waterloo at 3.44pm was unaltered and carried the name. The other titled Monday-Friday service dropped not only the Surbiton stop – and in consequence arrived at Waterloo five minutes earlier at 3.34pm – but also the title. The Saturday titled service from Bude left there, complete with restaurant car, at 11am and called everywhere to Halwill Junction where it joined forces with the 10am from Padstow – which also served Wadebridge, Port Isaac Road, Delabole, Camelford, Otterham and Launceston en route – and ran fast to Exeter St Davids. The train left Exeter Queen Street at 1.10pm, Salisbury at 2.55pm and was due in the metropolis at 4.29pm.

In pre-war years 2-6-0s were the mainstay for the *ACE* between Exeter and Ilfracombe and in this not untypical picture one such is assisted front and rear by M7 class tanks in lifting the down train up to the summit at Mortehoe. *By courtesy of National Railway Museum – M. W. Earley*

No particular attempt had been made to provide special or new stock for the train in 1926. It soon became apparent that new restaurant cars were required; six pairs of such cars, each consisting of a first class kitchen car and a third class open saloon, were ordered but although due for delivery in 1927 it was May 1928 before the first examples appeared in the train. Meanwhile the most noticeable feature of the train formation was the preponderance of brake composite coaches which were necessary for all the divisions. Each destination had to have first and third class accommodation each with smoking and non-smoking compartments. As many as eight out of ten vehicles were at times of this type so the traffic demands made for a cosmopolitan train make-up together with a disproportionate amount of luggage and guard space.

The main line locomotives might be pleasing enough but the ensemble was not very satisfying visually. From the passengers' point of view there was the niggling fear, at least on down trains, as to whether or not one was in the correct portion for Tavistock or Braunton or wherever. Once reassured by the travelling ticket inspector on this point each portion became something of a train within a train and social exchanges were encouraged by virtue of a common destination and dispelled doubt.

The pattern of winter operation was indicated by the timetable introduced on 20 September 1926; the 11 o'clock from Waterloo had a stop inserted at Sidmouth Junction to detach the Sidmouth and Exmouth coaches with Exeter being reached at 2.22pm. The Ilfracombe portion proceeded at 2.30pm and made similar stops as in the summer with arrivals at Ilfracombe at 4.29pm and Torrington at 4.15pm. The Plymouth portion followed from Exeter at 2.38pm arriving at Friary station at 4.40pm after casting off the Padstow and Bude portions at Okehampton. Those resumed their journey at 3.42pm and, with calls at all stations, Padstow was reached in one minute under seven hours from Waterloo and Bude in 62 minutes less. In the up direction the departure times from Plymouth Friary, Ilfracombe and Torrington were 10.15am, 10,22am and 10.25am respectively with Padstow being left at 8.35am and Bude at 9.45am in both of which cases the timetable omitted the train title. After uniting the Ilfracombe/Torrington and Plymouth/North Cornwall sections at Exeter Queen Street and attaching a restaurant car (for winter timings such amenities were confined to east of Exeter in each direction) a balancing call was made at Sidmouth Junction for the East Devon branch traffic and Salisbury was reached at 2.22pm. Here the through Brighton carriage from Ilfracombe was removed and the *ACE* then ran non-stop to London to arrive at 4 o'clock precisely.

So, with the two trains in summer, one train in winter schedules established this is a good point to note one or two underlying features of the operation of what was the country's most multi-portioned train. Firstly, it was always the Ilfracombe section, together with the attendant Torrington portion, that ranked as the main train and this was reflected in the timetable for some years in that the title would always be indicated for that section even if it did not appear in the North Cornwall route. The through carriage services to and from Lyme Regis, Seaton, Sidmouth and Exmouth seldom got any recognition in print and it is doubtful if carriage roofboards for these sections ever carried the train title. At the points where the through carriages were detached they were nearly always coupled to other vehicles to form a branch train and did not proceed independently. Portions breaking down at Exeter would sometimes have additional coaches added there.

Having said that, it must be conceded that when it suited authority the Saturday timetabled but untitled trains, such as the 10.45am Waterloo to Ilfracombe, would be referred to locally as a portion of the *Atlantic Coast Express* as indeed would any train put on as a relief to the *ACE* at times of heavy traffic. This is demonstrated by the announcement that so popular was the train proving that on Friday 2 September 1927 four portions had to be run, rising to six on the next day and that for these two days there had been 3,800 *bookings* for seats. Thus, when it was convenient, every relief would be an *ACE*!

Secondly, this was never a business train but fluctuated between one for occasional travellers for a great variety of destinations (which in the aggregate would warrant a complete train for about 150 miles and thereafter disperse its long-distance passengers down the various branches so that by the time, say, Torrington was reached the local traffic would outnumber those who entrained at Waterloo or Salisbury) and one which blossomed out on summer Saturdays with holidaymaking families occupying every seat into Devon and North Cornwall. This, in turn, does nothing to diminish the complications of chronicling its intricate history without wearying the reader – or writer.

Three out of the four Monday–Friday summer schedules for 1927 followed those of the previous summer, the 11 o'clock down having three minutes cut west of Salisbury and the up Plymouth and Torrington portions leaving five minutes earlier but arriving, as previously, in London at 3.44pm. The up North Cornwall/East Devon train got completely revamped: the summer Saturday of 1926 timing was taken en bloc from Padstow and Bude as far as the Exeter Queen Street departure of 1.10pm (the restaurant car was attached at Exeter instead of working from Bude) after which calls were made at Sidmouth Junction, Yeovil Junction and Salisbury with an arrival at Waterloo at 5.1pm. On Saturdays it was 1926 again except that the 10.45am from Waterloo was enhanced with the title while the 11.10am to Exmouth lost its restaurant car. In the up direction the named services were the 10.22am Ilfracombe-Waterloo and the 10am Padstow/10.58am Bude (restaurant car) – Waterloo, the 10.10am from Plymouth running without title as did the 10.39am restaurant car service from Exmouth.

The winter services from 1927/8 until 1938/9 ran without major adjustments: in the 1927/8 timetable the North Cornwall connection at Okehampton for Padstow and at Halwill Junction for Bude were each moved over a column to avoid any idea of a continuation of the *ACE* and were decelerated and slight adjustments were made to the up timings west of Exeter; in 1928/9 the Wrafton stop was omitted in both directions; the train title was restored in 1929/30 to the North Cornwall portions; as from the start of the 1932/3 timetable the Plymouth portion called additionally at Bow at 11.41am; a slight acceleration for the 1933/4 winter gave down arrivals of 4.18pm for Ilfracombe, Torrington 4.9pm, Bude 4.48pm, Padstow 6.9pm and Plymouth Friary 4.31pm; a conditional stop at Umberleigh of the up train to pick up was inserted for 1934/5; a further acceleration of five minutes to Exeter Central – the former Queen Street renamed – was reflected in booked arrivals in 1935/6 of 4.13pm, 4.4pm, 4.39pm, 5.37pm and 4.26pm for Ilfracombe, Torrington, Bude, Padstow and Plymouth Friary respectively with a conditional stop to pick up at Lydford in the up Plymouth portion and departures of 10.30am, 10.28am and 12.30pm from Ilfracombe, Torrington and Exeter Central to give an arrival at Waterloo of 3.55pm. Further cuts in timings continued in 1936/7 when the down train was booked into Exeter Central at 2.14pm, Ilfracombe at 4.7pm, Torrington at 3.59pm and Plymouth Friary at 4.22pm while in the up direction the previously conditional stops at Umberleigh and Portsmouth Arms became mandatory, departures from Padstow and Bude were altered to 8.40am and 9.40am respectively and the Waterloo arrival time was advanced to 3.50pm. The Mutley call for the down train disappeared in September 1937 when the timings reached a zenith in leaving Waterloo at 11am, calling at Salisbury 12.26–12.29pm, Sidmouth Junction at 1.54–1.56pm to arrive at Exeter Central at 2.12pm, Ilfracombe at 4.7pm, Torrington at 3.58pm and Plymouth Friary at 4.19pm. In the up direction the Salisbury stop was booked as 2.16–2.20pm and the Waterloo arrival became 3.49pm.

The changes and improvements in the summer schedules between 1928 and 1939 are summarised in tables 2 and 3. There are a few points which are not readily obvious from these tables: taking the down service first, in 1928, in the course of the recasting the times, the Surbiton and Wrafton stops were discontinued and the call at Yeovil Junction switched to Sidmouth Junction; from 1930 onwards the 11am departure from London serving the East Devon and Plymouth lines lost its title because its destinations were not of Atlantic nature and ran thereafter so shorn; 1935 saw the Fremington stop reintroduced and in 1936 the speed-up on the first stage of the 10.35am train's journey to 86 minutes to Salisbury brought its average speed for that length to 58.5mph, the fastest schedule on the Southern at that time; finally, in 1937 the Barnstaple Town stop was omitted.

In the up direction 1928 saw the elimination of the Wrafton stop, the

After World War II the *Atlantic Coast Express* had Merchant Navy class haulage east of Exeter. Here, on 16 November 1963, rebuilt MN Pacific No 35020 *Bibby Line* passes Woking with the down train with the exhaust building-up in front of the chimney, a curious phenomenon shared with one or two other express locomotive classes. *Author*

TABLE 2   DOWN ATLANTIC COAST EXPRESS 1928–1939 SUMMER SERVICES

PERIOD		Waterloo Dep. am	Salisbury pm	Sidmouth Jc pm	Exeter Arr. pm	B'staple Jc Arr. pm	Ilfracombe Arr. pm	Torrington Arr. pm	Bude Arr. pm	Padstow Arr. pm	Plym'th F Arr. pm	Rest. Car to	SATURDAYS Waterloo Dep. am	SATURDAYS
1928	17/6–8/7	11.0	12.30/34	2.3/5	2.22	3.36	4.27	4.17	—	—	4.40	Exeter	10.25	Bude(RC)/Padstow
	9/7–23/9	10.40	12.12/16	—	1.55	3.7	3.53	3.54	4.0	5.1	—	Ilfracombe	10.40	Ilfracombe(RC)/Torrington
		11.0	12.30/34	2.3/5	2.22	—	—	—	—	—	4.26	Exeter	11.0	Plymouth
1929	7/7–22/9	10.40	12.12/14	—	1.55	3.6	3.57	3.54	4.0	5.1	—	Ilfracombe	10.24	Bude(RC)/Padstow
		11.0	12.30/34	2.3/5	2.22	—	—	—	—	—	4.26	Exeter	10.40	Ilfracombe(RC)/Torrington
													11.0	Plymouth
1930	6/7–21/9	10.40	12.10/14	—	1.54	3.7	3.57	3.54	4.0	5.1	—	Ilfracombe	10.24	Bude(RC)/Padstow
													10.40	Ilfracombe(RC)/Torrington
1931	5/7–20/9	10.40	12.10/14	—	1.54	3.7	3.57	3.54	4.0	5.1	—	Ilfracombe	10.24	Bude/Padstow(RC)
													10.40	Ilfracombe(RC)/Torrington
1932	17/7–11/9	10.35	12.5/9	—	1.49	2.58	3.47	3.37	3.56	5.0	—	Ilfracombe	10.35	Ilfracombe(RC)
													10.45	Bude/Padstow(RC)
1933	16/7–10/9	10.35	12.5/9	—	1.49	2.58	3.47	3.37	3.56	5.0	—	Padstow	10.35	Ilfracombe(RC)
													10.45	Padstow(RC)
													11.0	Bude/Plymouth*
1934	8/7–30/9	10.35	12.5/9	—	1.49	2.58	3.47	3.37	3.56	4.53	—	Padstow	As 1933	
1935	7/7–29/9	10.35	12.3/7	—	1.47	3.2	3.47	3.40	3.33	4.31	—	Padstow	10.35	Ilfracombe(RC)
													10.45	Padstow(RC)
													11.0	Torrington/Bude/Padstow*
1936	5/7–27/9	10.35	12.1/4	—	1.42	2.47	3.32	3.26	3.33	4.31	—	Padstow	As 1933	
1937	4/7–26/9	10.35	12.1/3	—	1.41	2.52	3.35	3.30	3.26	4.24	—	Padstow	10.24	Ilfracombe(RC)
													10.40	Padstow(RC)
													11.0	Bude/Plymouth*
1938	3/7–25/9	10.35	12.1/3	—	1.41	2.52	3.35	3.30	3.25	4.24	—	Padstow	10.35	Ilfracombe(RC)
													10.35	Ilfracombe(RC)
													10.38	Padstow(RC)
													10.40	Bude*
													11.0	Plymouth/Padstow/Bude*
1939	2/7–10/9	10.35	12.1/3	—	1.41	2.52	3.35	3.30	3.25	4.24	—	Padstow	10.24	Ilfracombe(RC)
													10.35	Ilfracombe(RC)
													10.40	Padstow(RC)
													10.54	Padstow(RC)
													11.0	Plymouth/Padstow*

References to Exeter are to Queen Street to and including 1932 and to Central thereafter.
*Restaurant car to Exeter Central.

TABLE 3   UP ATLANTIC COAST EXPRESS 1928–1939 SUMMER SERVICES

PERIOD		Plym'th F. Dep. am	Padstow Dep. am	Bude Dep. am	Torrington Dep. am	Ilfracombe Dep. am	B'staple Jc. Dep. am	Exeter pm	Sidm'th Jc. Dep. pm	Salisbury pm	Waterloo Arr. pm	Rest. Car from	SATURDAYS	Departures am
1928	17/6–23/9	–	9.40	10.35	10.33	10.35	11.22	12.36/45	–	2.22/26	4.0	Ilfracombe	10.35 / 11.0	Ilfracombe(RC)/Torrington Bude(RC)/Padstow
1929	7/7–22/9 AND	–	–	–	10.23	10.25	11.11	12.26/30	–	2.10/14	3.46	Ilfracombe		As Mons-Fris with Restaurant car from Bude 10.35
1930	6/7–21/9	10.20	9.40	10.35	–	–	–	12.37/44	1.6	2.36/40	4.13	Exeter		
1931	5/7–20/9	–	9.40	–	10.23	10.25	11.11	12.25/30	–	2.10/14	3.46	Ilfracombe		As Mons-Fris with Restaurant car from Padstow 9.40
		10.20	9.40	10.38	–	–	–	12.39/44	1.6	2.36/40	4.13	Exeter		
1932	17/7–11/9	–	–	–	10.28	10.30	11.16	12.25/30	–	2.10/14	3.46	Ilfracombe	10.25 / 10.30 / 10.40	Padstow(RC) Ilfracombe(RC)/Torrington Bude(RC)
		10.20	9.40	10.38	–	–	–	12.39/44	1.9	2.36/40	4.13	Exeter	10.25 / 10.40	Ilfracombe(RC)/Torrington Bude(RC)
1933	16/7–10/9 AND	–	–	–	10.28	10.30	11.16	12.25/30	–	2.10/14†	3.46†	Exeter	10.25 / 10.30 / 10.40	Padstow(RC) Ilfracombe(RC)/Torrington Bude(RC)/Plymouth
1934	8/7–30/9	10.20	9.40	10.38	–	–	–	12.39/44	1.9	2.36/40	4.14	Padstow		
1935	7/7–29/9	–	–	–	10.28	10.30	11.15	12.24/30	–	2.8/12	3.40	Exeter	9.40 / 10.22 / 10.40	Padstow(RC) Torrington(RC)/Ilfracombe Bude(RC)/Plymouth
		10.20	9.40	10.38	–	–	–	12.40/44	1.9	2.36/40	4.13	Padstow		
1936	5/7–27/9 AND	–	–	–	10.28	10.30	11.12	12.24/30	–	2.8/12	3.40	Exeter	10.22 / 10.25 / 10.40	Torrington(RC)/Ilfracombe Padstow(RC) Bude(RC) A
1937	4/7–26/9	10.25	9.40	10.40	–	–	–	12.40/46	1.11	2.38/42	4.13Ø	Padstow		
1938	3/7–25/9	–	–	–	10.28	10.30	11.12	12.24/30	–	2.8/12	3.40	Exeter	10.30 / 10.40	As note A plus Ilfracombe(RC) Bude*
		10.25	9.40	10.40	–	–	–	12.40/45	1.11	2.38/42	4.12	Padstow		
1939	2/7–10/9	–	–	–	10.28	10.30	11.12	12.24/30	–	2.8/12	3.40	Exeter	10.10 / 10.22 / 10.25 / 10.30 / 11.0	Ilfracombe(RC) Torrington(RC) Padstow(RC) Ilfracombe(RC) Bude*
		–	10.25	11.25	–	–	–	1.23/30	1.52	3.22/26	4.58	Padstow		

References to Exeter are to Queen Street to and including 1932 and to Central thereafter.
*Restaurant car from Exeter Central   †One minute earlier in 1934   Ø4.11pm in 1937
A In 1937 and 1938 10.10am Ilfracombe(RC) 10.22am Torrington(RC) 10.25am Padstow(RC) 10.40am Bude(RC)/Plymouth

revision of the timings and the Plymouth and East Devon portions running as a separate untitled train. The timetable of 1929 then established a pattern that was to last for a whole decade; by 1930 the through Ilfracombe-Brighton coaches were reduced to Mondays, Fridays and Saturdays and by the next summer had disappeared from the *ACE*; in 1934 a conditional stop was inserted at Umberleigh and the next year another was introduced at Lydford following which, in 1937, those for Umberleigh and Portsmouth Arms became mandatory. The last revision, in 1939, involved the recasting of the North Cornwall service and the disappearance of the Plymouth portion.

From 1932 onwards there was a summer Sundays *ACE* and, curiously, also for the winter of 1933/4. The down train served Ilfracombe and Torrington and, in 1932, Plymouth also with the restaurant car going through to Ilfracombe. For 1933 the departure time was altered from 11am to 10.50am, Plymouth was dropped and the restaurant car came off at Exeter Central and, apart from a five minute earlier departure from 1937 onwards, so it remained. The up train originated from Ilfracombe and Torrington (plus Plymouth in 1933) and included a call at Crediton.

The typical winter formation of the train was ten carriages in each direction. In 1938/9 these were – from the engine – five corridor brake composites (each having one smoking and one non-smoking first class compartment and two smoking and two non-smoking third class compartments plus the guard's brake and luggage section) for Ilfracombe, Torrington, Plymouth, Padstow and Bude respectively. To alleviate the impression that one was travelling in a parcels train, there followed restaurant car 7934 and an open third both of which were detached at Exeter Central and then came three more corridor brake composites – one each for Exmouth, Sidmouth and Seaton, the last being detached at Salisbury and going forward at 12.38pm. The differences in the up train's composition were that the restaurant car would be either 7880 or 7969 and there would be two corridor brake composites one end of the train and six at the other end.

In summer matters were rather different. For 1939 the arrangements for the 10.35am from Waterloo were one corridor third and a four car dining set (restaurant cars 7867 or 7871) for Padstow; a corridor third and a corridor

The Ilfracombe portion of the up *Atlantic Coast Express* runs into Yeoford on 3 September 1959 behind Battle of Britain class No 34109 *Sir Trafford Leigh Mallory*, the customary post-war power west of Exeter. *Author*

The Saturday 10.48 a.m. ex. Torrington portion of the *Atlantic Coast Express* is accelerated out of Honiton tunnel by No 34054 *Lord Beaverbrook* on 4 July 1964. The third carriage is the buffet car attached at Exeter Central. Train identification numbers were not used west of Salisbury but one would be affixed to the smokebox door of the locomotive at that stop. *Author*

brake composite for Bude; a three corridor set (see appendix for SR carriage set formations) for Ilfracombe and, for Torrington, a repeat of the Bude portion, giving a total of 12 vehicles. In the up direction the 3.40pm arrival at Waterloo had an Ilfracombe three corridor set, a restaurant car (either 7933 or 7969), four corridor brake composites, one corridor third, one open third and a two corridor set, again a total of a dozen carriages. The 4.58pm arrival at Waterloo included the balancing Padstow and Bude sections plus four corridor brake composites, this totalling eleven coaches.

By this time the Lord Nelson 4–6–0s of Nine Elms shed had established themselves on the London-Salisbury part of the journey and the N15 class King Arthurs of Salisbury and Exmouth Junction depots still monopolised the Salisbury-Exeter Central length. West of Exeter, however, there was more variety. The Ilfracombe portion would be the duty of a Barnstaple based N class 2–6–0 which might have assistance over Mortehoe bank by a Class M7 0–4–4 tank or, less usually, by an E1R 0–6–2 tank rebuild from Barnstaple Junction shed. In the up direction an N class 2–6–0 would bank from Ilfracombe if required. The Torrington portion was booked for an E1R 0–6–2 tank (or, alternatively, an M7 class 0–4–4 tank on the down service). The Plymouth part was a round duty for a Class U1 2–6–0 which, until the introduction of this class to the West of England in late 1936/early 1937, had been the preserve of the ex-LSWR T9 4–4–0s. These game engines worked the Padstow section in each direction while the Bude coaches were handled by an M7 class tank to and from Halwill Junction. A few S11 class 4–4–0s were to be found in the mid-1930s on the North Cornwall route and one of this class – No E396 – appeared on the train regularly one summer.

September 1939, with war declared, brought with it drastic alterations which were to last too long. The title immediately disappeared from the timetables although the service ran, to slower timings and with additional stops, as the 10.50am from Waterloo. Eventually the new Merchant Navy class 4–6–2s were drafted on to the service between London and Exeter (with engine changes at Salisbury) and there were formations of 16 or more coaches which necessitated a cumbersome operation at Waterloo with the down train in two sections in adjoining platforms, the locomotive and front portion going out and then backing down and coupling up to the rear part before departing. In the up direction the train had to be split at Clapham Junction and an M7 class tank engine had the task of bringing in the rear portion to Waterloo after the main train, an operation commanding little commendation from the unfortunate passengers, of which a large proportion would be service personnel.

From 6 October 1947 the train reappeared in the timetables as the *Atlantic*

Coast Express. The times were Waterloo depart 10.50am; Salisbury 12.33–12.36pm (through coach to Seaton uncoupled); Sidmouth Junction 2.8–2.11pm (through coaches to Sidmouth and Exmouth detached); Exeter Central arrive 2.29pm where the restaurant car was cut out of the train. At 2.34pm the Ilfracombe and Torrington portion left and, after calls at Exeter St Davids and Eggesford, was due at Barnstaple Junction at 3.44pm. The Ilfracombe section proceeded as an all-stations train arriving at its destination at 4.36pm while the Torrington part doing likewise concluded its journey at 4.31pm. The Plymouth coaches left Exeter Central at 2.46pm and called at St Davids, North Tawton, Okehampton, Bridestowe, Lydford, Brentor, Tavistock, Devonport, Plymouth North Road and finished at Friary at 4.55 pm. The 3.55pm connection from Okehampton all stations to Bude and Padstow was not named.

In the up direction departure was from Padstow at 8.25am and Bude at 9.35am all stations, except Newton St Cyres, to Exeter Central (due 12.5pm). The Plymouth-Brighton train gave a connection at Exeter Central as it passed through (12.17 – 12.25pm). The main train's parts left Ilfracombe and Torrington simultaneously at 10.15am and served all stations en route to Exeter. There the restaurant car was inserted and departure was at 12.40pm; calls were made at Sidmouth Junction, Axminster, Yeovil Junction, Sherborne, Templecombe, Salisbury and Waterloo was reached at 4.41pm. So, despite the use of Pacific types both east and west of Exeter, the timings – the up one especially – with the many stops were hardly in the express category. C'est la guerre, of course.

Nationalisation in 1948 was of little immediate help. The train was used in both directions between London and Exeter in the interchange trials when LNER A4 Pacifics appeared as well as an LMS Pacific and a rebuilt Royal Scot locomotive. For the summer service on Mondays to Fridays the previous winter's timings were but slightly altered; the down North Cornwall service from Okehampton was moved over in the timetable to come into the column having the train's name (as well as the restaurant car right through to Padstow) and Newton St Cyres no longer was served in the up direction so that, with the restaurant car coming from Padstow, all times from Exeter Central to Waterloo were advanced by five minutes. On Saturdays departures from Waterloo were

  10.20am Bude and Padstow (restaurant car)
  10.35am Ilfracombe and Torrington (restaurant car to Exeter Central)
  10.50am Plymouth, Bude and Padstow (restaurant car to Exeter Central)

Up Saturday trains left Padstow at 8.25am and Bude at 9.30am (arrival at

For its last summer the *Atlantic Coast Express* suffered the indignity of haulage by Western Region diesel-hydraulic power as witness No D7100 (heading) and D7097 (banking) on the up service approaching Mortehoe on 29 August 1964. *S. C. Nash*

Waterloo at 3.40pm) and Ilfracombe at 10.15am running in the normal weekday timings. Locomotive buffer beam headboards were provided with the train's title in yellow lettering on a green ground as from the end of May 1948.

The following winter timetable had the restaurant car to and from Exeter Central rather than Padstow and the North Cornwall portions were confirmed as being part of the titled train. The summer 1949 timetable – which saw the introduction of the Tavern Cars – had the up train with 15 minute later departures from both Ilfracombe and Torrington which portions, after uniting at Barnstaple Junction, ran to Exeter Central calling only at Eggesford, Yeoford Junction and Exeter St Davids. Exeter Central was left at 12.30pm and with the same stops as previously Waterloo was reached at 4.26pm. In the following year from 5 June six minutes were knocked off the Salisbury-Waterloo length (increased to eight minutes in 1951) and from 25 September 1950 ten minutes reduction was possible by making the departure from Waterloo at 11 o'clock. For the first three months of 1951 the down train was withdrawn because of coal shortage.

Substantial accelerations were introduced in the summer of 1952 and these included the first mile-a-minute schedule on the Southern with the 11 o'clock booked into Salisbury in 83 minutes. Sidmouth Junction was reached at 1.48pm and Exeter Central at 2.5pm; there was a reduction in time to Ilfracombe (arrive 4.10pm), a 4.4pm arrival at Torrington and, with the deletion of calls between Okehampton and Tavistock, an arrival at Plymouth Friary at 4.30pm. Coming east improvements were even more radical with a Plymouth portion being introduced (leaving Friary at 9.50am and serving North Road, Devonport, St Budeaux, Bere Alston, Tavistock, Lydford and Bridestowe) and combining with the North Cornwall portion at Okehampton. Thence to Exeter Central it called at North Tawton, Bow, Yeoford, Crediton and St Davids. The complete train then left Exeter Central at 12.30pm and with calls at Sidmouth Junction (12.48 – 12.49pm) and Salisbury (2.9 – 2.13pm where through coaches from Lyme Regis and Yeovil Town were attached) was due at Waterloo at 3.40pm. In the winter 1952/3 timings Ilfracombe and Torrington arrivals became 4.2pm and 3.57pm respectively.

The winter timetable for 1953/4 had minor amendments with the stop at Maddaford Moor Halt on the down service being dropped and, in the up direction, the Plymouth portion leaving five minutes earlier. In June 1954 the stops between Okehampton and Tavistock were reinstated which lasted until June 1957 when they were again omitted. Friary station closed from 15 September 1958 and the train's terminus became that previously known as North Road (now simply Plymouth) with arrival at 4.21pm and departure at 10.2am. The stops at Bridestowe, Lydford and Brentor were reinstated for the summer 1959 timetable (arrival at Plymouth became 4.25pm) and the through Seaton coach which had been detached at Salisbury became advertised as to Exeter Central and, in November, to Honiton (although it actually still went through to Exeter Central as part of the stopping train).

11 September 1961 witnessed the final significant acceleration of the *ACE*. Eighty minutes to Salisbury (12.20 – 12.23pm), 160 minutes to Sidmouth Junction (1.40 – 1.42pm), two minutes under the three hours to Exeter Central, five minutes under the five hours to Ilfracombe were the principal features with arrivals at Torrington, Bude, Padstow and Plymouth at 3.49pm, 4.16pm, 5.21pm and 4.22pm respectively. In the up direction the speed-up was confined to east of Exeter, with calls at Sidmouth Junction at 12.47pm,

Salisbury from 2.3pm to 2.9pm, and Waterloo was scheduled to be reached at 3.29pm.

From September 1962 the through coach detachment and attachment at Salisbury was abandoned and then, as the Western Region took control west of Salisbury, the axe was used with a vengeance. In June 1963, instead of the down service being further accelerated – to reach Exeter Central at 1.50pm – as proposed by Waterloo, the train had two minutes cut from its schedule from Salisbury to Sidmouth Junction and the through coaches serving Torrington, Bude and Plymouth were all eliminated (connecting services were made available) just as the Southern Region was taking delivery of the long-awaited BR standard brake composite carriages for the service! In September the through Exmouth and Sidmouth coaches were also withdrawn which did away with the necessity for a little ritual peculiar to Sidmouth Junction whereby a flagman would position himself at the western end of the down platform and vigorously flag the train past the platform and over the level crossing until he adjudged that the rear coaches to be detached for the branches had cleared the points at the eastern end to allow the branch engine to back on and attach itself, at which juncture with military precision a rigidly held red flag would replace the green. It was nearby Feniton's equivalent of the Changing the Guard and used to entice enthusiasts from Exeter to witness it!

Details of the summer services have been tabulated (tables 4 and 5) for easy reference. The summer trains occupied about a quarter of each year and broadly followed the previous winter's timings although sometimes would introduce alterations to be followed in the autumn. Summer Saturday workings were complex and nearly every train from Waterloo between 10am and noon with a destination west of Salisbury tended to be termed a portion of the *ACE* whether or not it was so designated in the timetable.

It was common at periods of heavy loading out-of-season to find the down train run in two parts, the 11.5am from Waterloo being the untimetabled second part, usually calling at Axminster, on Mondays, Fridays and Maundy Thursdays and other days of pressure. An operating quirk in the up direction was that for the summers of 1949, 1950 and 1951 there were, Mondays to Fridays, through carriages from Exmouth (depart 11.50am) and Sidmouth (depart 12.20pm) which were attached at Sidmouth Junction but thereafter Lyme Regis and Yeovil Town had this facility in summer with carriages being attached at Salisbury. Titling of the Sunday service did not occur after 1939.

This all came to an abrupt end on 5 September 1964 with the final workings of the summer timetable and the downgrading of the Waterloo-Exeter route to secondary/alternative route status. Station, branch and trunk closures and singling of track followed as the ruthless work of rationalisation was done by

Padstow on the penultimate day. West Country class No 34015 *Exmouth* at the buffer stop beneath the Hotel Metropole, the stock British Railways standard type which carried the carriage nameboard beneath the roof gutter. *S. C. Nash*

Western Region. Even so with 20 years and more since closure and with no hope of ever reaching the Atlantic again, the trunk route Salisbury-Exeter survives and has seen some reinstatement of double track, reopening of closed stations, elevation to an Inter-City route and a progressive return from Salisbury westward to the Southern Region fold, so much so that more than 40 per cent has reverted to Waterloo's rule, and Network South East (ostensibly looking after the London commuter belt) extending to Whimple! All of which suggests much of the pruning bordered on the vindictive.

Post-war motive power for the train was invariably a Merchant Navy class 4–6–2 (large tender variety in later years) between London and Exeter Central (through engine workings were introduced as from 6 February 1950 as Nine Elms duty 5 and Exmouth Junction duty 497) and one of the smaller West

TABLE 4 DOWN ATLANTIC COAST EXPRESS 1948–1964 SUMMER SERVICES

PERIOD		MONDAYS TO FRIDAYS											SATURDAYS	
		Waterloo Dep. am	Salisbury pm	Sidmouth Jc pm	Exeter C Arr. pm	B'staple Jc Arr. pm	Ilfracombe Arr. pm	Torrington Arr. pm	Bude Arr. pm	Padstow Arr. pm	Plymouth Arr. pm	Restaurant Car to	Waterloo Dep. am	
1948	31/7–26/9	10.50	12.33/36	2.8/11	2.29	3.44	4.36	4.31	5.9	6.22	4.55	Padstow	10.20 / 10.35 / 10.50	Bude/Padstow(RC) / Ilfracombe/Torrington* / Plymouth/Bude/Padstow*
1949	23/5–25/9	10.35 / 10.50	12.14/18 / 12.33/36	— / 2.11 U	2.10 / 2.29	— / 3.44	— / 4.32	— / 4.31	4.20 / —	5.17 / —	4.34 / —	Exeter† / ExeterØ	10.20 / 10.50	Bude/Padstow* / Ilfracombe/Torrington*
1950	5/6–24/9	10.50	12.23/26	—	2.10	3.25	4.13	4.6	4.21	5.19	—	Exeter†	10.50	Ilfracombe/Torrington*
1951	2/7–9/9	10.50	12.23/26	—	2.10	3.25	4.12	4.6	4.21	5.19	—	Exeter†	10.50	Ilfracombe/Torrington*
1952	30/6–14/9	11.0	12.23/26	1.48/50	2.5	3.24	4.10	4.4	3.52	4.54	4.30	Exeter†	10.54	Ilfracombe/Torrington*
1953	8/6–20/9	11.0	12.23/26	1.47/49	2.5	3.25	4.11	4.5	4.4	5.0	4.25	Exeter†	10.35 / 11.0	Bude/Padstow* / Ilfracombe/Torrington*
1954	14/6–19/9	11.0	12.23/26	1.47/49	2.5	3.25	4.11	4.5	4.4	5.0	4.30	Exeter†	10.35 / 11.0	Bude/Padstow* / Ilfracombe/Torrington*
1955	13/6–18/9	11.0	12.23/26	1.47/49	2.5	3.25	4.11	4.5	4.4	5.0	4.30	Exeter	10.35 / 11.0	Bude/Padstow* / Ilfracombe(RC)/Torrington
1956	11/6–16/9	11.0	12.23/25	1.47/49	2.5	3.25	4.11	4.5	4.4	5.0	4.30	Exeter	10.35 / 11.0	Bude/Padstow* / Ilfracombe(RC)/Torrington
1957 1958	17/6–15/9 AND 9/6–14/9	11.0	12.23/25	1.47/49	2.5	3.25	4.11	4.5	4.4	5.0	4.21	Exeter	10.35 / 11.0	Bude/Padstow* / Ilfracombe(RC)/Torrington
1959	15/6–13/9 A	11.0 / 11.5	12.23/25 / 12.32/35	1.47/49 / —	2.5 / 2.16	3.16 / —	4.2 / —	3.54 / —	4.18 X / 4.18	5.7 X / 5.7	4.25 X / 4.25	Exeter / Exeter	10.35 / 11.0	Bude/Padstow* / Ilfracombe(RC)/Torrington
1960	13/6–11/9 18/7–11/9	11.0 / 11.5	12.23/25 / 12.32/35	1.47/49 / —	2.5 / 2.16	3.16 / —	4.2 / —	3.54 / —	4.18 X / 4.18	5.7 X / 5.7	4.25 X / 4.25	Exeter / Exeter	10.35 / 11.0	Bude/Padstow* / Ilfracombe(RC)/Torrington
1961	12/6–10/9 17/7–10/9	11.0 / 11.5	12.23/25 / 12.32/35	1.47/49 / —	2.5 / 2.15	3.16 / —	4.2 / —	3.55 / —	4.20 X / 4.20	5.3 X / 5.3	4.25 X / 4.25	Exeter / Exeter	10.35 / 11.0	Bude/Padstow* / Ilfracombe(RC)/Torrington
1962	18/6–9/9 16/7–9/9	11.0 / 11.5	12.20/23 / 12.30/32	1.40/42 / —	1.58 / 2.9	3.9 / —	3.55 / —	3.49 / —	4.12 X / 4.12	5.0 X / 5.0	4.22 X / 4.22	Exeter / Exeter	10.35 / 11.0	Bude/Padstow* / Ilfracombe(RC)/Torrington
1963	17/6–8/9 29/7–22/8 B	11.0 / 11.5	12.20/23 / 12.30/32	1.38/42 / —	1.58 / 2.9	3.9 / —	3.51 / —	— / —	— / —	5.0 X / 5.0	— / —	Exeter / Exeter	10.35 / 11.0	Bude/Padstow‡ / Ilfracombe(RC)/Torrington
1964	15/6–6/9 27/7–20/8 B	11.0 / 11.5	12.20/24 / 12.30/32	1.38/42 / —	1.58 / 2.9	3.9 / —	3.51 / —	— / —	— / —	5.0 X / 5.0—	— / —	Exeter / —	10.35 / 11.0	Bude/Padstow* / Ilfracombe(BC)/Torrington

From 1948 to 1958 Plymouth times are for Friary station and thereafter for previously named North Road Station.
A Mondays and Fridays; also Tuesdays, Wednesdays and Thursdays 21/7–3/9/1959. B Mondays to Thursdays inclusive.
U Picks up only. X Not when 11.5am ex. Waterloo operated. (RC) Restaurant car. (BC) Buffet car.
*Restaurant car to Exeter Central. †On Fridays to Exeter Central. ØOn Fridays to Padstow. ‡Buffet car to Exeter Central.

TABLE 5 UP ATLANTIC COAST EXPRESS 1948–1964 SUMMER SERVICES

PERIOD		Plymouth Dep. am	Padstow Dep. am	Bude Dep. am	Torrington Dep. am	Ilfracombe Dep. am	B'staple Jc Dep. am	Exeter C. pm	Sidm'th Jc Dep. pm	Salisbury pm	Waterloo Arr. pm	Restaurant Car from	SATURDAYS Departures am
1948	31/7–26/9	—	8.25	9.30	10.15	10.15	11.0	12.35	12.59	2.55/59	4.36	Padstow	8.25 Padstow/Bude* 10.15 Ilfracombe(RC)
1949	23/5–25/9	— —	— 9.52	— 10.58	10.30 —	10.30 —	11.16 —	12.30 12.50	12.54 —	2.47/50 2.57/3.0	4.26 4.36	Exeter Exeter	10.40 Ilfracombe(RC) 10.45 Padstow(RC)/Bude
1950	5/6–24/9	— —	— 9.52	— 10.58	10.30 —	10.30 —	11.16 —	12.30 12.50	12.54 —	2.45/50 2.55/3.0	4.20 4.36	Exeter Exeter	10.40 Ilfracombe(RC) 10.45 Padstow(RC)/Bude
1951	2/7–9/9	— —	— 9.52	— 10.58	10.30 —	10.30 —	11.16 —	12.30 12.50	12.54 —	2.45/50 2.58/3.2	4.18 4.36	Exeter Exeter	10.35 Ilfracombe(RC) 10.45 Padstow(RC)/Bude
1952	30/6–14/9 A	9.50	8.30 9.40	9.30 10.40	10.30 —	10.30 —	11.16 —	12.30 12.45	12.49 —	2.9/13 2.32/35	3.40 4.13	Exeter Exeter	10.30 Ilfracombe(RC) 10.45 Padstow(RC)/Bude
1953	8/6–20/9 A	9.50 X 9.50	9.35 X 9.35	10.20 X 10.20	10.30 —	10.30 —	11.16 —	12.30 12.16	12.49 —	2.9/13 1.57/2.0	3.40 3.32	Exeter Exeter	10.30 Ilfracombe(RC) 10.48 Torrington* 10.45 Padstow(RC)/Bude X Ø11.45 Bude†
1954	14/6–19/9 A	9.50 X 9.50	9.35 X 9.35	10.20 X 10.20	10.30 —	10.30 —	11.16 —	12.30 12.16	12.49 —	2.9/13 1.57/2.0	3.40 3.32	Exeter Exeter	10.30 Ilfracombe(RC) 10.48 Torrington* 11.0 Padstow(RC)/Bude X Ø11.45 Bude†
1955 1956	13/6–18/9 AND 11/6–16/9 AND	9.50 X	9.35 X	10.20 X	10.30	10.30	11.16	12.30	12.49	2.9/13	3.40	Exeter	10.30 Ilfracombe(RC) 10.48 Torrington* 11.0 Padstow†/Bude X
1957 1958	17/6–15/9 AB AND 9/6–14/9	9.50	9.35	10.20	—	—	—	12.16	—	1.57/2.0	3.32	Exeter	Ø11.45 Bude*
1959	15/6–13/9 C	10.2 X 10.2	9.35 X 9.35	10.20 X 10.20	10.30 —	10.30 —	11.16 —	12.30 12.16	12.49 —	2.9/13 1.57/2.0	3.40 3.32	Exeter Exeter	10.30 Ilfracombe(RC) 10.48 Torrington* 11.0 Padstow†/Bude X Ø11.45 Bude*
1960	13/6–11/9 18/7–11/9	10.2 X 10.2	9.33 X 9.33	10.20 X 10.20	1030 —	10.30 —	11.16 —	12.30 12.16	12.49 —	2.9/13 1.57/2.0	3.40 3.32	Exeter Exeter	10.30 Ilfracombe(RC) 10.48 Torrington* 11.0 Padstow(RC)/Bude X Ø11.45 Bude*
1961	12/6–10/9 17/7–10/9	10.2 X 10.2	9.33 X 9.33	10.20 X 10.20	10.30 —	10.30 —	11.16 —	12.30 12.16	12.49 —	2.9/15 1.57/2.0	3.38 3.32	Exeter Exeter	10.30 IlfracombeMBX 10.48 Torrington* 11.0 Padstow(RC)/Bude X Ø11.45 Bude*
1962	18/6–9/9 16/7–9/9	10.2 X 10.2	9.33 X 9.33	10.20 X 10.20	10.30 —	10.30 —	11.16 —	12.30 12.16	12.48 —	2.3/9 1.53/7	3.29 3.21	Exeter Exeter	As for 1960
1963	17/6–8/9 29/7–22/8 D	— —	9.33 X 9.33	— —	— —	10.30 —	11.16 —	12.30 12.16	12.48 —	2.3/9 1.53/7	3.29 3.21	Exeter Exeter(BC)	10.30 Ilfracombe(BC) 10.48 Torrington BCX 11.0 Padstow(BC)/Bude
1964	15/6–6/9 27/7–20/8 D	— —	9.33 X 9.33	— —	— —	10.30 —	11.17 —	12.30 12.18	12.49 —	2.3/9 1.53/7	3.29 3.21	Exeter —	10.30 Ilfracombe 10.48 Torrington BCX 11.0 Padstow/Bude

From 1948 to 1958 Plymouth times are for Friary station and thereafter for previously named North Road station.
A Mondays and Fridays: also Tuesdays, Wednesdays and Thursdays 5–28/8/1952, 28/7–27/8/1953, 27/7–26/8/1954 and 26/7–28/8/1955.
B Mondays to Fridays 23/7–24/8/1956, 22/7–30/8/1957, 21/7–29/8/1958 and Mondays and Fridays thereafter each year.
C Mondays to Fridays 20/7–7/9 and Friday 11/9. D Mondays to Thursdays. X Not when other service operates.
*Restaurant car from Exeter Central. †Restaurant car from Okehampton. ØFrom mid-July: at other times combines with Padstow portion. (RC) Restaurant car. (BC) Buffet car. BCX Buffet car from Exeter Central. MBX Miniature buffet car from Exeter Central.

Country or Battle of Britain 4–6–2s would take charge of the portions to and from there serving Ilfracombe, Padstow and Plymouth as well as sometimes appearing on the lesser workings between Exeter and London. The modified light Pacifics were, however, never permitted to work the route from Coleford Junction to Ilfracombe nor that from Meldon Junction to Padstow. The faithful M7 class 0–4–4 tanks did duty on the Exmouth, Sidmouth, Torrington and Bude branches and assisted over Mortehoe summit as well as banking up from Exeter St Davids to Central. In the early 1950s LMR and BR standard 2–6–2 tanks took over much of the M7 class work although the latter held sway on the Seaton branch until at least the end of the through *ACE* coaches to that resort. From late 1962 the BR standard 2–6–4 tanks progressively replaced the BR standard 2–6–2 tanks throughout the area. The E1R 0–6–2 tank class banked trains up to Exeter Central from St Davids although in the last years first Z class 0–8–0 tanks and then W class 2–6–4 tanks, both of Southern Railway origin, as well as BR standard tanks undertook this duty. The T9 4–4–0s and N class 2–6–0s worked the up Plymouth portion from time to time.

Unusual locomotive workings included a BR Britannia from Exeter Central to Waterloo in 1953 when the Merchant Navy class was temporarily withdrawn for investigation, SR diesel-electric No 10203 regularly for a period in 1954, BR standard 2–6–4 tanks occasionally on the Exeter Central-Ilfracombe portion in late days and for the final three weeks diesel-hydraulic Warship class locomotives took over the up service from Exeter to Waterloo. On Saturdays sometimes a King Arthur 4–6–0, either of true Southern Railway lineage or of the BR standard Class 5 type which had abducted some of the King Arthur names, would appear on one of the titled portions east of Exeter.

The prowess of the Pacifics between Waterloo and Exeter on the *ACE* is legendary, with maxima of 100mph and high average start-to-stop runs. More often than not this high level of performance was maintained on the train's other sections with the smaller motive power. So far as performance was concerned the *ACE* was certainly the Southern's 'flagship service'.

A choice of 65 destinations without change was offered the traveller from Waterloo in the eleven coach formation of a typical (1955/6) winter service. Working from the ticket barrier at Waterloo, the first carriage was a brake composite for Seaton which would be detached at Salisbury and added to the four coach slow train to Exeter and again detached at Seaton Junction and be worked singly to its destination. Next came two more brake composites, one for Sidmouth, the other for Exmouth. Together they would be detached at Sidmouth Junction and coupled to two other coaches and the whole worked to Tipton St Johns where the Exmouth coach would be uncoupled and the other coaches proceed to Sidmouth; a two-coach set would then be coupled to the

The nameboard on the smoke deflector shows to advantage in this shot of Merchant Navy 4-6-2 No 21C7 *Aberdeen Commonwealth* climbing Honiton bank with a full-length *Devon Belle*, the first four Pullmans of which are destined for Plymouth. *Author's collection*

through coach at Tipton and the three would proceed to Exmouth. Open saloon 7834 and kitchen buffet car (tavern type) 7897 *The Three Plovers* came next in the formation and these would be removed at Exeter Central. A two-set for Plymouth and four brake composites (one each for Bude, Padstow, Torrington and Ilfracombe) completed the train. At Exeter Central another coach was shunted on to the front two carriages, usually by the train engine propelling in from the siding on the south side at the head of the bank from St Davids, and the three would go to Barnstaple Junction where the first two carried on to Ilfracombe; the Torrington coach had another added before proceeding to its destination. The four coach Plymouth/Bude/Padstow formation had an extra one added at Exeter; at Okehampton the Plymouth pair

The sanders on No 35008 *Orient Line* are being freely used as the engine draws away from Wilton South with the down *Devon Belle* in August 1949. *Brian Reed*

went their own way while at Halwill Junction the Bude coach would be dropped allowing the other two to go to Padstow; then, with two more added, the Bude coach would leave.

In the reverse direction a building-up rather than a breaking-down process was observed and for 1955/6 the allocated tavern car for the up service was 7895 *The Bull* and saloon 7839 which alternated with 7892 *The White Horse* and saloon 7838. By complete contrast the 1955 summer Saturday four up trains started and finished thus:

Train	Coaches at start	Coaches at Waterloo
10.30am Ilfracombe	11	13
10.48am Torrington	6	12
11.0am Padstow	9	12
11.45am Bude	7	10

That is when the light Pacifics came in particularly useful in North Devon and North Cornwall. Now by-passes have to be built in the Dartmoor National Park to get the motorists to the destinations once served by the *ACE*!

Devon Belle

In complete contrast to the *ACE* was the *Devon Belle* – an elegant all-Pullman formation, including an observation car, seasonal timings and completely lacking in tradition save that of the Pullman Car Company. Such was the interloper that appeared on the scene in the summer of 1947, when the Southern Railway was trying to restore facilities to something approaching pre-war standard; the shortage of ordinary coaching stock could be alleviated by the availability of the long-stored Pullman vehicles and so the opportunity

The four-coach portion for Plymouth of the down *Devon Belle* provides little problem for No 34011 *Tavistock* as it leaves Okehampton on 19 June 1949. *S. C. Nash*

was taken to utilise these in making up two trains for the summer holiday traffic, giving the advantage of seat reservations which were not then available on ordinary trains.

Two Pullmans were converted at Preston Park works to observation cars. Each seated 27 passengers in single and double tub-type seats, cunningly designed to be uncomfortable for anything other than a short sitting, thus ensuring a good turn-over of passengers wishing to view the passing scene from the rear of the train. Bar, pantry and lavatory were also incorporated in these cars, together with a curved wall mural map of the route to Devon designed by Miss Eleanor Esmonde-White.

Starting on 20 June 1947, the train ran on Mondays, Fridays, Saturdays and Sundays, the schedule being:

		noon					am	
Waterloo	dep	12.0		Plymouth Friary	dep	11.30		
Sidmouth Junc	arr	3.16		Plymouth N Road	dep	11.40		
	dep	3.18		Devonport	dep	11.47		
Exeter Central	arr	3.36 pm		Okehampton	arr	12.43		
	dep	3.39	3.48		dep	12.45 noon		
Exeter St Davids	dep	3.45	3.52	Ilfracombe	dep		12.0	
Okehampton	arr	4.25		Mortehoe	dep		12.12	
	dep	4.27		Braunton	dep		12.23	
Devonport	arr	5.16		Barnstaple Town	dep		12.32	
Plymouth N Road	arr	5.25		Barnstaple Junc	arr		12.36	
Plymouth Friary	arr	5.36			dep		12.37	
Barnstaple Junc	arr		4.49	Exeter St Davids	dep	1.23	1.33	
	dep		4.51	Exeter Central	arr	1.27	1.38	
Barnstaple Town	dep		4.55		dep		1.40	
Braunton	dep		5.5	Sidmouth Junc	arr		2.2	
Mortehoe	dep		5.23		dep		2.3	
Ilfracombe	arr		5.32	Waterloo	arr		5.20	

Supplementary fares were levied, ranging from 3s6d for third class between Waterloo and Exeter to 8s for first class from London to Ilfracombe, although no extra charge was made for use of the observation cars. Clearly the train was aimed to appeal to holidaymakers who were prepared to indulge themselves at the beginning and end of their vacation.

Engine changes were made each way at Wilton (the first station west of Salisbury) and at Exeter Central, the first because water capacity of the Merchant Navy class tenders was insufficient for a non-stop public timetabled run and the latter because of route restrictions on the Merchant Navy engines. For the inaugural run, which was typical for this train, Nine Elms engine No 21C15 hauled the train each way between Waterloo and Wilton, No 21C3 (on a

Salisbury duty) from Wilton to Exeter and No 21C4 (an Exmouth Junction shed engine) from Exeter to Wilton. West of Exeter No 21C103 *Plymouth* dealt with the Plymouth portion in each direction and No 21C117 *Ilfracombe* likewise the Ilfracombe portion. Banking assistance on the Ilfracombe branch was given, usually by N class 2–6–0 and M7 class 0–4–4 tank locomotives. The standard formation was the four leading cars for Plymouth and the remaining eight for Ilfracombe. It was this Ilfracombe portion that No 21C161 took out on a press run into Surrey on 19 June immediately before commencement of the public service.

In addition to the engine buffer beam nameboard, wing plates with the train title were carried on the smoke deflectors of the locomotive for which purpose various members of the Pacifics were fitted with a batten at the top of the deflector plates. One of these plates became dislodged on the locomotive of the up train on 22 September 1947 between Sidmouth Junction and Honiton and hit the engine of the down *Atlantic Coast Express*, thankfully without causing grave injury to anybody. These lasted until the end of the 1952 season, the next year seeing just the BR (SR) standard smokebox type nameboard.

The train formation for the first season was:

Portion	Train 1	Train 2	Type	Seats
Plymouth	36	208	3rd Parlour	36
	Iolanthe	*Argus*	1st Kitchen	22
	61	33	3rd Kitchen	36
	55	54	3rd Brake	30
Ilfracombe	*Minerva*	*Princess Elizabeth*	1st Parlour	24
	Cynthia	*Rosamund*	1st Kitchen	22
	Fingall	*Geraldine*	1st Kitchen	22
	35	34	3rd Parlour	42
	169	249	3rd Kitchen	30
	60	32	3rd Kitchen	36
	65	27	3rd Brake	30
	14	13	Observation	27

Additional, or substitute, cars could be taken from the Pullman pool as required. This formation – and more particularly when increased to its maximum by the addition of a couple more cars for Ilfracombe – provided a good test for the Merchant Navy class locomotives especially when there was time to be recouped on the up run after the not very generous time allowance for joining the two sections at Exeter Central had been exceeded.

Particular attention was given to the observation cars with a porter delegated to clean the windows during the engine change at Wilton. These cars had, of course, to be turned for each journey. At Ilfracombe this was done on the

The *Devon Belle* observation cars had to be turned at each end of the journey. Here the operation at Ilfracombe engine shed is depicted. *Robin Russell*

locomotive turntable and similarly, after the empty stock had been taken back to Clapham Yard from Waterloo. An M7 class tank engine was rostered to take the observation car up to Waterloo for turning on the turntable there, an operation which could be witnessed between 9 and 9.15pm in the evening of the days the train ran, and return it to Clapham Yard.

By August 1947 demand was heavy enough for the Ilfracombe portion to be loaded, at least on Saturdays, to ten cars giving a fourteen-coach formation east of Exeter Central. The next year, 1948, a stop was inserted each way at Tavistock (12.14pm up and 4.53pm down) and the down train was extended to run on Thursdays and the up service on Tuesdays, when a Salisbury engine worked the train from Wilton to Waterloo. By now seat reservations had returned for selected ordinary passenger trains but not on Saturdays or

Sundays; it was to be 1949 before this facility was restored for the weekends.

Somewhat understandably, since the destination was not a fashionable resort, the Plymouth portion was seldom heavily patronised (it was very popular at the beginning with Plymouth and Cornish passengers who could not reserve seats on the Paddington services) and for the summer of 1950 it was discontinued which allowed the Ilfracombe arrival time to be advanced to 5.27pm. The cars which had previously gone through to Plymouth were now detached at Exeter Central. The restoration of seat reservations generally also seemed to have some effect on patronage and there were proposals not to operate the train for the summer of 1952. However, it was not the end; the days of operation were limited to Fridays, Saturdays and Sundays for the down train and to Mondays, Saturdays and Sundays for the up service and this was repeated in 1953. In 1954 the days remained the same but the Friday departure was retimed to 4.40pm and gave two additional stops at Salisbury (6.5pm) and Axminister (7.16pm). The arrival time at Ilfracombe was 9.48pm which was a 19 minute acceleration on the usual timing of nearly 5½ hours. The engine

The changeover of locomotives at Wilton South has been completed and Merchant Navy 4-6-2 No 35009 *Shaw Savill* is about to set off for Sidmouth Junction and Exeter Central after which No 35013 *Blue Funnel*, which had brought the *Devon Belle* from London, will leave the siding and run back to Salisbury shed for servicing and turning before returning to take over the up train. The oblong smokebox headboards are in use without the 'wings' on the smoke deflectors indicating the picture was secured in the last years of the service. *Robin Russell*

TABLE 6 DEVON BELLE DATES OF OPERATION

YEAR	TIMETABLE STARTED	DOWN SERVICES	UP SERVICES	LAST SERVICE	TIMETABLE ENDED
1947	Monday, 16 June	Mondays, Fridays and Saturdays 20 June to 27 October; Sundays until 26 October	Mondays, Fridays and Saturdays 20 June to 27 October; Sundays until 26 October	Down and up Monday 27 October	Sunday 5 October
1948	Monday, 31 May	Mondays, Thursdays, Fridays and Saturdays until 25 October; Sundays until 24 October	Mondays, Tuesdays, Fridays and Saturdays until 26 October; Sundays until 24 October	Up Tuesday 26 October	Sunday 27 September
1949	Monday, 23 May	Mondays, Thursdays, Fridays and Saturdays from 26 May; Sundays until 18 September	Mondays, Tuesdays, Fridays and Saturdays from 27 May; Sundays	Up Sunday 25 September	Sunday 25 September
1950	Monday, 5 June	Mondays, Thursdays, Fridays and Saturdays from 8 June; Sundays until 17 September	Mondays, Tuesdays, Fridays and Saturdays from 9 June; Sundays	Up Sunday 24 September	Sunday 24 September
1951	Monday, 18 June postponed to 2 July (but see text)	Mondays, Thursdays, Fridays and Saturdays from 22 June; Sundays until 2 September*	Mondays, Tuesdays, Fridays and Saturdays from 23 June; Sundays	Up Sunday 16 September*	Sunday 9 September*
1952	Monday, 30 June	Fridays; Saturdays; Sundays until 7 September	Mondays from 7 July; Saturdays; Sundays	Up Sunday 14 September	Sunday 14 September
1953	Monday, 8 June	Fridays; Saturdays; Sundays until 13 September	Mondays from 15 June; Saturdays; Sundays	Up Sunday 20 September	Sunday 20 September
1954	Monday, 14 June	Fridays; Saturdays; Sundays until 12 September	Mondays from 21 June; Saturdays; Sundays	Up Sunday 19 September	Sunday 19 September

*The train overran the revised ending of the summer timetable period (amended from 23 to 9 September) by one week at least, being noted on 15 September. It presumably operated on 16 September in the up direction but certainly no later.

change at Wilton obviously was not required on Fridays because water could be taken at Salisbury and consequently the Nine Elms Merchant Navy on duty 6 worked right through to Exeter Central.

The final down run turned out to be on Saturday 18 September 1954 and the last time the *Devon Belle* drew into Waterloo was the day following. At the time it was not known these trips would mark the passing of the train but eventually the decision was taken not to continue this summer all-Pullman service into 1955 and beyond. Table 6 sets out the dates of operation of the train during its existence; it may be said that despite the postponement of the start of the summer timetable in 1951 some services did operate in June. It is known that the trains operated on Saturday 23 June and 30 June and therefore it is reasonable to assume that down trains ran on 22/24/29 June and 1 July and up trains on 24 and 25 June and 1/2 July. Devonshire has never sustained a Pullman service for any length of time although perhaps it is fair to state that the *Devon Belle* experiment arose as an expedient to overcome a temporary stock shortage: it certainly lasted much longer than the Great Western's *Torquay Pullman*.

CHAPTER THREE

Into Wessex

The Bournemouth Limited

For a few years before the First World War Bournemouth had enjoyed a fast two-hour train to and from London, despite some shortcomings in the timekeeping qualities of the service. With the war over and grouping accomplished, it was not unnatural that the townsfolk of the resort in the mid-twenties urged upon the Southern Railway the desirability of the reintroduction of this facility.

The railway company was not entirely unmindful of this but had many calls for improvements. Newly-built King Arthur class engines had been drafted to Bournemouth and new carriage stock was on order for the route. So deserving, however, were Bournemouth's claims that it was decided to accelerate the Bournemouth and Weymouth services in the summer of 1929, rather than wait for the new coaches to be delivered. Two long standing weekday trains serving Weymouth – the 7.30am up, calling at Bournemouth Central at 8.43am, as well as Southampton, and arriving at Waterloo at 11am and the 4.30pm down, which was due into Weymouth at 7.56pm – were earmarked for improvement and two new services, the 10.30am from Waterloo and 5.15pm up from Bournemouth Central, were introduced, all to two-hour non-stop schedules east of Bournemouth.

The 7.30am from Weymouth and 4.30pm return were very much trains for Bournemouth, Poole, Dorchester and Weymouth residents, enabling them to make a day trip to the capital. Commuting from Bournemouth to London at that time was unheard-of (leaving aside that such terminology was then unknown): nonetheless a director could be in his office in late morning, visit his club for luncheon, make a return to the office to sign correspondence and then return by the 4.30pm, while his wife busied herself with visiting Harrods or a gallery, lunching with friends, inspecting new fashions and the like before rejoining her husband at Waterloo. The very popularity of the service to some extent posed a problem and it was decided to make the accelerated service a limited formation train with an indicative title, hence the *Bournemouth Limited*.

Bookmark from the summer timetable of 1929 advertising the new *Bournemouth Limited*. The locomotive represented bears more resemblance to a Lord Nelson rather than the King Arthur type actually used at first. *Author's collection*

On and from July 8th.

THE NEW "BOURNEMOUTH LIMITED"

Corridor Restaurant Car
non-stop express between

**WATERLOO AND BOURNEMOUTH
IN 2 HOURS**
15 minutes faster!

SOUTHERN RAILWAY
quickest way to sunshine
Full details in folder at S R stations

See Coloured Supplement and pages 154 to 163 of this Time-table

Timings were (Sunday excepted):

		pm		
Waterloo	dep	4.30		
B'mouth Central	arr	6.30	pm	
	dep	6.32	6.38	
B'mouth West	arr	6.43	—	
Poole	dep		6.52	
Wareham	arr		7.4	pm
	dep		7.6	7.17
Dorchester	dep		7.27	—
Weymouth	arr		7.44	—
Corfe Castle	dep			7.30
Swanage	arr			7.41

		am	
Swanage	dep	7.20	am
Weymouth	dep	—	7.32
Dorchester	dep	—	7.49
Poole	dep	8.3	8.16
B'mouth West	arr	8.19	—
	dep	8.26	—
B'mouth Central	arr	8.34	8.28
	dep	8.40	
Waterloo	arr	10.40	

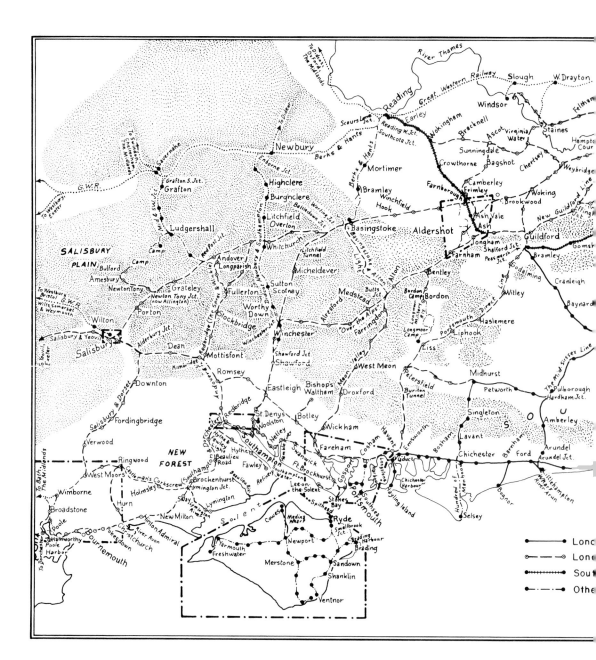

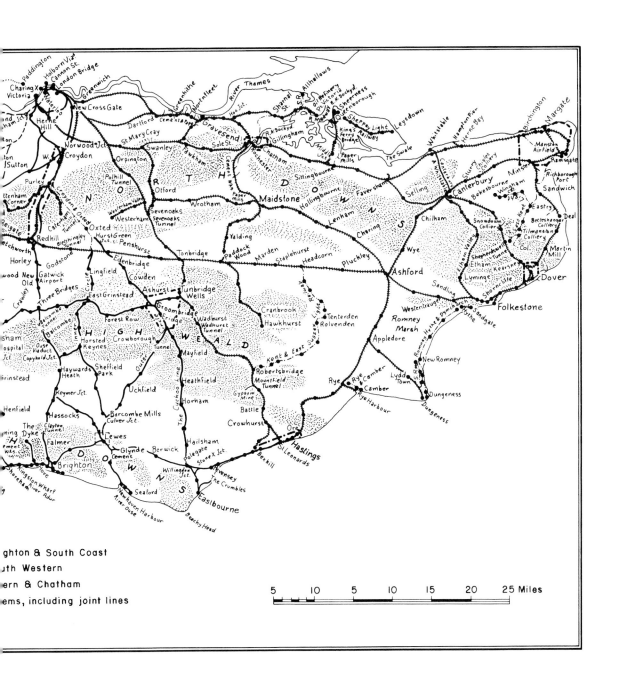

5   10   5   10   15   20   25 Miles

To enable the Bournemouth based King Arthur class locomotives to keep time the load was restricted to ten vehicles (or approximately 330 tons empty). Of these ten coaches, four (two corridor brake thirds, one corridor composite and a dining car) formed the Weymouth portion, two (one corridor brake third and one corridor brake composite) served Swanage and the remaining four – the only ones, incidentally, to carry *Bournemouth Limited* roofboards – consisting of two corridor brake thirds, one corridor third and a corridor first made up the Bournemouth West part. The modus operandi was for the King Arthur engine to work to and from Bournemouth West and for a smaller locomotive, such as a D15 class 4–4–0, to take the Weymouth portion. In the down direction the Swanage coaches were detached at Wareham although in the morning these coaches were worked through to Bournemouth West, joined to the four coach portion there, and worked round to Bournemouth Central, where the Weymouth section was shunted on to the rear.

A non-typical thirteen-coach preview train ran non-stop from Waterloo to Bournemouth Central on 4 July 1929 hauled by No E860 *Lord Hawke* in the two-hour timing without a balancing return trip. On the following Monday, 8 July, the *Bournemouth Limited* commenced its life. Apart from increased loading (such as an extra dining car) from time to time, contrary to the supposedly limited formation, the train had for its first five years a sedate existence, the sole amendment being a two-minute speed-up of the down Swanage portion in September 1933. Punctuality sometimes left something to

Schools class No 932 *Blundell's* climbs Pokesdown bank with the down *Bournemouth Limited* on 20 May 1939 made up to twelve coaches. *G. O. P. Pearce*

be desired; despite this the summer timetable of 1934 introduced a schedule of exactly three hours each way between Weymouth and Waterloo, the minutes being adjusted west of Bournemouth giving arrival and departure times at Weymouth of 7.30pm and 7.40am respectively. In October 1934 the restaurant car was curtailed to run between London and Bournemouth West and, apart from the summer timetables of 1936 and 1937 when it once again reached Weymouth, this came to be the regular working. At about this time through running of the King Arthurs on the up train from Weymouth was instituted but the D15 engines still did the honours in the reverse direction from Bournemouth.

As from 8 July 1935 two more minutes were clipped off the timings throughout on the down train and between Bournemouth and Waterloo on the morning service. A year later, starting on 6 July, the *Limited* reached its zenith so far as schedules were concerned with these times:

		pm				am	
Waterloo	dep	4.30	pm	Swanage	dep	7.17	am
B'mouth Central		6.26/29	6.34	Weymouth	dep	–	7.45
B'mouth West	arr	–	6.44	Dorchester	dep	–	7.59
Poole	dep	6.41	pm	Poole	dep	7.56	8.24
Wareham		6.52/53	6.57	B'mouth West		8.12/20	–
Dorchester	dep	7.12	–	B'mouth Central		8.28	8.35/40
Weymouth	arr	7.24	–	Waterloo	arr		10.38
Corfe Castle	dep		7.11				
Swanage	arr		7.21				

Another year passed and Schools class 4–4–0s Nos 924–933, displaced from their duties at Fratton shed because of the Portsmouth Direct line electrification, were transferred to Bournemouth shed and took over the duties, the *Bournemouth Limited* among them, which had been the preserve of the King Arthurs and soon began to discharge the tasks with distinction, even though the *Limited* loading limit had been been increased to 365 tons.

The final timetable alteration became effective on 4 July 1938 when, to give Swanage passengers a better up connection (the Swanage portion had always called at all stations to Bournemouth West and, indeed, still did), a stop was inserted at Wareham so that a cross-platform change could be made from the 7.44am pull and push train from Swanage, allowing such passengers nearly half-an-hour longer in bed than hitherto if they wished to take this option. The departure from Weymouth had to be three minutes earlier to offset the Wareham stop. To coincide with this the coaching stock and six of the Schools class engines were repainted in the new Bournemouth, or (as it later became to be known) malachite, green livery, the first such complete named train to be treated on the railway. Not only were the coaches redecorated externally but refitting internally was done, with the seats having individual backs, compartment advertising giving way to pictures and the decor in general following a lighter touch.

The coaching stock formation was a three corridor set (221 or 232) for Weymouth, a two corridor set (180 or 199) for Swanage and a six dining set (241 or 243), having two third brakes, two open thirds, a corridor first and a restaurant car (either 7940 or 7943), for Bournemouth West. This eleven coach rake was expanded on Fridays when a loose corridor third (either 1802 or 1803) specially painted in the new livery would be added for Bournemouth West.

In the up direction the Schools class engine worked right through from Weymouth to Waterloo but going down it went to Bournemouth West and a U class 2–6–0 took the Weymouth part on from Bournemouth Central. Other motive power was M7 class 0–4–4 tanks on both Swanage portions and a T9 4–4–0 from Bournemouth West to Central in the mornings.

Sadly these improvements were to be short-lived. War was declared on 3 September 1939 and with the abandonment of the summer timetables the *Bournemouth Limited*, as such, ran for the last time on 9 September 1939. At first the wartime timetables dispensed with the service altogether but after a short while the train, now nameless, could be traced as leaving Bournemouth Central at 8.40am for London and returning to Bournemouth at 4.35pm (instead of 4.30pm) with various intermediate stops, such as Southampton and Winchester, and it continued thus throughout the war and into nationalisation days.

The Royal Wessex

After the war there was no move to restore the name *Bournemouth Limited* nor to give Bournemouth a regular non-stop London service; indeed, there was never to be such a service again. With nationalisation of the railways in its fourth year and standard coaching stock just coming into production, British Railways decided to mark the Festival of Britain year of 1951 with the introduction of five special trains of the new stock. For the Southern Region the choice fell upon the 7.38am Weymouth-Waterloo and return 4.35pm services and these trains were christened *The Royal Wessex*, not inappropriately because Wintoncester, Sandbourne, Casterbridge and Budmouth, all from Thomas Hardy's Wessex novels, were among the towns served.

Inauguration day of the Festival trains was 3 May, before the summer

As one of the Festival trains the *Royal Wessex* had its own brochure but seldom, if ever, had one of the Britannia class depicted thereon to haul it. Waterloo station was cheek-by-jowl with the main Festival of Britain exhibition and so it was fitting that one of its expresses should be designated a Festival Train. *Author's collection*

timetable came into force, and so the *Royal Wessex* came into being on an existing timing, rather than as an innovation. The times were, of course, of the direct lineage of the *Bournemouth Limited*; the down train left Waterloo at 4.35pm, Winchester City at 5.58pm, Southampton Central at 6.18pm and Brockenhurst at 6.41pm with an arrival at Bournemouth Central at 7.3pm. The front portion went forward at 7.5pm – leaving the rear section to go round to Bournemouth West – calling at Poole at 7.18pm to arrive at Wareham at 7.29pm, where the *Swanage* portion was detached (arrival at Corfe Castle was at 7.50pm and Swanage at 8pm); Dorchester was reached at 7.50pm and the journey was concluded at 8.3pm at Weymouth. In the up direction the stops were similar except that Wool was added and Brockenhurst omitted, nor was there a through coach attachment at Wareham, the 7.47am pull and push train from Swanage merely giving a cross-platform connection. Departure of the combined train from Bournemouth Central was at the time-honoured hour of 8.40am, from Southampton Central at 9.16am, Winchester City at 9.38am to give an arrival at Waterloo at 10.54am.

For the inaugural trains West Country class engines, which customarily were employed on the service, were used. No 34105 *Swanage*, a

The inaugural run of the *Royal Wessex*. West Country class 4-6-2 No 34105 *Swanage* restarts the up train from Bournemouth Central on 3 May 1951. *G. O. P. Pearce*

Bournemouth-shedded engine, worked the up train and Nine Elms based No 34008 headed the down service. The timings and motive power were no different from usual: the great difference was in the train itself for, instead of eleven coaches, it now became a thirteen-coach formation with a tare weight of 446 tons. This arose not because of larger or heavier coaches, for the new BR stock was the same length and width as the last Southern stock and a little less in weight, but from the third-class compartment seating being three aside instead of four and, to make matters worse, the inclusion of a three-vehicle dining set in the formation. Six coaches comprised the Bournemouth West portion, with five for Weymouth and two for Swanage. To begin with the Swanage portion was formed of Southern Bulleid type stock painted in the BR cream and crimson lake coaching livery to match the remainder of the train.

The summer timetables for 1951, due to come into operation on 18 June, were postponed until 2 July, when the schedules were tightened up and through Swanage coaches joined the up train at Wareham. The full timings then became:

		pm					am
Waterloo	dep	4.35		Weymouth	dep		7.34
Winchester City	dep	5.50		Dorchester South	dep		7.49
Southampton Cen		6.8/10		Wool	dep	am	8.1
Brockenhurst		6.31/33 pm		Swanage	dep	7.36	–
B'mouth Central		6.55/57 7.5		Corfe Castle	dep	7.47	–
B'mouth West	arr	– 7.13		Wareham		7.59	8.10/13
Poole	dep	7.10 pm		Poole	dep	am	8.25
Wareham		7.21/23 7.30		B'mouth West	dep	8.20	–
Dorchester South	dep	7.42 –		B'mouth Central		8.28	8.35/40
Weymouth	arr	7.55 –		Southampton Cen			9.13/15
Corfe Castle	dep	7.42		Winchester City	dep		9.37
Swanage	arr	7.52		Waterloo	arr		10.50

The detaching of coaches at Bournemouth Central and Wareham was a simple enough business, although the Swanage portion did involve sandwich working with the M7 class 0–4–4 tank propelling a two-coach pull and push unit and pulling the two through coaches behind it. On the up working the through portions at both Wareham and Bournemouth Central would arrive in advance of the Weymouth section and then be pulled back into a siding and propelled forward to couple up to the main train after its arrival.

For the West Country class locomotives powering the train the sterner test was the up working which involved restarting the heaviest regular train on the Western Section of the Southern Region on the long rising gradient at Winchester and resulted in a somewhat indifferent punctuality record at

Waterloo. When it was established that the name was not just to grace the train for the Festival year of 1951 but to continue as a regular feature the operating department had to consider how to make the working of the train less onerous. The answer was to dispense with the BR standard three-unit restaurant set (kitchen only car No 80009 with open first No 9 and open third No 1006) and replace it with kitchen buffet car No 7898 – the tavern car *The Green Man* in fact – and refreshment saloon No 7840. This change was effected at the beginning of 1952 and at the same time diesel-electric locomotives Nos 10201/2 were rostered (singly) for the down working; the up train continued with Bournemouth shed's light Pacifics.

Matters continued thus with varying degrees of success – such as No 10201 bursting into flames on approaching Beaulieu Road on the down train on 5 June 1952. The London Midland Region diesel-electric locomotives Nos 10000 and 10001 also joined in the duty and these too had successes and failures, as on 7 July 1954, when No 10001 gave up the ghost near Eastleigh. Meanwhile, in February 1954, Merchant Navy class Nos 35008, 35011 and 35012 were transferred to Bournemouth to provide greater power for duty 381 which encompassed the up working of the train. Notwithstanding, it is the West Country class that one principally associates with the up train over the years.

For the summer of 1957 the stock was repainted green complete with new BR crests. The formation remained almost the same: five coaches for Weymouth (corridor brake second 34157, corridor second 24169, corridor composites 15023, 15021 and corridor brake second 34158), two for Swanage (corridor composite 15022 and corridor brake second 34155) and the remainder for Bournemouth West (corridor brake second 34159, kitchen buffet tavern 7892 *The White Horse*, refreshment saloon 7838, corridor first 13003, open second 3914 and corridor brake second 34156). This formation afforded exactly 400 seats and continued to give a poor seat/weight ratio in excess of one ton. Overcrowding persisted and timekeeping of the up service could hardly be termed exemplary. Nonetheless the situation appears to have been accepted by management and, under protest, by the travelling public. As from 5 January 1959 a call at Wool on the down train was made because the 7.12pm train from Bournemouth Central following the *Royal Wessex*, which had given a connection, had been withdrawn.

It took until 1962 for the obvious remedy to be applied and then, from 2 April, the *Royal Wessex* reverted to the Bulleid stock that it had before being named. Lancing carriage works had just previously completed overhauling six-dining set No 291, three-set 864 and three-set 858 and these formed the Bournemouth West, Swanage and Weymouth portions respectively. This

On a summer Saturday in 1962 the *Royal Wessex* with its recently restored Bullied stock. No 34065 *Hurricane* sets forth purposefully through Pokesdown with the up service. The locomotive headboard, it will be noticed, includes the definite article in the title. *Author*

formation gave 514 seats for one coach less (because the second class compartments seated eight and there were extra compartments in the brake seconds than in the BR stock) and sent the seating capacity soaring by over twenty-five per cent and the seat/weight ratio down by about the same percentage to a more acceptable figure of threequarters of a ton. It was a solution which should have been adopted years previously. The Swanage portion was short-lived in its new guise because it ran for the last time on 8 September 1962, a connection at Wareham thereafter having to suffice for Corfe Castle and Swanage passengers.

Apart from this and the stop at Wool introduced at the beginning of 1959 the schedule remained virtually unchanged from July 1951 although it was about

1960 that the down *Royal Wessex* started calling at Hinton Admiral on Mondays, Tuesdays, Thursdays and Fridays to allow a passenger who was attending a course of lectures in London to alight and save twenty minutes and a change of trains at Brockenhurst that otherwise would be necessary. This was possible because of a right to stop one train (not booked to call) in each direction daily at Hinton Admiral which was the subject of an agreement made many years before between Sir George Meyrick and the LSWR. Eventually all these private rights on BR were extinguished by an Act of Parliament but at least the authorities could be thankful that it was the down train on the sharp down gradient which was involved rather than the up service.

A decline set in with the introduction of the 24-hour clock timetable on 14 June 1965 which took into account the allowances necessary for electrification works. The 16.35 was slowed to arrive at Bournemouth Central at 19.09 and Weymouth at 20.15. In the up direction the train left Weymouth at 07.32, Bournemouth Central at 08.33 and got into Waterloo at 11.02. The Bournemouth West portion of the train ran for the last time on 4 September 1965, because of the closure of that terminus (there was a road motor coach connection for another four weeks), after which the coaches were simply added or detached at Bournemouth Central. From 18 April 1966 a stop was inserted in the up timing at Southampton Airport. At the end of August that year an inspection saloon was attached for about ten days to the rear of the down train and season ticket holders were invited to travel in it to see the progress of the electrification works.

Diesel-electric traction reappeared after an absence of over eleven years (the units Nos 10000/1 and 10201–3 had left the Region in the Summer of 1955) from 3 October 1966 when six Brush type 4 machines, then numbered D1921–6, were allocated to Eastleigh and undertook various Bournemouth line duties, one of which involved the down working of the *Royal Wessex*. These locomotives proved to be none too reliable and in the spring of 1967, after the live rail had been energised, gave place to electro-diesel locomotives hauling non-traction electric stock on the down service. Steam still held sway on the up train although that was supposed to have type 3 diesel-electric traction on Saturdays commercing 17 June 1967 but by that time the locomotive duties were in such a state of flux that rosters were being made up almost on a day-to-day basis and certainly on that particular day the *Royal Wessex* was headed up to London by light Pacific No 34013.

Thus, by the time electrification was introduced, the train had become a mere shadow of its former self, lacking its regular coaching stock each way. Perhaps the final day, 8 July 1967, came as a happy release from the uncertainties of the preceding two years' purgatorial progress of modernisation. The train never captured the imagination nor attention in quite the same way as had the *Bournemouth Limited*, even though it had enjoyed a longer existence. Possibly, this was because the *Limited* became the sole non-stop train between London and Bournemouth to a fast timing whereas the *Royal Wessex* differed little from other services on the route and eventually was eclipsed by regular two-hour schedule trains to and from Bournemouth, and was simply a name applied to one of a number of broadly similar services.

The Bournemouth Belle

If the *Bournemouth Limited* could be said to be a train for Bournemouth residents, the *Bournemouth Belle* was the opposite: a train to convey people to Bournemouth and return them to London. The denizens of Bournemouth seldom travelled on the *Belle* for the perfectly good reason that the times of the train were not suitably orientated for them.

The train was introduced at what might have been thought to be an impropitious time, the early 1930s, with the slump and attendant unemployment which seemed incompatible with an all-Pullman train. Be that

Pre-second war *Bournemouth Belle* hauled by King Arthur class locomotive. No 773 *Sir Lavaine* heads a nine car train on the down service near Battledown. *L & GRP/David & Charles*

as it may, the Southern Railway directors launched the train in 1931 and persevered with it until it came to prove a sound proposition. Pullman cars had been seen on the route in London & South Western Railway days but, over the years before the World War I, had given place to conventional restaurant cars.

Initially the train was to operate for the period of the 1931 summer timetable to serve Southampton and Bournemouth daily and on weekdays Poole, Wareham, Dorchester and Weymouth in addition. On weekdays the train was divided at Bournemouth Central, the front portion of five coaches going forward and the remainder proceeding to Bournemouth West, which station was the terminus for the whole train on Sundays. This procedure had its counterpart in the up direction.

Ten Pullmans, first-class cars *Flora, Montana* and *Aurelia* and third-class cars Nos 40, 41, 60, 81, 82, 83 and 84, comprised the first train. Of these, the last four had been recently constructed and were specially allocated to the service. The accommodation offered was 314 seats, of which 74 were in the first-class vehicles. Supplementary fares, ranging from one shilling and sixpence third class Waterloo-Southampton for four shillings first class Waterloo-Weymouth, were payable for travel on the *Belle*. The train was timed to leave Waterloo at 10.30am and run to Southampton West (as Central station was then known) in eighty-nine minutes and, including a two minute halt there, arrive at Bournemouth Central two hours and nine minutes after leaving London. The weekday Weymouth portion left Bournemouth at 12.41pm and took sixty-four minutes to its final destination calling at Poole, Wareham (where a non-Pullman connection for Swanage was available) and Dorchester. In the opposite direction Weymouth was left at 4pm and with calls corresponding to the down service the train was booked to arrive at Bournemouth Central also in sixty-four minutes. The Bournemouth West portion, which started its journey at 4.50pm was attached to the rear and the combined train left at 5.10pm for a thirty-five minute run to Southampton West. Arrival at Waterloo was scheduled for 7.18pm, ninety minutes being the running time from Southampton.

Sunday, 5 July 1931 saw the inaugural train leave Waterloo behind King

Another version of the pre-war *Bournemouth Belle* with the same load, same duty number (55) and at the same location but with Lord Nelson class No 852 *Sir Walter Raleigh* doing the work. *L & GRP/David & Charles*

By the time this picture of the down *Bournemouth Belle* was taken at Fleet in July 1939 the Lord Nelson class was receiving large diameter chimneys and improved exhaust arrangements. In this instance the engine is No 851 *Sir Francis Drake*. *Author's Collection*

Arthur class No E780 *Sir Persant*, a late substitute for a Lord Nelson class engine. Unfortunately the journey to Bournemouth was delayed by excursion trains and a late arrival ensued. On the return run a dead stand outside Eastleigh imperiled a punctual trip but, by dint of a forty-six minute run in from Worting Junction, arrival was one minute early and set a performance example which was to be emulated by other drivers of the train through the years.

The popularity of the Sunday train was quickly established and encouraged the company to announce the continuation of the service for that day in the 1931/2 winter timetable. Publication of the summer timetable for 1932 revealed that eleven weeks of running the previous year had been sufficient to confirm that the service to Weymouth (which also embraced Poole, Wareham and Dorchester) could not attract enough patronage and, accordingly, Bournemouth was to be the western terminus of the *Belle*. Disappointed as the civic fathers of Weymouth might be (one had expressed his hope for the Sunday train also to serve Weymouth) it was obvious that a stay of just over two hours was not worth the comparatively long total journey time for the day tripper. This was also recognised in the case of Bournemouth because the departure time from Bournemouth West became 6.8pm with an arrival at Waterloo at 8.30pm.

This schedule continued until July 1934 for the winter Sundays only service as well as the daily summer trains of 1933. Then the evening departure was put back to 7.20pm from Bournemouth West to give a rather late arrival, at 9.40pm, at Waterloo. The weekday train of 1934 operated until 8 September and thereafter until the end of that month ran on Fridays and Saturdays. Difficulty was being encountered in determining the most suitable timing for the up train for with the publication of the 1935 summer timetable it was advertised to leave Bournemouth West at 4.35pm and terminate in London at 6.55pm; the Sunday up train, however, clung to its 6.8pm departure from the coast. The running of Friday and Saturday trips in September, introduced the previous year, was repeated in 1935.

With the worst of the slump in trade over the *Bournemouth Belle* became a daily train in winter, as well as in summer, as from New Year's Day 1936 and the timings of the previous summer were continued. Six months later the schedule was pared and the weekday up train offered a two-hour service from Bournemouth Central with an arrival at Waterloo at 6.45pm. The down train was now booked into Southampton Central (as West had become) at 11.57am and Bournemouth Central at 12.36pm. These timings were stabilised and the alteration, from July 1937, of the Sunday up train leaving Bournemouth West at 6.30pm and arriving at Waterloo at 8.45pm proved to be the sole amendment of any consequence thereafter until the service was suspended because of the war on 10 September 1939.

Motive power provided for the train in the 1931–39 period was either King Arthur or Lord Nelson class engines. Provided delays did not exceed five minutes, the former type could competently deal with the train and good performances were recorded from time to time with them. Towards the end of the period modifications had been made to the Lord Nelsons and these locomotives were to be seen regularly at the head of the *Belle* and came to set a surer standard of running with the train than had been evident in the earlier

Post-war but still in Southern Railway days the *Bournemouth Belle*, now complete with square engine headboard, runs down through Eastleigh on 5 July 1947 headed by then un-named Battle of Britain class No 21C158. *Author*

part of their career. The loading of the train varied according to the season and day of the week and the rake thus fluctuated from eight to a maximum of twelve cars although on occasion it had dropped to as low as six vehicles.

Resumption of the service after the war was not delayed, despite the difficulties of the times, and with the energetic planning typical of the Southern Railway after the war the *Bournemouth Belle* was recommissioned on 7 October 1946. Ten cars, some refurbished specially for the service, formed the train that day; the first-class cars were *Philomel*, *Lydia* and *Rosemary*, the third-class brakes Nos 94 and 95 and the other third-class cars being Nos 31, 32, 34, 35 and 60, affording 66 seats in the superior class out of a total of 302 for the whole train. The most noticeable difference in the first post-war *Belle* was the motive power – No 21C18 *British India Line* of the Merchant Navy class, which carried the train nameboard on its front buffer beam. The timings adopted (both weekdays and Sundays) were:

		pm			pm
Waterloo	dep	12.30	B'mouth West	dep	7.15
Southampton Central		1.57/59	B'mouth Central		7.23/25
B'mouth Central		2.35/37	Southampton Central		7.58/8.0
B'mouth West	arr	2.46	Waterloo	arr	9.25

Reintroduction of the service did much to alleviate the austerities of the period insofar as the passenger was concerned, for not only could he reserve a seat in advance but also enjoy the comforts of Pullman opulence and for two hours forget the rigours of such matters as bread rationing, for the very small outlay of three shillings (15p) above the cost of the ordinary fare. The railway authorities for their part were glad to be able to use Pullman vehicles so easing the strained rolling stock position caused by hostilities.

At the conclusion of the currency of the 1946/7 winter timetable the hours of the up train were revised to bring it into London at 6.45pm with the two-hour schedule from Bournemouth Central ruling. This finally severed the day excursion facility which had prevailed – certainly on Sundays – for much of the existence of the train, a two-hour sojourn hardly being attractive to the day tripper. In the summer of 1948 deceleration of the schedules took place, five minutes being added in each direction: minor variations occurred without restoration to the two-hour schedule (not even in 1957 when several other trains on the route were elevated to that basis) until the introduction of the 1963 summer timetable. This was comparatively short-lived, however, because of the universal decelerations of 1965 brought by pre-electrification works. Nonetheless, the 12.30pm departure from Waterloo and the (about) 4.30pm return from Bournemouth were maintained.

The cars making up the formation of the *Bournemouth Belle* were taken from the general pool of Pullman vehicles but each season the rake would be set out in the Appendix to the Carriage Working Notice. For example, as from 15 September 1952 the winter formation was noted as:

Coach Letter	Car	Description	Seats 1st	Seats 3rd	Weight Tons
M	95	3rd Brake	–	22	40
L	96	3rd Parlour	–	36	40
K	*Sorrento*	1st Kitchen	16	–	31*
J	*Sunbeam*	1st Parlour	26	–	40
H	*Hibernia*	1st Kitchen	20	–	40
G	*Glencoe*	1st Parlour	26	–	40
E	98	3rd Parlour	–	38	40
D	47	3rd Kitchen	–	35	44
C	7	3rd Kitchen	–	35	40
B	45	3rd Kitchen	–	35	44
A	94	3rd Brake	–	22	40
		Totals	88	223	439

*Eight-wheeled car (all others twelve-wheeled). Cars E and G were provided on Fridays, Saturdays and Sundays, also on other days when required.

In contrast the summer 1958 formation (by which time third class had been redesignated as second) was set out as:

Coach Letter	Car	Description	Seats 1st	Seats 2nd	Weight Tons
M	41	2nd Brake	–	29	39
L	98	2nd Parlour	–	38	40
K	*Rosalind*	1st Kitchen	16	–	43
J	*Sunbeam*	1st Parlour	26	–	40
H	*Hibernia*	1st Kitchen	20	–	40
G	*Topaz*	1st Parlour	24	–	31*
F	96	2nd Parlour	–	36	40
E	17	2nd Kitchen	–	32	44
D	45	2nd Kitchen	–	35	44
C	294	2nd Parlour	–	36	40
B	47	2nd Kitchen	–	35	44
A	95	2nd Brake	–	22	40
		Totals	86	263	485

*Eight-wheeled car (all others twelve-wheeled). Car F was provided when traffic demanded.

The authorities disliked empty Pullman car trains being brought into Waterloo with the locomotive's chimney next to the coaches and here, at Clapham Junction carriage sidings, Feltham shed's 4-6-2 tank No 30518 waits – correctly chimney-first – on a summer Saturday to head the *Bournemouth Belle* the few miles into Waterloo to receive its patrons. *Author*

During the last decade of the train's existence it became increasingly common to find one or both of the Pullman brakes missing, because of repair or withdrawal, and, to meet the luggage requirements of the service, it then became necessary to attach a bogie passenger brake van. At one period the Southern even managed to requisition a Western Region vehicle in chocolate and cream livery to 'do this duty and so avoid the sore thumb effect another colour would have had when contrasted with the Pullman livery.

Pre-electrification works caused a truncation of the service at Bournemouth Central from 6 September 1965, although passengers using Bournemouth

For a short time a few British Railways Britannia class 4-6-2s were allocated to the Southern Region. No 70009 *Alfred the Great* waits at Waterloo with the down *Bournemouth Belle* complete with the second type of headboard. *Robin Russell*

West station were conveyed by motor coaches (Pullman perhaps?) to and from the Central station up to and including 2 October, after which the West station was officially closed to passengers. This was but the harbinger of delays, re-routeings and cancellations of the service because of engineering works until the end came on Sunday 9 July 1967 when diesel-electric locomotive No D1924 hauled the last up *Bournemouth Belle* made up of nine Pullmans (including cars *Aquila*, *Lucille*, *Phyllis* and *Ursula*) and two brake vans, one from the Eastern and the other from the London Midland Region!

At first, not unlike pre-war days, the haulage of the train from 1946 had little to show in the way of variety, it being confined to the two types of Pacific locomotives of the Southern with the emphasis on the Merchant Navy class. Lord Nelsons did sometimes appear before Nine Elms shed got the light Pacifics. Diesel-electric traction was introduced in 1952 but, like the *Royal Wessex*, the flirtation with main line diesels Nos 10000/1 and 10201–3 turned out – to the relief of the admirers of Southern steam – to be commendably brief with steam reigning supreme from the summer of 1955. Diversity of locomotive types was achieved when the modified members of the Southern Region's Pacific classes appeared on the duty (the preserve of Nine Elms shed

With a good head of steam modified Merchant Navy class No 35022 *Holland America Line* climbs through Clapham cutting on 25 July 1964 on the down *Bournemouth Belle* with the train identification number (423) board chalked-up '12.30' taking the place of the customary nameboard. *P. H. Groom*

Like the *Atlantic Coast Express* the *Bournemouth Belle* towards the end had non-steam haulage. Brush Diesel-electric No D1926 climbs up through Micheldever with the train, which includes an ordinary bogie luggage van, on 2 July 1967. *S. C. Nash*

mostly, although there was a period when it fell to Bournemouth, and even Salisbury shed provided an engine on Sundays in the 1956 summer) and ex-LNER V2 class 2–6–2s deputised on one or two occasions in 1953 while the Merchant Navy class was temporarily withdrawn for special examination. Of British Railways standard classes to work the train, Britannia class 4–6–2 No 70009 had a spell when the Southern had a small allocation of the class in 1951 and, in an emergency, a Class 5 4–6–0 has stood in.

Diesel-electric traction re-appeared on summer Sundays in 1966, two type 3 machines (then numbered in the D65XX series) being used in multiple and this was followed in January 1967 by Brush type 4 locomotives rostered for the working. Availability of these machines was not good and frequent steam substitutions took place; indeed, in May the train had two (one in each direction) unmodified light Pacifics on one occasion, while one day in June unmodified No 34023 appeared instead of the rostered diesel locomotive in both directions. The plan to have the last run worked by steam was wrecked by the veto emanating from the general manager's office, which action not only caused alienation of goodwill but also revealed a sad lack of sense of occasion.

To see this train in pre-war days headed by an immaculate malachite green Lord Nelson glide into Bournemouth Central – or even weave over the crossover into the western end of the down platform to deposit its passengers a long way from the exit – was to be impressed by the sheer elegance of the train. Even under nationalisation much of this lived on but it was clearly incompatible with the egalitarian policy pursued by British Rail and the pull and push concept of the electric service and it was perhaps fitting that the *Bournemouth Belle* should pass into history at the same time as its faithful associate – Southern Steam.

CHAPTER FOUR

Outward Bound

Normandy Express	**Brittany Express**
Cunarder	**Statesman**
Union-Castle Express	**Holland-American**
South American	**Greek Line**
Arosa Line	**Springbok**
Sitmar Line	**Union-Castle Safmarine**

The completion of Southampton docks, begun in London & South Western Railway days and carried on energetically by the Southern Railway, was marked on 31 July 1950 with the formal opening of the Ocean Terminal in the Old Docks, a project which had been conceived before nationalisation. By 1950 Southampton had became the country's premier passenger port and the railway was servicing it by two types of train – the boat trains for its own traditional Channel Islands, Le Havre and St Malo routes and the Ocean Liner expresses for the passenger liners plying the seven seas.

Already a link had been established between the shipping lines and the railway in the names given to the Merchant Navy class of locomotives but no train having a title, as opposed to the general term of Continental Express, passed through the dock gates. However, with the introduction of a new vessel – SS *Normannia* – for the Le Havre service in 1952, someone had the inspiration to bestow a title on the connecting boat trains of *Normandy Express*. The Le Havre route had an all-year service, outwards on Monday, Wednesday and Friday with inward arrivals on Wednesday, Friday and Sunday; the connecting boat train left Waterloo at 9pm and arrived back a minute or two after the same hour of the morning. The same departure served the Channel Islands service and since these islands had once formed part of Normandy there was no inconsistency in the naming but enthusiasm for the title did run riot when the 6.35pm departure from Waterloo for the St Malo service also acquired the designation because that port was part of, as well as the gateway to, Brittany. Although the maiden voyage of SS *Normannia* was made on Monday 3 March 1952 and at the same time Pullman cars were introduced into the boat train the title *Normandy Express* does not appear to

The *Brittany Express* gallops past Surbiton on the down through line en route for Southampton Docks worked by King Arthur class 4-6-0 No 30744 *Maid of Astolat* on 5 August 1955. *J. N. Faulkner*

have come into use until the start of the summer timetable on 30 June.

A couple of years passed before it was decided to give the St Malo service the title *Brittany Express*. Whereas the *Normandy Express* could lay claim to being a service for the businessman wanting to go to Rouen or as an alternative to the *Night Ferry* service to and from Paris, this was a summer-only service running in high season (end June to end September) on Monday, Wednesday and Friday outward with arrivals on Wednesday, Friday and Sunday at Waterloo at 9.34am for a quality clientele holidaying in the resorts west of St Malo. The first of the St Malo sailings of SS *Falaise* scheduled for 1954 was on Tuesday 18 May, repeated each Tuesday for a month until the three per week sailings started on 21 June: presumably the inaugural date for the *Brittany*

Express should have been 18 May. However the first reference to the title that can be traced was in a special traffic notice which had the 6.35pm from Waterloo on 8 June indicated as being allocated the title.

Meanwhile some of the Ocean Liner expresses had been receiving titles. First of these was the *Cunarder* applied to the principal first class (often, but not necessarily, all Pullman stock) boat train run in connection with RMS *Queen Mary* and RMS *Queen Elizabeth* sailings. For the inaugural trip, the 7.5pm from Waterloo on 2 July 1952, No 35004 *Cunard White Star* hauled the train. Hard on the heels of the *Cunarder* came the all-Pullman *Statesman* on 8 July for the maiden voyage of SS *United States*; because No 35012 *United States Lines* was under repair at the time in Eastleigh works West Country class No 34007 hauled the train rather than a Merchant Navy type carrying the name of a rival line. It was at this time that the Blue Riband of the North Atlantic was to pass from Cunard to the United States Lines.

Not unnaturally there was no denying other flags using Southampton the prestige of a titled train and foremost among these was the Union-Castle Line with its regular 4 o'clock Thursday afternoon sailing to South Africa. So in the summer of 1953 there appeared the *Union-Castle Express*, the *Holland American* and, for Royal Mail Lines, the *South American* first noted on 9 October. *Greek Line* and *Arosa Line* followed in 1954 and 1955 respectively. In 1957 the train for the weekly South African mail sailing of Union-Castle was allocated the name of *Springbok* but the *Union-Castle Express* continued to be seen from time to time, possibly on other sailings. A latecomer to the range of titles was *Sitmar Line* which appeared in 1960 in connection with the sailings of SS *Fairsea*. At a late date a headboard with *Union-Castle Safmarine* appeared as well as some for P&O Orient Lines cruises with just the ship's name, such as *Canberra* or *Oriana* appearing above the line's title but these last would not appear to be train titles as such.

Locomotive smokebox headboards and carriage roofboards were provided for the trains and were complemented at Waterloo by appropriate indicator boards at the platform entrance. These various boards were usually finished in the house colours or carried a motif or insignia of the line concerned. Roofboards in many cases included the ship's name; for the *Cunarder* these had *Queen Mary* one side and *Queen Elizabeth* on the other face to be used as appropriate.

There the similarity between the trains for the Channel services and the Ocean Liner expresses ended, although it is conceded that the *Brittany Express* did share the feature of a non-stop run between London and the docks. The Ocean Liner trains were leisurely affairs carrying not only passengers but also friends and relatives to wave or weep farewells at the dockside, where the period between arrival of the trains and the departure of the ship could be several hours. The cross-channel sailings were conducted on a much more brisk basis because the voyage was in hours rather than days. The Le Havre service leaving Waterloo at 9pm called at Basingstoke and Winchester City and in the up direction at Eastleigh, Shawford and Micheldever as well, both trains being available to ordinary passengers; in the winter months from 1955 onwards the outward sailing was advanced by an hour and accordingly coaches were attached to the regular 7.30pm Bournemouth service from Waterloo and detached at Southampton Central to be worked round to the docks as a separate train.

A distinction was also made in the coaching stock. For several years there were five sets, 350 to 354, each of eight coaches, allocated for working Ocean Liner Boat Trains (the term 'boat' is peculiar to the railway authorities for a seafarer will say boats were what were slipped from their davits when a ship was sinking!) and four sets known as 10 Pullman Buffet Sets for Waterloo-Southampton Docks workings of the cross-channel traffic, augmented as necessary with additional vehicles in either case; whereas the 10 Pullman sets worked to pre-determined rosters the Ocean Liner sets would be diagramed as required.

As an illustration of working in the heyday of liner traffic Thursday 23 June 1955 will serve. On that particular day the conditional if required path of 8.15am from Waterloo to Southampton New Docks was taken by train B56 named *Greek Line* consisting of ten vehicles (set 350 augmented to two brake composites, five open thirds, one first, one Pullman and a corridor van) for TSS *Columbia*. Then came un-titled trains from Waterloo at 9.15am, 9.21am and 10.2am formed of sets 351, 352 and 354 respectively, all strengthened with additional stock, the middle one (B60) being for RMMV *Arundel Castle* and the others (B57 and B58) for RMS *Queen Elizabeth*. At 10.20am the *Union-Castle Express* (train B61) left for the New Docks, being the main train for the 4 o'clock sailing of *Arundel Castle* and made up of seven vehicles (two brake firsts, one open third, two firsts, one Pullman and a corridor van) to be followed 15 minutes later by train B59, the *Cunarder*, consisting of ten Pullmans, a first and a corridor van bound for the *Queen Elizabeth* at the Ocean Terminal in the Old Docks. In the afternoon at 2.20pm the *South American* set out, consisting of two brake firsts, three open thirds, three Pullmans, three firsts and a corridor van, for the Old Docks with passengers for RMS *Andes* as train B62.

The engine workings for the two types of train were also in contrast. With the exception of the Thursday Union-Castle trains from Waterloo (which were Nine Elms duties for light Pacifics) the engine workings for the ocean liner

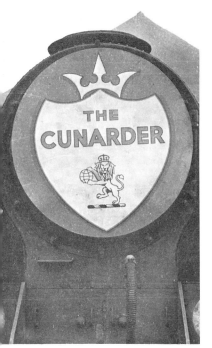

When the *Cunarder* and *Statesman* were inaugurated large circular locomotive smokebox type headboards were used. During 1953 the oblong type of board, easily adjustable to a variety of locomotive classes by utilising smokebox door lampirons, became the standard for Ocean Liner expresses in common with the majority of Southern Region titled trains. A selection of these painted boards shows a pleasant diversity of styles. *Holland American, Robin Russell,* all others *L. Elsey*

trains were special duties usually powered by Eastleigh-based Lord Nelson class locomotives up to London. These engines would then await a balancing turn on a similar train back. The Merchant Navy class were kept off these trains except for special occasions because the greater power they could provide was not necessary and it saved embarrassments such as *Elders Fyffes*, which would be equated with banana boats, heading the *Cunarder*. *Lord Anson* or *Sir John Hawkins* were much more acceptable! The exception to this was when, because of a tug strike at Southampton, the *Cunarder* ran from Plymouth on 20 April 1953 and No 35004 *Cunard White Star* worked the train of 14 vehicles including 10 Pullmans, between Exeter and Salisbury.

Of the regular timetabled trains the 6.35pm from Waterloo to Southampton Old Docks and the 7.50am up (*Brittany Express*) formed the major part of Eastleigh shed's duty 256, at first a King Arthur class engine and then, from 1956 a Lord Nelson job; the 7.3am from the Docks (Le Havre service) was duty 252 booked for an Eastleigh Lord Nelson (West Country in 1955); the 9pm from Waterloo started as a Nine Elms duty (31) for a Lord Nelson then, in the summer of 1954, formed part of Dorchester duty 426 when some Lord Nelsons were shedded there, then was incorporated in Bournemouth's duty 395 and from the winter of 1957 reverted to Nine Elms having become a West Country class booking in 1956.

Liner traffic reached its peak at Southampton in the mid 1950s. During the 24-hour period ending 16 September 1955 thirteen liners entered or left the docks and this involved nine down special trains and no fewer than eighteen up, two of which had to be diverted to Victoria because of congestion at Waterloo, a ploy which was used subsequently at times of pressure. Although there was a move in 1956 to discontinue the Le Havre service BR was prevailed upon not to break the tradition of over a century. The port continued for a year or two to be used intensively but the zenith had passed and soon the motor car and the aeroplane would together alter the whole aspect of the traffic. The car started to be used increasingly as the family holiday carrier on the one hand and on the other jet aircraft were to capture the North Atlantic and other passenger traffic. In 1957 one million trans-Atlantic passengers were carried by sea and air alike but so dramatic was the decline that in 1962 the figure for sea had fallen to 42,000 – less than five per cent of that five years previously. By 1968 there was no winter ocean service at all to the USA.

So, in less than a decade, the Southampton passenger traffic had plummeted. The emphasis, so far as liners were concerned, had shifted from trans-Atlantic and far haul sailings to cruise traffic and to car carriers elsewhere.

Down the years there had been various alterations to the continental services. The seasonal *Brittany Express* started with first and third class Pullman accommodation but in 1955 it had an unclassed refreshment car and in 1956 that became a buffet car which then lasted throughout the train's career. From 17 June 1956 the departure time from Southampton Docks was put back to 8.5am and the arrival at Waterloo was due at 9.55am. In 1964 the alternative Wednesday sailings went from Weymouth and so for 3 and 17 June, 1, 15 and 29 July, 12 and 26 August and 9 and 23 September the *Brittany Express* could be found going both up and down on those dates via Poole. It was retimed to leave Waterloo at 9.15pm, call at Basingstoke, Southampton Central and Bournemouth Central and arrive at Weymouth Quay at 12.50am. In the up direction it left Weymouth at 6am making the same calls plus one at Poole and arriving at its normal time of 9.55am at Waterloo. The long-standing statutory stop at Poole had by this time been rescinded which explains the absence of a call there in the down direction. The final outward journey was on 25 September 1964 and the last inward working two days later both via Southampton (the train's appearance in the 1965 timetable arose from withdrawal agreement being given after the book had gone to press).

The *Normandy Express* had a rather more complicated life. When it started, the down service appeared in the general public timetable as an ordinary train – untitled – and it ran thus, in conjunction with the Channel Islands service, until 3 October 1955 when, because of time difference between France (which used Central European time) and the United Kingdom it was attached to the rear of the ordinary 7.30pm Bournemouth train and detached at Southampton Central from where it was worked via the curve at Northam to the Old Docks by a Q or 700 class 0–6–0 to make the earlier ship connection. This procedure held until 9 April 1956 and was repeated every winter thereafter. From 18 May 1956 the 9pm train was deleted from the general public timetable and at the same time, in company with the *Brittany Express*, received a buffet car to serve for refreshment purposes but that did not last long for it was taken out of the train for the 1959 summer. From 11 April 1960 the Waterloo departure was altered to 9.15pm and then to 9.5pm from 12 June 1961. In the up direction the buffet car remained in the formation until the summer of 1961 after which it was omitted for the summer seasons but reappeared each winter.

The inward service appeared in the general timetable starting at 7.22am from Eastleigh calling all stations to Basingstoke and then Waterloo, although for Sundays it was shown leaving the Docks at 7.3am and advertised a refreshment car service. If the ships were late on weekdays, Eastleigh had to provide a covering train and locomotive and this explains why a refreshment car was not advertised in the general timetable. However, from the summer of 1954 the Docks departure did enter the timetable and then each winter from

Prominent among locomotive headboards in the depths of Nine Elms shed in January 1967 is that for *Union-Castle Safmarine*, with rather-worse-for-wear examples of *Cunarder* and *Statesman*, as well as those used for sailings of the *Canberra* and *Oriana*. Shipping lines not having titled trians did nonetheless have distinctive carriage boards, such as *British India Co's Boat Train* with flags at each end and the whole rendered in proper house colours. *B. I. Fletcher*

1954/5 on Sundays the train also called all stations Basingstoke to Woking giving a 9.13am arrival at Waterloo. On Sundays the Shawford and Micheldever stops were not made. For the winter of 1963/4 the service was reduced to Monday and Thursday outward with arrivals at Waterloo on Wednesday and Saturday with the last outward run being made on Friday, 8 May 1964 and the final, inward, trip on Sunday 10 May 1964. Both SS *Normannia* and SS *Falaise* were converted to vehicle ferries being withdrawn in September 1963 for that purpose.

By 1964 the ocean liner trains had fallen on evil times; Pullman cars had been withdrawn, engine headboards forgotten, the coaches were dirty and punctuality was poor but, despite all this, premium fares were still charged, all of which caused discontent within shipping circles. The regular Thursday sailing to South Africa finished on 8 July 1965 and by the end of 1968 only the mail service remained. It would be convenient to conclude that the 1967 electrification saw the end of the named trains to and from Southampton Docks; perhaps it did so far as engine headboards and carriage roofboards were concerned but a special traffic notice as late as July 1971 did indicate one train as the *Springbok* and that seems to have gone during the late summer/early autumn of that year even though the ships continued on that route until September/October 1977 when they succumbed to air competition.

Like old soldiers the ocean liner express titles, with their trains, simply faded away. None, of course, appeared in the public timetables nor did the Brittany and Normandy names, the more strangely because the timings of those trains were clearly indicated in the continental section and one would have expected uniform treatment with the other named boat trains of the railway. Finally, in April 1983, the Ocean Terminal station was demolished. So the last vestige of travel glamour was swept away – are we better off with the car seat belts or suffering from jet-lag?

CHAPTER FIVE

To Sussex-By-The-Sea

Brighton Limited

Unlike some railway companies the London, Brighton & South Coast Railway was not renowned for its advanced passenger rolling stock for even by grouping the number of main-line corridor coaches it owned could be counted on the fingers of one hand. For the superior class passenger however it did provide a luxury not often seen elsewhere – Pullman cars. At first it relied on such cars to provide not refreshment but comfort and would insert single cars in various services: these American built vehicles, with their huge clerestories, looked almost comically ponderous amid a train of low roofed LBSCR stock but, no matter, they did prove sufficiently popular to proliferate on the principal routes.

The first Pullman car arrived on the LBSCR in 1875 and by 1881 the first all-Pullman train was inaugurated with day cars *Maud, Louise, Victoria* and *Beatrice*. This started the weekday service on Monday 5 December running in the times of previously first class accommodation trains from London (Victoria) to Brighton at 10am (calling at Clapham Junction and Preston Park) and 3.50pm (non-stop in 1¼ hours) and returning from Brighton at 1.20pm (calling at Grosvenor Road) and 5.45pm with stops at East Croydon, Clapham Junction and Grosvenor Road. On Sundays, from 11 December 1881, there was a non-stop down train from Victoria at 12.30pm, again in 1¼ hours, and the return was made at 9.30pm with a halt at Grosvenor Road (outside Victoria) for ticket inspection.

These trains continued with occasional variations and, in the case of the Sunday service, breaks (there was, for example, only weekdays running during 1883) for a long time and for this purpose we pick up with them again in 1898 by which time there had been stock changes (in 1888 when three cars and a couple of six wheel vans, one each end, known as 'Pullman Pups' were introduced) and the weekdays 10am had been put back five minutes throughout, the up 1.20pm had stops inserted at East Croydon and Clapham Junction and both up trains had dispensed with the Grosvenor Road halt. On Sundays the London departure was 10.45am and the return 5pm with calls

90

The down *Southern Belle*, with LBSCR Atlantic No 39, on the Quarry Line, its normal route, crossing the line serving Redhill at Star Bridge. *Lens of Sutton*

each way at East Croydon and Clapham Junction. The trains were indicated as being either Pullman Limited Express or Pullman Limited Fast.

Timetable alterations were made for October 1898. The Sunday trains were scheduled non-stop between London and Brighton in an hour leaving at 11am and returning at 9pm and on weekdays the 3.50pm service was accelerated to arrive at Brighton at 5pm and the 1.20pm and 5.45pm up were both made non-stop in 1¼ hours. There was no alteration in the timetables of the train description, the note Pullman Limited Express remaining. The inaugural Sunday train on 2 October was made up of cars *Victoria, Beatrice, Princess of Wales, Duchess of York* and *Her Majesty* with a baggage car each end and was hauled by B2 class 4–4–0 No 206 *Smeaton*. It is on record that a one minute early arrival was made at Brighton and all seats were taken on this, the first 60-minute express to Brighton. But it had to wait until 1 January 1899 for the title *Brighton Limited* to appear in the timetables and the facility of a twelve shilling day return ticket to be advertised.

Of all the titled trains encompassed within this volume the *Brighton Limited* is probably the least complicated in its timetable. It ran on Sundays from October to June each year leaving Victoria at 11am and Brighton at 9pm, except in June when departure from Brighton was at 10pm, all journeys being run in the hour. During July, August and September each year there were trains running a few minutes later which did include Pullmans but not exclusively. So it was a nine-months-a-year train in contrast to the weekday all-Pullman services which operated throughout the year but were never titled. It restarted as usual on the first Sunday in October 1908 and then made its final run as the *Brighton Limited* on 25 October 1908.

Southern Belle

'The King is dead – Long live the Queen!' best describes the metamorphosis of the *Brighton Limited* to the *Southern Belle*. After a trial run with special guests on 31 October, the new *Southern Belle* train entered service on 1 November 1908, being hauled on its inaugural journey by 4–4–2 No 39. The new seven car first class only Pullman train consisted of four parlour cars (*Belgravia, Bessborough, Cleopatra, Princess Helen*) one buffet (*Grosvenor*) and two brake

Another picture of the *Southern Belle* in LBSCR days with B4 class 4-4-0 No 46 *Prince of Wales* hauling the train of 1908 Pullmans south of Coulsdon towards the coast. *Author's collection*

parlour smoking cars (*Alberta* and *Verona*) and was described as being 'exquisitely upholstered, lighted by electricity' – the 1889 train had also had electric lighting – 'comfortably warmed and ventilated and fitted with all the latest improvements.' The cars, built by Metropolitan Amalgamated Railway Carriage & Wagon Company Ltd at Lancaster and fitted out by W.S. Laycock Ltd of Millhouses, Sheffield, were the first of their line to have elliptical, rather than clerestory, roofs and formed the first all-Pullman car train to be constructed in England. Of Edwardian opulence all these cars were twelve-wheelers and became renowned on the service with their beautiful mahogany panelling inlaid with satinwood, the fine soft coloured carpeting, damask silk blinds and settees in green morocco. The French renaissance style was employed for the 31 seat parlour smoking cars, the Adams style for the 33 seat parlour cars *Bessborough* and *Princess Helen* and the 25 seat buffet car with the other two 33 seat parlour cars being decorated in the style of Pergolesi. Total seating accommodation was 219 and there was the refinement – for railway travel – of separate toilets for the sexes. Small wonder this train was variously described as a 'Chain of Vestibuled Luxury', or 'The Most Luxurious Train in the World'.

The tradition of restricting the title to the Sunday service was abandoned and the first daily all-Pullman train in the country was introduced. Initially the timings were:

		am	
London (Victoria)	dep	11.0	
Brighton	arr	12.0	
		SuX	SuO
		pm	pm
Brighton	dep	5.45	9.0
London (Victoria)	arr	6.45	10.0

From 6 December 1908 the Sunday services were doubled each way with departures from Victoria at 11am and 6.30pm, the return trips being made at 5pm and 9pm, in every case to a 60 minute schedule. From 6 June 1909 the 9pm train was altered to 9.30pm. Popularity of the train grew and starting in June 1910 there was an additional pair of services on Mondays to Fridays, at 12.20pm from Brighton and 3.10pm from Victoria; these were extended to include Saturdays in the following October. Two more twelve wheel cars,

As the years passed the *Southern Belle* had various types of locomotives entrusted to haul it; here, in early Southern Railway days, LBSCR J 4-6-2 class tank No 325 passes milepost 19 on the Quarry line, just south of Quarry tunnel, with the down service. *Lens of Sutton*

parlour *Vivienne* having 28 seats and buffet *Myrtle* (23 seats), were built by Cravens and furnished by Laycocks and added to the fleet of cars in 1911.

The all-Pullman nature of the train was rudely shattered in 1913 when, from 1 January, the 12.20pm up and 3.10pm down trains ran with third class ordinary carriages. Matters continued thus until the outbreak of war in 1914 and the withdrawal of all Pullman services for September. Understandably, Bradshaw's timetable suffered a whole crop of omissions or errors in the early months of the war due to the sheer number of alterations that had to be made but what appears to have happened was that in October the *Southern Belle* reverted to the timetable in force in August apart from the curious feature of the Sunday 6.30pm operating without any Pullman cars. This is thought to have been an error of omission for by December they were once more advertised. However, by March 1915 the 11am and 5.45pm weekday trips were also conveying ordinary third class passengers and from 1 October all the weekday runs offered first and third class Pullman and ordinary third class accommodation. Sundays remained first class Pullman only.

More adjustments were indicated in Bradshaw during 1916: for January and February the Sunday 6.30pm and 9.30pm trains were omitted and on weekdays in February the ordinary third class accommodation was dropped but all returned in March and continued for the rest of the year and then entirely disappeared. In October 1917 there was an unnamed first class Pullman car train on Sundays from Victoria at 11am (arrive Brighton 12.5pm) returning at 5pm in 65 minutes which lasted for five months.

Nothing more happened until March 1919 when the *Southern Belle* suddenly returned for Sundays – first class Pullman only as usual – with an 11 o'clock departure from Victoria (arrive Brighton 12.8pm) and a return from Brighton in 70 minutes at 5pm. In May the weekday service was reinstated for first and third Pullman and ordinary third class; from Victoria at 11am and back from Brighton pretty smartly at 1.20pm, the schedules being 68 and 70 minutes respectively. In February 1920 the Sunday service was increased by a return evening working at 6.30pm from London and 9.30pm back both in 78 minutes. November 1920 saw further improvements with all services being speeded up to one hour and the addition of weekday trains at 3.10pm from Victoria and 5.45pm from Brighton.

During the coal strike in the spring of 1921 all the services were suspended.

River class 2-6-4 tank No.A790 *River Avon* near Mertsham with the down *Southern Belle* circa 1926. *Author's collection*

The up *Southern Belle* near Patcham in 1931 with U class 2-6-0 No A633 at the head. *Lens of Sutton*

From 1 December 1921 the *Belle* resumed its all-Pullman nature after the ordinary third class carriages on weekdays were cut out. No further alterations took place until 14 July 1924 when the weekday schedules were recast:

		Weekdays		Sundays	
		am	pm	am	pm
London (Victoria)	dep	11.5	3.5	11.0	6.30
Brighton	arr	12.5	4.5	12.0	7.30
		pm	pm	pm	pm
Brighton	dep	1.35	5.35	5.0	9.30
London (Victoria)	arr	2.35	6.35	6.0	10.30

First class Pullmans only remained the order of the day for Sunday with both classes of Pullman available on weekdays.

Various adjustments to the Sunday timings occured. From 17 June 1928 the down evening service was altered to a 7.5pm departure; starting on 7 July 1929 the 11am from Victoria was altered to 11.5am and the 9.30pm return to 10pm; finally, in October 1932, the 7.5pm and 10pm services were dispensed with.

Announcement of electrification of the London-Brighton route preceeded the coming-of-age celebrations for the *Belle* on Friday 1 November 1929 by a few weeks. The Southern Railway sought to make the most of the twenty-first birthday celebrations and decked out the train engine King Arthur class No E 793 *Sir Ontzlake* with a smokebox headboard and a beflagged buffer beam and arranged for the fireman on the inaugural run, W. Coughtray, to be the driver for the 11.5am trip from Victoria as well as other members – driver, guard and conductors – of the first day to be on one of the anniversary trips. A small commemorative brochure was issued jointly by the Pullman Car Company and Southern Railway which included a silhouette of a King Arthur type locomotive with an eight-wheel tender (artist's licence – though they did have eight-wheel tenders on the Western ex LSWR routes) hauling eleven 12-wheel Pullmans.

Until the introduction of ordinary third class carriages into the train the *Southern Belle* had presented a uniform appearance but even with the restoration of the all-Pullman train after the war it lost something of its unique Edwardian charm. With the train loading up to ten or more cars at times and third class Pullmans having to be inserted, vehicles other than the 1908 and 1911 cars appeared. These included the American cars as well as new (1925) cars *Fingall*, *Octavia*, *Plato*, *Rainbow* and *Rosamund* and gave a rather cosmopolitan air to the *Belle*.

Motive power was seldom lacking in interest. In LBSCR days there were the Atlantics, magnificient in their umber livery which went so well with the cars,

Steam haulage of the *Southern Belle* climaxed in the King Arthur class. The 5.35pm service leaves Brighton on 30 April 1932 with No 767 *Sir Valence* laying a smokescreen over the town. H. C. *Casserley*

the smaller B4 class 4–4–0s, the I3 4–4–2 tanks and – going up the scale – the two J class 4–6–2 tanks to the ultimate in the huge L class Baltic tanks. In Southern Railway times the 4–6–4 tanks carried on but were assisted by the River class 2–6–4 tanks, the U class 2–6–0s and, lastly, by some of those members of the King Arthur class fitted with six-wheel tenders (those of the class with eight-wheel tenders were unacceptable to the Civil Engineer although the turntables at Victoria and Brighton could accommodate them).

Steam bowed out in style. For the last down run Baltic tank No 2333 *Remembrance* was imaginatively booked to haul a heterogeneous eight-car train consisting of first class cars *Myrtle* and *Vivienne*, third class American clerestory cars 9 and 18, third class cars 17, 26 and 35 and third class brake car 25. It ran before time all the way on this final day of 1932 and although it arrived at Brighton 1¼ minutes early, if it had not been for signal checks it would have got down in 55 minutes – a schedule time 25 years in the future!

For electrification the order for new rolling stock included three five-coach all-Pullman multiple-units to continue the *Southern Belle* service. These introduced the first motor Pullman cars in the world which were also the heaviest coaches, at 62 tons each, to run on British metals. The three units, because the other new units for the Brighton line express service were made up of six coaches, had the highest power/weight ratio of all those constructed at the time, with four motors each rated at 225 horsepower per motor coach, a total of 1800hp per unit or equal to 360hp per car of the unit. The Metropolitan-Cammell Carriage & Wagon Company built the Pullmans each of which were finished in the traditional umber and cream externally and inlaid panelling of individual design internally. Pressure ventilation equipment was provided to circulate the air in the cars; the kitchens were, as would be expected, all-electric but apart from the driving ends of the motor coaches, which were embellished with the Pullman coat-of-arms below the route number indicator, there was not a lot to distinguish between these and steam hauled cars constructed at about the same time. The total seating capacity of each unit was 192 of which 40 was in the first class cars. The total tare weight of each five car unit was 249 tons. The composition of the units was:

Unit 2051   Motor brake third 88, kitchen firsts *Hazel* and *Doris*, parlour third 86 and motor brake third 89

Unit 2052   Motor brake third 90, kitchen firsts *Audrey* and *Vera*, parlour third 87 and motor brake third 91

Unit 2053   Motor brake third 92, kitchen firsts *Gwen* and *Mona*, parlour third 85 and motor brake third 93

The cars, of steel construction, were 68ft 8¾in long over buffers and were the longest of their type to have been built in the country at the time. The weight of the parlour (56 seats) and kitchen cars was 56 and 43 tons respectively and the formation of the stock meant that third class seats were made available on Sundays for the first time, thus shattering the Sabbath first class exclusiveness. A difficulty arose when units were coupled together because the motor coaches did not have corridor connections at the driving ends and, consequently, two conductors had to travel for the one service.

Coincident with the introduction of electrification and this stock on New Year's Day 1933 the *Southern Belle* service was increased to three trips daily in each direction at 11am, 3pm (except Sundays) and 7pm from Victoria, returning at 1.25pm (not Sundays), 5.25pm and 9.25pm all on a public schedule of one hour although the working timetable was one of 58min in the down direction with the aim of attaining a high standard of punctuality. The majority of journeys were made with two units, that is a total of ten cars; never was there a fifteen car train, although one unit of five cars was the usual formation when loadings were not heavy such as early afternoon up and mid-afternoon down services mid-week (or in latter days the late night down trip) this being sufficient to accommodate the patrons presenting themselves. The Southern Railway did not bother going into detail about the *Southern Belle* now being the first all-electric all-Pullman service in the world or anything of a technical nature but advertised it very simply as 'The finest Train in Britain!'

Brighton Belle

On Friday, 29 June 1934 the *Southern Belle* became the *Brighton Belle*. This date, of course, did not coincide with the introduction of a new timetable but was chosen because the world's largest covered sea-water swimming pool was being opened at Brighton that day and the opportunity was taken to link the

In British Rail days the old Pullman livery was swept aside, the car names and numbers removed externally but the world's only all-Pullman electric multiple-units could not be mistaken for anything but the *Brighton Belle*. Unit No 3052 leads the 14.00 service from Victoria past South Croydon in 1971. *Author*

two ceremonies. The 11am train from Victoria arrived at Brighton complete with a headboard bearing the town's coat of arms and the new title and the Mayor re-named the train at the station before the company adjourned to the swimming pool for the proceedings there.

The three trains each way on weekdays (11am, 3pm and 7pm from Victoria and 1.25pm, 5.25pm and 9.25pm from Brighton) continued without alteration as did the two each way on Sundays and apart from the three units being renumbered from 2051, 2052 and 2053 to 3051, 3052 and 3053 in 1937, there were no alterations until the outbreak of war in September 1939. Then, in company with all the other titled trains, the name was dropped. The units were then used minus carriage roofboards coupled to six-coach units on services to and from Brighton until May 1942 when all Pullman cars were withdrawn. Unit 3052 had been damaged by bombing while standing in No 17 platform at Victoria at about 10.30pm on 9 October 1940 during an air raid and was immediately taken out of service.

Had not this unit required extensive repair after this damage it is likely that the *Brighton Belle* would have been reinstated from 6 May 1946. As it was Pullman facilities were available from that date in the pre-war *Belle* timings and from 7 October these services usually included one of the two available 5BEL units. The all-Pullman nature of the train was restored on 6 October 1947 when the proud name re-appeared in the timetable to the almost identical timings as pre-war except that on Sundays the service was 11am from Victoria and 5.25pm return. The difficulties of the period was reflected in the menu but the Pullman Car Company put a good face on matters, not least of all by adding dignity to one otherwise plebeian dish by describing it as 'baked beans *upon* toast'. The supplementary charges were now three shillings for first class and half that for third class.

With the summer timetable of 1948 the position reverted exactly to pre-war, the 7pm from Victoria and 9.25pm from Brighton Sunday trips being restored. For 26 September 1949 the last up service was advanced one hour to leave Brighton at 8.25pm both weekdays and Sundays and, except for the summers of 1950, 1951 and 1952 when the departure was back to 9.25pm, this became the normal timing.

There followed a long period without any alterations until the autumn of 1963 when, from 9 September, two extra trips were inserted in the timetable – 9.40am daily from Brighton and 11pm weekdays from Victoria. The train forming the late evening service was placed in the platform at 10pm each night to allow meals to be taken at leisure. The 9.40am departure did not have to wait long before it was slotted into a 9.25am departure (from 15 June 1964). These extra workings had, incidentally, altered the overnight stabling of the units from London to Brighton. The long standing tradition of non-stop running was broken from 4 November 1964 when the 11pm service from London called at Haywards Heath at 11.44pm and arrived in Brighton at two minutes past midnight.

Withdrawal in the mid-1960s of the sister stock built for the Brighton main line electrification at the same time as the 5BEL units was a reminder of advancing years. The wartime break and the less intensive use of the stock, as compared with the ordinary units, clearly allowed some grace in this matter but the vintage of the train was emphasised when compared with new standard CEP and VEP units in which company it now sped the line, especially as the umber and cream seemed to be a greater contrast to the rail blue.

Recasting of the timetables to take effect from 10 July 1967 brought with it an acceleration of the Brighton non-stops to 55 minutes and as the supplementary fare all-Pullman service could hardly be seen to lag behind, the old dowager *Brighton Belle* had to lift her skirts and follow the trend. So the public timetables which now sported 24 hour times for the service became:

			SuX	SX	SO	SuX
Victoria	dep	11.00	15.00	19.00	19.00	23.00
Haywards Heath	arr	—	—	—	—	23.42
Brighton	arr	11.55	15.55	19.56	19.55	23.58
	SO	SSuX	SuO	SuX		
Brighton dep	9.20	9.25	9.45	13.45	17.45	20.45
Victoria arr	10.18	10.24	10.40	14.40	18.40	21.40

From 6 May 1968 the 13.45 up and 15.00 down services were put forward by one hour thus breaking the four-hour interval sequence. The Sundays 22.00 departure from Victoria (due Brighton at 22.55) became a *Brighton Belle* service as from 12 October 1969 and with the introduction of the new timetable on 4 May 1970 came some niggling alterations. One minute was added to the journey time for the 11.00 and 14.00 departures from Victoria and the 12.45, 17.45 and 20.45 departures from Brighton and the 9.20 Saturdays from Brighton ran from mid-June to early September (in 1970 but not in 1971) but at other times was retimed to leave at 9.45 arriving at Victoria at 10.41. At the same time the timetable columns dropped the title in favour of Pullman Limited Train, the sole reference anywhere to *Brighton Belle* being in a footnote under seat reservations. This came as a straw in the wind. Because the BEL units were limited to 75mph, compared with the top speed of 90mph by the newer trains, coupled with a desire to avoid the worst effects of rough riding the train had been given one minute longer for the journey than the

other hourly non-stops and it was clear that if the premium service was to continue then new stock would have to be provided. Despite this the supplements were raised to 30p for first and 20p for second class in 1971.

Meanwhile the units had a facelift. In the six months between December 1968 and May 1969 all three were decked out in BR blue and grey and lost their names and numbers on the waist panels these being replaced by the train title. A BR logo appeared also at waist level at the outer ends by the driver's cab doors balanced at the inner end by the car number; the intermediate cars had their numbers similarly at each end and in the case of the first class cars the class numeral also. All the car numbers were increased by 200, the first class cars being numbered 279 (*Hazel*), 280 (*Audrey*), 281 (*Gwen*), 282 (*Doris*), 283

Vale! *Author's collection*

(*Mona*) and 284 (*Vera*). The yellow ends to the cabs had the train title across them and the carriage roofboards were dispensed with as was the word Pullman at fascia level. Internal refurnishing took place at the same time with the distinctive old style table lamps disappearing. Unfortunately not long afterward, on 15 September 1969, car 279 of unit 3051 suffered an electrical fire in Brighton station before the morning up working the damage being accentuated by firemen wielding axes on the panelling to get to the seat of the outbreak.

Electric multiple-unit stock on the Southern has always had a reputation for lively – some would say rough – riding and, despite its Pullman character, the *Brighton Belle* was no exception, but for the habituees this seemed to endear it all the more to them. It is well-known that members of the theatrical profession who resided at Brighton used the train extensively for their journeys to and from London. No less a person than Sir Laurence (as he then was) Olivier managed to get kippers restored to the breakfast menu after their sudden deletion. It has been said that the train was famous for the sheer social quality of its passengers and there is more than a grain of truth in this assertion, but, nevertheless, there was a good cross-section of life to be sampled on it from the famous right down to the day tripper to Sussex-by-the-Sea. Even HM Queen Elizabeth The Queen Mother travelled to an engagement in it by an ordinary service run on one occasion.

It was one thing to get the kippers back but quite another to obtain a replacement train. Various proposals were made such as diesel Pullmans, dedicated electric units or electric locomotive hauled stock but all to no avail, because, to quote the then Divisional Manager '. . . the over-riding factor . . . was the economic one – better utilisation of stock.' At least it was an honest admission that the trains were run to suit the railway operators', rather than the travellers', convenience.

The last day of the *Brighton Belle* on 30 April 1972 included 'Cheese and Wine' and 'Champagne' specials at inflated fares and it was the previous day that some passengers, eschewing the final junketings, elected for their last journey to take farewell of, and make their salute to, a gracious tradition stretching back over 70 years. So popular was the train that all fifteen cars were sold to various purchasers, none being scrapped by BR.

City Limited

Very different, in every respect, was the other named train connecting London and Brighton or, as it might be better described, connecting Brighton with London for that was what its function was – the *City Limited*. It originated in a first class only train which, before World War I, ran non-stop from Brighton to

London Bridge in the morning to convey Brighton businessmen to the City of London and returned at 5pm from London Bridge (which, incidentally, was situated on the wrong side of the river to be included in the city boundaries; Cannon Street station did qualify and by a quirk of history did host the service from October 1867 to July 1868 long before the title became official) and become popularly known as the *City Limited*. After the cessation of hostilities restoration of services throughout the country was not particularly swift; the London, Brighton & South Coast Railway, however, went a long way towards a return to pre-war timings with its timetable introduced on 7 February 1921. The 5pm (Saturdays excepted) from London Bridge to Brighton was accelerated to become a sixty minute train and the 8.45am up was altered to leave at 8.48am and to arrive at London Bridge at 9.50am, each train being non-stop and officially designated *City Limited* as well as offering both classes of accommodation but no refreshment facilities. Neither service, of course, operated on Sundays.

The train was unique in that a special rake of wide 'balloon roof' coaches having recessed doors was used. Three of the coaches were gangwayed together (a practice not common on the Brighton line except for Pullmans), one being of the then-normal side corridor type, another having an open gangway and the third, a brake, being a saloon with armchairs in the centre and fixed seating at the ends.

The couple of minutes needed to be clipped from the up schedule to give a timing of one hour was made effective from 14 July 1924 but proved to be short-lived, for the 8.50am departure was back to 8.48am by 13 July of the following year, as part of a general retrenchment from over-optimistic schedules on the route.

At the end of 1925 Lancing carriage works turned out an eleven coach corridor set for the service, providing 312 first class and 192 third class seats, which underlined the heavy patronage by first class ticket holders. This set was numbered 471 and consisted of seven first class compartment coaches, one third, one composite and two third brakes. In the spring of 1926 one of the vehicles was replaced by the first class Pullman car *Princess Patricia* and the timetable was amended to announce a First Class Pullman Breakfast (up train)

LBSCR 4-6-4 tank No 333 *Remembrance*, perhaps the most famous of later LBSCR locomotives, passes Honor Oak Park with the up *City Limited*, the sixth vehicle of which is the Pullman car. *Author's collection*

The down *City Limited* in the summer of 1932 near Salfords in charge of Baltic tank No B328. *Dr. Ian C. Allen*

108   *To Sussex-By-The-Sea*

or Tea (down service) Car. Motive power was invariably one of the LBSCR L class 4–6–4 tank engines.

A more successful attempt was made in 1928 to get the morning train down to a timing of one hour. As from 9 July the timetable was altered to give a departure from Brighton at 8.45am and an arrival at London Bridge exactly an hour later. This timing, together with the 5pm down service in one hour, remained in force until the final up journey was made on Saturday 31 December 1932. The previous day the last down trip had been made with Baltic Tank No 332 in charge.

For electrification the Southern Railway decided to build special stock, in the same way as the 5BEL units were constructed for the *Belle* services, for the *City Limited*. This consisted of three six-coach electric mulitple-units – known as 6CIT units – having a high ratio of first class seating so that in a twelve coach train accommodating approximately 520 passengers there were no fewer than 276 first class seats. Having done this it was all the more curious to find that the train title of the up service was dropped from the first day of the electric service but that the 5pm from London Bridge continued to be so indicated in the timetable until deleted in July 1934. No carriage roofboards were provided in any case and although it might be tempting to state that the *City Limited* lasted in the down direction until Friday 6 July 1934 it does seem

The Eastbourne Pullman Limited in its customary 1910 period formation of four Pullmans (which in earlier years had done duty in the *Brighton Limited*) two vans and 2-2-2 No 329 *Stephenson* passes Purley on the down service. *Pamlin Prints*

that this was an oversight and that the name should have lapsed entirely as from 1 January 1933.

For a long time the trains remained in public esteem as *City Limited* so reverting to the situation before World War I but by the second conflict not only had the special first class character of the train been submerged in the prevailing uniformity of operation but in later years the timings passed into oblivion.

Eastbourne Pullman Limited

Brighton was not unique among Sussex resorts in having an all-Pullman train serving it, for, hardly had the *Southern Belle* been inaugurated than the Train Alteration Notice for December 1908 included the information that 'Every Sunday a new non-stop train consisting of Pullman cars only will run' leaving Victoria at 10.45am and returning from Eastbourne at 5.20pm to a ninety minute timing in each direction, the day return fare being twelve shillings and sixpence. No title was assigned to the working in the notice.

This really was an extension of, or alteration to, a service introduced on 5 July that year. This also was a Sunday-only train running to and from Eastbourne in 1½ hours leaving London (Victoria) at 10.15am and arriving back in London at 6.45pm. Patronage of the service was sufficient for it to be

Gladstone class 0-4-2 No 172 *Littlehampton* on the down service of the LBSCR *Eastbourne Pullman Limited* just east of Lewes. The Pullman 'Pup' van will be noted at the rear of the train. *Lens of Sutton*

converted to all-Pullman (the class was never stated, though nominally first, because the return day fare was the ruling factor) as soon as the *Southern Belle* had been launched, using the Pullman vehicles cascaded – as present day terminology has it – from the previous Brighton Pullman service.

The commencing day of the new service was 6 December 1908 which Eastbourne itself chose to ignore because the train would bring the dreaded day trippers – albeit of superior class! – on a Sunday to the town rather than residential visitors and, furthermore, it did little to improve the London train service for which there was agitation in some quarters. It was June 1909 before the service appeared in the LBSCR public timetable (there had been no issue since the previous October) when it was designated *Eastbourne Pullman Limited* and at the same time there was a reversion to a 5.15pm departure from Eastbourne. Officially, therefore, the title was applicable from 6 June. Loading for the service was, understandably, not heavy and the four Pullmans and two vans were entrusted to the Gladstone class 0–4–2, following the pattern set on the July 1908 service, and for many of the trips during the period 1910–2, the train was often headed by Battersea shed's No 329 *Stephenson*, a G class 2–2–2 type. There were not many examples of an all-Pullman train being booked for haulage by a 'Single'! *Stephenson* last officiated on the train in September 1912 and the following year the service, under the title *Eastbourne Pullman Limited*, ceased with the final run on 25 May.

Eastbourne Sunday Limited

The summer timetable coming into force on 1 June 1913, a Sunday, introduced the *Eastbourne Sunday Limited* which was the previous Pullman Limited train but with the addition of some ordinary third class accommodation – hence the reason for the title change – running to the same timings. A rather more radical alteration was made in 1914 when, from 7 June, the departure from Victoria was earlier at 10.40am and the train included a portion for coastal stations to West Worthing which was slipped at Haywards Heath. The overall 90-minute timing to Eastbourne was maintained as indeed was the return day Pullman fare. Third class Pullmans were introduced on 3 October 1915 (those already in the train then being classed as first) and then abruptly at the end of 1916 on 31 December came the last run, the whole service including the outwards slip portion being axed and nothing put in its place.

The vacuum continued until the equally sudden reappearance, on 7 October 1917, of an un-named service for third class ordinary and first class Pullman passengers of a Sunday non-stop train from Victoria at 10.40am with arrival at Eastbourne at 12.10pm. The return was given as 9.10pm from Eastbourne with an appearance, after a call at East Croydon, at Victoria at

By 1933 former LSWR locomotives were at work on the *Eastbourne Sunday Limited*. On June 4 that year T9 class 4-4-0 307 approaches Clapham Junction with the down service. *H. C. Casserley*

10.45pm. Just what motivated this late departure time is not clear (were there some powerful preachers in Eastbourne's churches or chapels at that period?!) but whatever it was the decision seems to have been a misjudgement because by December the train was leaving at 5.25pm. For four years it ran to various permutations – first and third class Pullmans and ordinary third class; third class Pullman and ordinary class; no Pullmans at all; either at 10.40am or 10.45am from Victoria; returning at 5.15pm or 5.25pm – but steadfastly with a call at East Croydon in the up direction and never with a title.

Eventually, starting on 4 December 1921 the train became the *Eastbourne Sunday Limited* again and the accommodation all-Pullman (both classes) to a ninety minute non-stop booking each way, departures being at 10.45am and 5.15pm. For the remainder of the train's existence the departure and arrival times at the London end remained constant at 10.45am and 6.45pm (except for a curious 6.46pm arrival in 1932 which might have been a mistake); the schedules, however, were gradually tightened up, first to an 85-minute journey from 7 October 1923 and then, from 1 January 1933, to eighty minutes each way.

The loading was usually moderate at five or six Pullman cars although on occasion might be increased to as many as eight or nine. With the lighter loads no problem was posed for the motive power but the combined down service of the 1914-1916 period might have taxed the locomotive as far as Haywards Heath and an eight coach formation on the 1933 timing would have called for a good effort from the T9 class 4—4—0s used at that time.

After the war the I3 class 4—4—2 tanks held the stage still hauling the old American cars, until, in 1924, the B4X class 4—4—0s took over. After grouping, when there appeared to be some uncertainty as to the title (*Eastbourne Sunday Limited* in the main timetable columns with *Eastbourne Sunday Pullman* in the summary tables) there was a great variety of motive power. In 1927 the formation was designated, because it was equipped with vacuum brakes only (instead of the LBSCR's Westinghouse brake), for working by King Arthur 4—6—0 or L12 class 4—4—0s and it got the latter ex LSWR type much to the annoyance of devotees of the old LBSCR who were particularly sore to see No E424 with its similarity of number with their beloved Atlantic No B424! Some of the batch of Battersea's King Arthurs with six-wheel tenders (within the

Towards the end of its existence the *Eastbourne Sunday Limited* had U1 class 2-6-0 haulage on the up journey. One Sunday in 1935 No 1907 of the class heads the train near Horley. *Dr Ian C. Allen*

The Eastbourne Belle that never was! One of the *Brighton Belle* electric multiple-unit sets, 3052, shorn of carriage roofboards, works the Sundays-only summer all-Pullman service down through Polegate in June 1948. *S. C. Nash*

number range E763 to E772) also appeared followed by the then new A630 series of 2–6–0s.

With the acceleration of 1933 and the transfer of the 1925 *Southern Belle* Pullmans to the service, the haulage task reverted to four-coupled locomotives in the shape of Battersea's allocation of ex LSWR T9 class. A youthful observer at Eastbourne was gratified that year to note most of these London based engines making at least one appearance on the train. Towards the end of 1933 King Arthurs reasserted themselves only to give way in the summer of 1934 to Atlantics based at New Cross Gate. Their reign was short for, by autumn, the 4–6–0s had returned; these in turn were ousted in April 1935 by the Schools class 4–4–0s – because of the prohibition of heavier types on the damaged Southerham Bridge near Lewes – which type saw matters through to the end, No 902 *Wellington* being at the head of the last down train on 30 June 1935.

In the final years the engine workings were not the same out and return but involved Eastbourne shed, which provided either a Schools or an ex LBSCR 4–6–4 tank for the up duty, although in the last weeks the U1 class 2–6–0s took over and so it fell to No 1908 to work the last up journey before the train, which had always used cast-off stock, was swept into memory by the Eastbourne electrification on 7 July 1935.

That might be thought to be the end but there was to be an echo thirteen years later. Immediately after nationalisation, but undoubtedly part of the old company's post-war enterprise, came the resurrection of the Sunday only all-Pullman service to Eastbourne, now confined to the duration of the summer services. Using one of the 5BEL units of the *Brighton Belle*, it first ran on 6 June 1948, leaving Victoria at 10.40am and arriving, after a non-stop run, at Eastbourne at noon. The return was at 5.45pm with an arrival in London, without intermediate call, at 7.5pm. These timings, except for an odd deduction of one minute each way in 1949, went unchanged until 1954 when the departure from Victoria was brought forward to 10.12am (arrival in Eastbourne at 11.38am), this being the sole major change until the train's demise on 15 September 1957. Essentially a day excursion train with a third class return fare, including Pullman supplements, of well under £1, it never had a title of any description inserted against its timing in any timetable – although some timetable leaflets did bear a display panel for it as the *Eastbourne Belle* – nor did the stock carry roofboards proclaiming a name.

CHAPTER SIX

Through the Garden of England

Granville Special Express

The first titled train in Britain was operated by the South Eastern Railway – the *Granville Special Express*. Such was the conclusion drawn by contributors and editor of the *Railway Magazine* during a series of discussions in the Pertinent Paragraphs section of that journal in the early 1930s. It was argued, in the main by erudite clerics, that, appellations like 'Excursion', 'Limited Mail' or 'Irish Mail' were descriptive of the function of the train rather than of a titular nature and that the first officially titled train was the *Granville Special Express* which appeared in March 1877.

It is, perhaps, unfortunate that the contributors to this review did not examine the case rather more widely than Bradshaw because a different conclusion might well have resulted. Certainly the *Granville Special Express* first appeared as a train in Bradshaw in March 1877 and at that time the London & South Western Railway ran a Day Mail, the London & North Western had an Irish Mail, a Special Scottish Mail and a Limited Mail which last term was also used by the North British and Caledonian companies and the Midland and North Eastern railways each operated trains designated Scotch Express. Further consideration might have been given to the name being purely functional in nature because it can be shown that it started as a special, although not exclusive, express for the Granville Hotel at Ramsgate. Additionally, it first ran not in March 1877 but in the final month of the previous year.

The Granville Hotel in Ramsgate, or rather more grandly St Lawrence-on-Sea, opened on 31 July 1869 but did not long remain under one ownership. By 1876 Mr Edmund F. Davis had acquired it and inserted an announcement in *The Times* of 20 November 1876 that it had opened under the managership of Mr G. F. Verini and offered covered sea swimming bath, Turkish bath, sitz double ozone and sulphur baths, skating rink, American bowling alleys and billiards rooms among its attractions. The next month a further advertisement appeared in the same newspaper, under the heading GRANVILLE SPECIAL EXPRESS, which intimated that arrangements had been made with the South

Eastern Railway to run a First-Class Special Private Express to Ramsgate every Friday on and after 22 December until further notice, leaving London Charing Cross at 3.45pm and Cannon Street at 3.50pm arriving at Ramsgate at 6pm, with a return from Ramsgate on 27 December at 8.30am giving an arrival at Charing Cross at 10.45am. Return tickets were thirty shillings (£1.50) each and mention of an allowance of twelve shillings and sixpence being made for those staying at the hotel was indicative that the service was not solely for the hotel's clientele.

Inauguration of this train was sufficient to merit the attendance of a reporter from the *Thanet Advertiser* at the station to witness its arrival. Owing to unforeseen circumstances he was discomforted in giving as full an account of the occasion as he would have wished as witness . . . 'A moment or two after the signal had been given that the special had passed St Lawrence, the lights at the Ramsgate station suddenly lowered and, in a minute or so went entirely out, leaving the place in complete and most unpleasant darkness. As quickly as possible lamps were obtained from the lamp room and, after being lighted, placed along the arrival platform, and as the last of these was being deposited on the ground the special glided into the station. Owing to the darkness which prevailed, we were unable to estimate the number of passengers but the train consisted of seven 1st class carriages and one saloon.' No matter, because at the hotel table d'hôte awaited the guests, a private band was in attendance and the final piece of the special pyrotechnic display that evening had the words 'Honour to the Granville Express' – surely the first train to be so saluted with its title!

After the Christmas period the train settled down to a regular Friday afternoon departure from London and a Monday morning return in the same timings as the inaugural service – shades of winter weekend breaks popular a century later – not appearing in Bradshaw until March 1877 when it included a call at Canterbury at 5.30pm and was indicated as SPECIAL EXPRESS as was the Monday 8.30am return shown as arriving at Cannon Street at 10.45am and Charing Cross at 10.55am. April saw the Ramsgate departure altered to 8.40am and then in May came the first entry of *Granville Special Express* the schedule being:

		pm		am
London (Charing Cross)	dep	3.45	arr	10.50
(Cannon Street)	dep	3.55	arr	10.40
Ramsgate	arr	5.40	dep	8.40

In June it appeared as first class down but first and second class up but this is

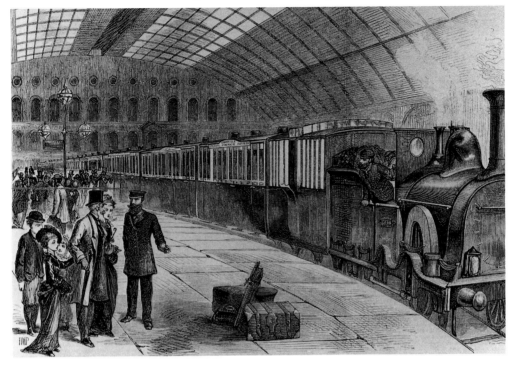

At first sight this illustration from the Granville Illustrated News (the house journal of the Granville Hotel at Ramsgate) of October 1879 would appear to relate to the Granville service from Victoria at the time of publication. However, the setting is clearly Charing Cross as the detailing of the end wall and distinctive lamp standard indicates and, apart from the added initials of LCDR on the locomotive cab side, represents – as well as the artist's talents allow – the early days of the service on the South Eastern Railway, even to the saloon in the train. The locomotive would appear to be one of the 2-4-0s of the 118 class. Reissue of the drawing with the LCDR initials would have been made when that company was providing a daily service in competition with the SER weekly train. *Kent County Library, Ramsgate*

thought to have been an error of omission in the case of the down train for by July it was certainly both classes each way (probably because of the rival London, Chatham & Dover Railway special of copy-cat nature) and also served Margate arriving at 5.55pm and leaving there at 8.30am. On 2 March the train was credited with running from London to Ramsgate in 1¾ hours, the quickest journey ever made between these points, obviously to cock-a-snook at the LCDR train, which started that day and was advertised to take that length of time to Margate.

Minor amendments followed: the departure time from Margate was advanced to 8.25pm from January 1878 and the next month all three classes were accommodated with an arrival in London a couple of minutes later. April 1878 brought a rather more radical change in that the service combined in both directions with an unnamed Dover service so that a stop was made at Ashford Junction at 5.2pm going down to give arrivals at Ramsgate and Margate at 5.45pm and 6pm respectively. The up service called at Ashford Junction at 9.21/5am and was due in London at 10.45am (Cannon Street) and 10.56am (Charing Cross). Calls were also made at London Bridge in both directions. At Easter the services operated on Maundy Thursday and the following Tuesday. Adjustments in times were made from July when Ramsgate and Margate arrivals became 5.50pm and 6.5pm respectively and the departure from Margate amended to 8.30am and a call inserted at Waterloo Junction at 10.52am.

An attempt to widen the range of the train's activities came in October 1878 when a Deal portion was included in the down train and a call at Canterbury West was booked for 5.25pm. The Deal portion was detached at Minster Junction at 5.42pm with the main train arriving at Ramsgate at 5.53pm and Margate ten minutes later. The Deal coaches arrived at their destination at 6.7pm having called en route at Sandwich at 5.55pm. Up timings were Margate 8.25am, Ramsgate 8.35am and Canterbury West 8.58am. The arrangement of combining the service with one to and from Dover ceased at the end of 1878.

For the months of July, August and September 1879 the down train was booked to call at Waterloo Junction at 3.47pm and New Cross at 4.7pm additionally and then run non-stop to Canterbury West (5.52pm) finishing at Margate at 6.40pm and Deal at 6.38pm. In the up direction there were departures from Margate at 8.15am, Ramsgate at 8.30am, Deal at 8.12am, Sandwich 8.21am, Minster Junction 8.37 am, Canterbury 9am, Ashford Junction 9.32am (after a 12 minute wait) to arrive at London Bridge at 10.40am, Cannon Street 10.53am, Waterloo Junction 10.59am and Charing Cross at 11.4am.

With the introduction of the October 1879 timetable the down train became the *Granville Express* but the up train's title remained unchanged as the *Granville Special Express*. The New Cross stop was omitted and the down times reverted to those introduced twelve months previously. As from January 1880 all down arrival times were extended by seven minutes. However, the two once-a-week titles were discarded at the end of May 1880, the *Granville Express* fading away at the conclusion of its run on 28 May and the *Granville Special Express* three days later. An ordinary daily up service in similar timings came into force in June followed in July by one, also daily, in the down direction.

Granville Express
Granville and Walmer and Deal Express
Granville and Deal and Walmer Express
Granville and Walmer and Deal, Shorncliffe, Folkestone and Dover Express
Granville and Walmer and Deal, Sandgate, Shorncliffe, Folkestone and Dover Express
Granville and Dover, Folkestone, Shorncliffe, Sandgate and Hythe Express
Granville and Dover, Folkestone, Shorncliffe and Sandgate Express

When the South Eastern Railway revived the title *Granville Express* from 1 April 1884 it was on daily – except Sundays – basis and was applied to services already in existence. The outward train left Charing Cross at 3.45pm, Cannon Street at 3.55pm and London Bridge at 3.58pm and ran non-stop to Canterbury (5.30pm) and then called at Minister Junction, where the Sandwich (arrive 6.2pm), Deal (6.12pm), and Walmer (6.19pm) portion was detached, to arrive at Ramsgate at 6pm and Margate at 6.10pm. In the up direction Margate was left at 9.30am, Ramsgate at 9.40am, Minister at 9.48am (the Walmer portion had started at 9.18am calling at Deal and Sandwich en route), Canterbury at 10.8am with arrivals in London at 11.38am (London Bridge), 11.43am (Cannon Street), and 11.53am at Charing Cross.

All this was short lived because in June the Saturday schedule in the down direction was altered and the title dropped and for July, August and September it was not used at all. However, it bounced back in October to the schedules ruling in April plus the addition of an Ashford call for the up train at 10.30am with two minutes added to the arrival times in London and, from November, this service also stopped at Waterloo Junction with the arrival at the terminus becoming three minutes before noon. From February 1885 a balancing stop at Ashford was made for the down train and the following calls were seven minutes later. July, August and September 1885 followed the pattern of the previous year with the title discontinued. On its reappearance in October the down train had its times altered to a 3.40pm departure from Charing Cross (Cannon Street and London Bridge 12 and 17 minutes later respectively), Ashford was called at between 5.23pm and 5.25pm, Canterbury at 5.45pm, Minister Junction 6.2pm, Ramsgate 6.15pm to finish at Margate at 6.25pm (Walmer 6.33pm).

January 1886 saw an acceleration in the down service of ten minutes and the introduction of a Dover portion which was detached at Ashford and came to receive the description of Fast Train rather than the main title. After the three month break in July, August and September the services continued as previously right round to and including the three month cessation in 1887 and then on until May 1888 when the titles were changed to *The Granville and*

Walmer and Deal Express in the down direction and *The Granville and Deal and Walmer Express* for the London bound service. In June the down train had a new schedule: Charing Cross 3.25pm, Cannon Street 3.33pm, London Bridge 3.38pm, Ashford Junction 5pm, Canterbury 5.20pm, Minster Junction 5.37pm, Ramsgate 5.50pm, Margate 6pm with the part to Walmer finishing its journey at 6.7pm. In July it was the turn of the up train to be amended – rather drastically for a completely new service. The train now left Margate at 8am, Ramsgate 8.10am, Walmer 7.44am, Minster Junction 8.18am, Canterbury 8.38am and arrived at Cannon Street at 10.15am and Charing Cross at 10.25am. By October, however, this 8am service from Margate took the title of *Kent Coast Express* and the *Granville and Deal and Walmer Express* title was dropped in favour of simply *Granville Express* which was applied to the 9.30am Margate-Charing Cross service with virtually all the previous calls and timings including the Dover portion with London being reached at noon.

More revisions came in 1889. In June the down train left Charing Cross at 3.15pm and ran about ten minutes earlier than previously with the same calls and including a Dover portion. In July the up service ousted the *Kent Coast Express* from the 7.55am Margate working (same stops and portions and arrival times in London) for a three month period after which the status quo was re-established.

The *Granville and Walmer and Deal Express* from the beginning of December was retimed to fifteen minutes later (Charing Cross depart 3.30pm and Margate arrive 6.5pm) and during 1890 the up train's arrival drifted back to 12.5pm at Charing Cross and then, from January 1891, to 12.10pm. From June 1892 the down service ran five minutes earlier throughout and from 1 October that year called at St Lawrence Junction with arrivals at Ramsgate and Margate a couple of minutes later than hitherto.

For the summer timetable of 1893, starting 1 June, the schedules were recast. The down train now left Charing Cross at 3.15pm, called at Cannon Street at 3.23pm, London Bridge at 3.28pm and then ran without further call to Ashford Junction (4.45pm) after which it served Canterbury (5.8pm), Minster Junction, St Lawrence Junction, Ramsgate (5.40pm) and Margate (5.50pm). The Walmer portion – calling en route at Sandwich and Deal – reached its destination from Minster Junction at 5.56pm. No Dover portion was carried. In the up direction the *Granville Express* left Margate at 9.35am, Ramsgate at 9.45am, collected its Walmer portion (which had started at 9.22am) at Minster Junction and then called at Canterbury at 10.14am and Ashford Junction at 10.37/40am (where the Dover portion was attached) and set out for a non-stop run to London where it was due to appear at London Bridge at noon, Cannon Street four minutes later, Waterloo Junction at 12.11pm and Charing Cross at 12.15pm.

Come the winter and the down service was decelerated and had a Dover Town portion again. Scheduled times were Charing Cross 3.25pm, Cannon Street 3.33pm, London Bridge 3.38pm, Ashford Junction 5.3pm, Canterbury 5.26pm, Minster Junction 5.43pm, St Lawrence Junction 5.53pm, Ramsgate 5.58pm and Margate 6.8pm (Walmer 6.12pm and Dover Town 5.55pm).

For the summers of 1894 and 1897 the 3.15pm London departure timetable of June 1893 was used from June to October inclusive while for 1895 and 1896 this timetable spanned the months of June, July, August and September. During these summers it was customary for the up service to operate without a Dover portion. However, for the up service a new schedule was introduced for July, August, September and October 1897 when Margate was left at 10.10am, Ramsgate at 10.18am, Minster Junction 10.29am (Walmer portion started at 9.55am), Canterbury 10.49am, Ashford 11.12am and the last of the four London stops, Charing Cross, was reached at 12.44pm.

Once more the November 1893 schedule in the down direction was used, this time for the winter of 1897/8; for the up service there was a reversion to the 9.35am departure from Margate, the Dover portion being joined at Ashford with Charing Cross expecting the train at 12.17pm. May 1898 saw the down train advanced to leave London ten minutes earlier with corresponding earlier calls down the line and then, in June, take up the summer schedule of June 1893 again. In July the up train followed course with a 10.10am departure from Margate and 12.46pm arrival at Charing Cross. In November both went back to the winter times and the arrangement of being combined with a Dover portion.

From June to October 1899 the usual summer procedure of the Dover portions not being combined was followed with departures from Charing Cross at 3.15pm and Margate at 9.35am. When the winter timetable resumed in November to the customary times the down train was saddled with the unwieldy title of *Granville and Walmer and Deal, Shorncliffe, Folkestone and Dover Express* while the up train was called nothing more than the *Granville Express*. The June-October 1900 down train had its title clipped to *Granville and Walmer and Deal Express* because the Dover portion was no longer carried. But in November even more grandiose titles appeared: *Granville and Walmer and Deal, Sandgate, Shorncliffe, Folkestone and Dover Express* from London and *Granville and Dover, Folkestone, Shorncliffe, Sandgate and Hythe Express* in the up direction. Imagine the reaction of the foreman charged to produce carriage roofboards for these trains!

These title amendments, of course, reflected the situation of the newly formed South Eastern & Chatham Railway operating two *Granville* services by different routes from London and indirectly were a tacit admission that the main thrust of the Charing Cross orientated services would be in the

Hythe-Dover-Deal arc rather than Ramsgate and Margate which could be better served from Victoria.

The usual summer arrangements applied in 1901 from June in the case of the down train and from July for the up until October when they once more rejoiced in the extended titles although the up train – now leaving Margate Sands at 9.30am – did dispense with Hythe.

Again in 1902 the down train shed its Dover portion in June and the up service did likewise in July and at the same time included a call at Tonbridge at 11.15am without amendment to the arrival time in London, although there was a temporary block in Chislehurst tunnel in late summer/early autumn which must have disrupted expectations of scheduled arrival times. In September the down train was decelerated with calls at Ashford at 5.3pm, Canterbury West 5.28pm, Minster Junction 5.49pm, Ramsgate Town 6.3pm and Margate Sands 6.15pm. The Walmer portion was due there at 6.26pm. The next month it ran with the Dover portion and cumbersome title. In November the up service had minor timing amendments (Ashford 10.38am, Tonbridge 11.13am, Charing Cross 12.10pm) and the down service likewise in January 1903 (Ramsgate Town 5.51pm, Margate Sands 6.3pm, Dover Town 5.55pm, Walmer 6.8pm). The summer 1903 timetable gave some improvement from June to the outward train; after calling at Waterloo Junction at 3.17pm, Cannon Street at 3.23pm and London Bridge at 3.28pm the next stop was Ashford (4.45/50pm) and, after the usual calls, Margate Sands should have been reached at three minutes before 6pm.

Extended titles were reintroduced in October and arrivals were altered to Margate Sands 5.54pm, Walmer 6.2pm and Dover Town 5.49pm. Whether the titles indicated in the timetable were carried in full or abbreviated form, such as *Granville Express*, may be a moot point. Anyhow after 30 June 1904 it mattered no more for that was the last time either long or short titles were used. The 3.15pm from Charing Cross gave way in favour of a similar service at 3.22pm while the up train had various alterations made to its operation. The name *Granville*, so far as Charing Cross was concerned, was dead having made a small mark in railway history.

Kent Coast Express

For July, August and September 1888 the *Granville and Deal and Walmer Express* had been given a new timing up from Margate at 8am instead of the customary 9.30am. From 1 October the *Granville Express* reverted to its previous timings and the title *Kent Coast Express* was then allocated to the weekday 8am from Margate which called at Ramsgate at 8.10am, Minster

Junction at 8.18am (where a portion which had left Walmer at 7.44am, calling at Deal and Sandwich, was attached), Canterbury at 8.38am and then ran without further stop to Cannon Street where it was due at 10.15am. Charing Cross was reached at 10.25am. It continued thus until June 1889 when the departure times (except from the Walmer branch) were advanced by five minutes and the train received a portion from Dover which left the Town station at 8.5am and called en route at Folkestone, Radnor Park, Shorncliffe Camp and Sandling Junction and then joined the main train at Ashford. No call was advertised for either portion at Ashford and the arrival times in London were not affected. Initially this arrangement was short-lived because the title was dropped for July, August and September (the *Granville* service took over the timing) but it came back into force in October.

Commencing in February 1890 Chilham was afforded the facility of an 'on request' stop for the train and after avoiding the previous summer's confusion of title alteration, the October timetable indicated a call at Waterloo Junction at 10.22am and an arrival at Charing Cross at 10.27am. A portion from Dover Town (8.5am) and intermediate stations (Folkestone, Radnor Park, Shorncliffe Camp and Sandling Junction) was introduced in May 1889 and combined with the main train at Ashford Junction which was left at 8.54am. By August 1893 Bradshaw gave this part independent status with the title in its own column. From 2 November 1896 a call was introduced at Grove Park at 10.2am and arrivals at the London destinations were two minutes later in consequence. In July 1901 there was a deceleration with departures put back to 8am at Margate Sands, 8.11am at Ramsgate Town, 8.40am at Canterbury West and 9.7am at Ashford (where the 8.5am from Dover Town joined) and the arrivals in London became 10.31am at Cannon Street, 10.39am at Waterloo Junction and 10.43am at Charing Cross.

Paddock Wood got its only titled train service although admittedly as part of an arrangement to give a Maidstone connection on 2 June 1902 when the train included a call there at 9.38am to compensate for which the Grove Park halt was no longer made. The Chilham conditional stop appears to have been dropped just for the month of June (it was back by July) but this could well have been an error of omission on the part of the timetable compilers or printers. From 1 October 1903 another conditional stop, at Wye, was included so that the service afforded the curiosity of a number of one-way titled train calls for unusual stations – Chilham, Wye and Paddock Wood. Like the other titled train on this route, of which it had been an offshoot, the *Kent Coast Express* was shorn of its name as from 1 July 1904 although the service continued to operate.

ton 124 *Through the Garden of England*

Man of Kent

The last title to be bestowed on an ordinary steam passenger train on BR Southern Region was that of *Man of Kent*. With the start of the summer timetable on 8 June 1953 a couple of the London – Folkestone Central trains was accelerated over the seventy miles to the pre-war eighty minute timing of the unofficially so-called 'Folkestone Flyers'. These were the 4.15pm from Charing Cross, calling at Waterloo at 4.17pm and arriving at Folkestone Central at 5.35pm and Dover Priory at 5.49pm and then serving all stations to Margate which was reached at 6.54pm. In the up direction the 9.40am from Margate made the same calls to leave Folkestone Central at 11.10am and arrive at Waterloo at 12.26pm and Charing Cross at 12.30pm. Both these services ran every weekday and included refreshment cars throughout their journeys.

By reason of their timings, these trains were of little use for London commuters nor yet for businessmen out and back from London in a day; most of the passengers (apart from local traffic north of Dover) therefore were making irregular journeys and were mainly residents of, or visitors to, Folkestone, Dover, Deal and Sandwich. No through London traffic from Ramsgate, let alone Margate, was to be expected, the trains merely running to those towns for operating convenience.

After the first summer the up train was given an easier timing on summer Saturdays with a 9.28am departure from Margate and a ninety minute schedule from Folkestone into Charing Cross (arrival 12.26pm) and this pattern persisted thereafter with, from 1957 onwards, a ninety-seven minute booking from Folkestone to London.

The extension of the title to another pair of trains came about in a curious way. Carriage workings were altered with BR Mark 1 stock displacing the SR Bulleid type; with the latter the carriage nameboards were on the roof so that on arrival of the up train at Charing Cross a man simply walked along the carriage roofs turning the boards round to ensure the name was not displayed on the outgoing service. The Mark 1 stock, however, followed the LMS practice of having the nameboards on the carriage sides immediately above the windows and the turning of the boards had to be done from platform level. As the track which served platform 6 at Charing Cross, which the up train used, had a wall on its west side and no staging available the boards on that side of the train did not get dealt with and, consequently, the 1.15pm departure went out and passed the headquarter offices at Waterloo flaunting a purloined title. To overcome this problem the management decided that the easiest solution was to ennoble the balancing workings and this, in due time, was done.

So from 11 June 1956 the title was applied to the 1.15pm (Saturdays excepted) from Charing Cross, which called at Waterloo at 1.17pm, Ashford

The *Man of Kent* originally had locomotive headboards without embellishment but later, as in this instance, the white horse shields with *INVICTA* under for Kent, were added. Schools class 4-0-0 No 30927 *Clifton* passes through Paddock Wood with the up morning service on Saturday 29 August 1959. *Author*

(2.21 – 2.24pm), Shorncliffe and then all stations, except Folkestone Junction, to Margate where it concluded operations at 4.10pm. On Saturdays the train left Charing Cross at 12.55pm and ran fast in eighty minutes to Folkestone Central after which it called everywhere to Ramsgate which it reached at 3.32pm. In the up direction the mantle of *Man of Kent* fell upon the 12.40pm departure from Margate which picked up at all stations to Shorncliffe and then Ashford, departing at 2.35pm, running non-stop to Waterloo (3.42pm) and Charing Cross (arrival 3.46pm) daily except, of course, on Sundays.

The following summer the timings became eroded: the 1.15pm was advanced to 1.8pm, the 4.15pm to 4.10pm and so on and the eighty minute

The afternoon up service of the *Man of Kent* entering Walmer with modified West Country class No 34017 *Ilfracombe* in charge on 30 April 1960. *Author*

schedules were lost. In the autumn of that year the refreshment cars which all four services carried were redesignated buffet cars.

There came a brief resurgence between November 1959 and mid-June 1960 when the 4.10pm from Charing Cross was due to put in an appearance at Folkestone Central at 5.30pm and in the opposite direction the 11.8am from Folkestone was booked into Charing Cross at 12.28pm. With the Kent electrification works nearing completion the schedules for the final year of operation were again lengthened. The quartet last ran on Saturday, 10 June 1961 just over eight years from the day the name *Man of Kent* was first carried. Electrification brought no substantial benefits in acceleration of these services and now even the buffet facilities have gone, so that progress is questionable to say the least.

Eleven coaches were the customary loading on the main part of the journey. In the summer of 1957, for example, the 12.39pm up and 4.10pm down were made up of one corridor second and seven corridor set 278 (which included a refreshment car) with a three corridor set added (or detached) at Folkestone Central. The 9.38am up and the 1.10pm down likewise had a corridor second and seven corridor set (either 277 or 279), and a three corridor set which was attached at Folkestone Central and detached at Dover Priory. The seven coach corridor sets were composed of a corridor brake second each end (35004 to 35009), two corridor composites (15906 to 15911), a buffet car and two open seconds (4373 to 4378) while the three corridor sets (559 and 560) each had two corridor brake seconds with a corridor composite between, the coach numbers running on consecutively from the seven coach corridor sets.

Apart from the last year of operation when, from July 1960, diesel-electric locomotives of D50XX and D65XX series worked either singly or in tandem, the motive power was either Schools class 4–4–0s or the light 4–6–2s. In the winter of 1957/8 all duties were booked for the Pacifics, Ramsgate shed being responsible for the two up trains (duties 472 and 475) and the first down train (duty 469) with Dover's duty 434 embracing the 4.10pm from Charing Cross. Perhaps this last was the most exacting of the four duties and it was this train that frequently had Schools class haulage. The smaller engines seldom disgraced themselves when called upon to head the *Man of Kent* through the Garden of England.

Outwardly no different from other trains on the route the *Conqueror*, composed of 4CEP units 1598 and 1519 in the so-called 'Jaffa-cake' livery, nears the end of its journey as it approaches West St Leonards on 4 June 1987. *Author*

Conqueror

During the 1980s British Rail stepped up its marketing efforts by giving certain routes distinctive names and also by increasing the number of titled trains it operated, even to the point of having a title applying in one direction only.

The route from London to Hastings via Battle was, during November 1984, designated 'The 1066 Route' and the diesel multiple-unit sets working over it acquired a suitable logo and this was carried over to the electric multiple-unit stock when, in May 1986, electrification between Tonbridge and St Leonards was completed. The new timetable included one down train in the morning which was faster than any other service and this, slightly speeded-up, was accorded the title of *Conqueror* from 11 May 1987. This title, it was explained in the timetable, was chosen to commemorate the 900th anniversary of the death of William Duke of Normandy. The following winter timetable, although retaining the service, did not perpetuate the title which accordingly lapsed after the run on 2 October.

Departure from London Charing Cross was at 09.15, Waterloo East at 09.18 and a call was made at Orpington, in the outer suburbs, at 09.37; the train next called at Tonbridge (09.54), Tunbridge Wells (10.02) and Battle (10.24) to arrive at St Leonards (Warrior Square) at 10.33 and, finally, Hastings at 10.35 in a total of 80 minutes for the 62½ mile journey. There was no balancing up titled service.

The customary train formation was two 4CEP (411/2 class) type electric multiple units giving an eight coach formation all usually in the brown livery nicknamed 'Jaffa Cake' which had persisted on the route to the exclusion of the later Network South East colours. An ambulatory refreshment service was provided.

CHAPTER SEVEN

Via Chatham with the Kent Coasters

Westgate-on-Sea and Granville Special Express
Granville and Westgate-on-Sea Special Express
Westgate-on-Sea, Cliftonville and Granville Special Express
Granville, Cliftonville and Westgate-on-Sea Special Express
Granville Express
Granville Limited Express

Imitation is said to be the sincerest form of flattery although it is perhaps questionable if the London, Chatham & Dover Railway would have copied the South Eastern Railway if it had subscribed to that statement. Anyhow the SER had launched the special express for the Granville Hotel at Ramsgate for the Christmas of 1876 and so there was not much surprise when the LCDR did for Margate what the SER had done for Ramsgate.

Keble's Gazette of 3 March 1877 gave the news that arrangements had been made between the proprietor, one John Grieve, of the Cliftonville Hotel at Margate and the LCDR by which a special fast express train was to run to Margate every Friday in connection with the Cliftonville Hotel, leaving Victoria at 3.15pm and arriving at Margate at 5pm. If this had been at the sole instigation of the Cliftonville's proprietor it was poor reward for him that a rival in Ramsgate – the Albion Hotel – should try to seduce guests there by the same service by inserting advertisements in *The Times*.

The LCDR started the Friday outwards, Monday return service on 2 March 1877 with accommodation for all three classes. There were connections for Holborn Viaduct and Ludgate Hill and stops at Herne Hill, Margate and Broadstairs the arrival and departure times at Ramsgate Harbour being 5.15pm and 10am respectively, with an overall schedule of two hours. There had been nothing comparable previously and the innovation merited the term Special Express Train. In July additional stops were inserted and the journey time extended and 'Fast' took the place of 'Express' in the description; in October it reverted to the first timing, only to be amended the next month.

On Monday 1 April 1878 the LCDR suddenly blossomed forth with a daily (except Sundays) first, second and third class *Westgate-on-Sea and Granville*

Special Express and *The Granville and Westgate-on-Sea Special Express* the first in the down and the other in the up direction. The timings were much the same as the special express train of 1877 but included a call at Westgate each way, the down one taking the path of a Saturdays-only service and the up one the Mondays-only train:

		pm		am
London Victoria	dep	3.15	arr	12 noon
Holborn Viaduct	dep	3.10	arr	12.5
Ludgate Hill	dep	3.12	arr	12.2
Herne Hill	dep	3.25	arr	11.50
Westgate-on-Sea	arr	4.57	dep	10.18
Margate	arr	5.0	dep	10.14
Broadstairs	arr	5.10	dep	10.7
Ramsgate Harbour	arr	5.15	dep	10.0

In the up direction there was an unadvertised stop at Grosvenor Bridge for ticket collection purposes.

The train enjoyed a long period with nothing more than minor alterations. From June 1884 the titles had Cliftonville inserted between Granville and Westgate-on-Sea although Bradshaw got muddled at first and called the up train the *Cliftonville, Granville and Westgate-on-Sea Special Express* but corrected its error in its July issue. It was not until November 1889 that there was an alteration in schedule and that a straight-forward ten minute later running of the down train (Victoria depart 3.25pm) followed by, in October 1891, three minutes being added to the Ramsgate arrival time making it 5.28pm. The Ludgate Hill call was dropped at the beginning of 1891.

From July 1894 the title of the down service was contracted to *Granville Express* and on 2 June 1900 the *Granville Limited Express* was introduced as a Saturdays-only summer service (June to September inclusive) leaving Victoria at 3.15pm and Holborn Viaduct at 3.13pm, the portions (each consisting of one first, one second, two thirds and a van) joining at Herne Hill for departure at 3.25pm on a non-stop run to Margate West (4.59pm), Broadstairs (5.8pm) and Ramsgate Harbour (5.15pm). The 3.25pm Victoria departure continued to run on Saturdays under its usual title, the 3.15pm train being in the nature of a titled relief service.

For the same four-monthly period in 1901, 1902 and 1903 the *Granville Limited Express* ran on Saturdays to the original 1900 schedule. At other times of heavy patronage the departures from Victoria and Holborn Viaduct would run independently with the main (Victoria) service omitting the call at Herne Hill and proceeding in advance. The *Granville Limited Express* title did not reappear in June 1904 and the down *Granville Express* and up *Granville, Cliftonville and Westgate-on-Sea Special Express* titles ceased to apply after 30 June 1904 although both services ran otherwise unaltered. The trains had a timetable note of 'West End to Margate, Ramsgate &c Express' and vice versa. There had been occasions when variations on the title of the up train appeared, such as the summer of 1902 when it was rendered as *Granville and Cliftonville Special Express* and in 1899 – when *Granville Special Express* was used – but these could well have been printers' contractions.

Resurrection of the title, in whatever form, had to wait until 11 July 1921 when the same pair of trains regained the appellation *Granville Express*. Again it was a weekdays service, the Victoria departure being at 3.15pm with arrivals of 4.47pm at Margate West, 4.59pm at Broadstairs and 5.6pm at Ramsgate Harbour. Coming up the train continued to leave Ramsgate Harbour at 10am, then called at Broadstairs, Margate West, Westgate-on-Sea and, surprisingly, Sittingbourne (11.2am) reaching London at 12.8pm. There were no City portions but the luxury of a first class Pullman (described as tea car going down and buffet car inwards) was available on payment of a two shillings supplement. The Sittingbourne call was not made from 2 October

The LCDR *Granville Express* headed by 2-4-0 No 53 *Europa* near Shortlands. *L & GRP*

1922 and, in consequence, Victoria was reached at 12.3pm. The seven coach train formation, the same in each direction, consisted of a three coach non-corridor set, a Pullman, a couple of ten compartment thirds and a bogie composite, all in the charge of a D1 or E1 4–4–0 locomotive.

The Sittingbourne call of the up service was revived with the timetable of 9 July 1923 and for that summer the down train on Saturdays arrived in Thanet about ten minutes later than on other days. The winter 1923/4 timings perpetuated the Sittingbourne call but not the longer running time on Saturdays. With effect from 14 July 1924 the down train lost its title on Saturdays and the up train ceased calling at Sittingbourne and was speeded up to arrive in London at noon, except on Saturdays when the arrival was booked for 12.7pm despite the omission of the Westgate-on-Sea call in addition to that at Sittingbourne. Although in subsequent summer Saturdays the down train carried its title the omission of the Westgate stop of the up train remained. Commencing 12 July 1925 the departure from Ramsgate Harbour was moved to 10.5am with a London arrival at 12.10pm. The next summer came the opening of Dumpton Park and the train called there in both directions and, of course, used the new Ramsgate station which replaced the original LCD and SER stations. On Saturdays that summer the departure times were Victoria 3.5pm and Ramsgate 10.10am.

The title was dropped for the summer of 1927, the last day it was carried being 9 July; the services, nevertheless, continued for another dozen years. Sixty years after the title died there was a down train approximating to the *Granville* – leaving Victoria at 15.20 (Ramsgate 17.07) – and, although serving more intermediate stations, it offered no significant improvement in overall times and lacked the consolation of a Pullman car. Such is progress!

Kent Coast Express

Five years after the London, Chatham & Dover Railway had first given a train a title it introduced a new weekdays service for expanding residential business traffic. This, starting in April 1882, left London (Victoria) at 5.15pm and called at Herne Hill to attach the City portion (Holborn Viaduct 5.10pm, Ludgate Hill 5.12pm) after which it ran fast to Chatham (6.10/3pm), Herne Bay 6.52pm, Westgate-on-Sea 7.9pm, Margate 7.12pm, Broadstairs 7.19pm and finished at Ramsgate at 7.26pm. Two months later, on 1 June, it received the title *Kent Coast Express*. Presumably because not enough traffic was being generated, the schedule was altered so that from October calls were made at Faversham (arrive 6.39pm) and all stations, apart from Margate East, to Ramsgate, which was reached at 7.40pm and the train then settled down to a period of consolidation.

The Saturdays-only 1.15pm ex Cannon Street *City Express* leaving Broadstairs in the early 1920s in charge of the then recently rebuilt D1 class 4-4-0 No 487. Non-gangwayed 'Trio C' three coach set next to the engine, Pullman car fourth. *Lens of Sutton*

For the months of July, August and September 1885 the title was transferred to the 7.15pm from Victoria which ran precisely two hours later throughout than the 5.15pm. In October 1885 the 7.15pm disappeared and the 5.15pm once more became the *Kent Coast Express*. In the summer of 1886 a similar transfer of title occurred, this time to the 6.25pm from Victoria which called at Brixton (an unusual station to have a titled train service) and Herne Hill and then ran non-stop to Westgate-on-Sea, where it was due at 8.7pm, calling next at Margate at 8.10pm and Broadstairs at 8.20pm, concluding its run at 8.25pm at Ramsgate. After this July to September interlude the title again reverted to the 5.15pm from Victoria which then took five minutes longer to its destination.

This one-way title suddenly had its counterpart in April 1887 when an up *Kent Coast Express* was introduced: this left, except Sundays, Ramsgate at 8am, Broadstairs 8.7am, Margate 8.15am, Westgate-on-Sea 8.20am,

Birchington 8.25am, Herne Bay 8.39am, Whitstable 8.47am and then ran without further call to Herne Hill (due 10.2am) to finish at Victoria at 10.12am.

An uneventful period then followed until the autumn of 1891 when, as from October, the up train called at Faversham and consequently arrived at Victoria at 10.15am; the next month the down train called at Rochester and finished at Ramsgate at 7.50pm and at the same time combined with the Ostend boat train dividing at Faversham. From April 1892 the call at Rochester was altered to Rochester Bridge. The combination with the boat train, together with the Rochester Bridge call, was dropped at the beginning of June for the summer period until October when both were resumed. In December the Rochester Bridge call was altered back to Rochester and then from March 1893 both stations were served by the train. For the summer (July – September) of 1893 the Ostend boat train again ran separately but when, in October, the two services once more joined forces it was to a different timetable. Victoria was left at 5.30pm and Herne Hill at 5.40pm (Holborn Viaduct at 5.25pm and St Pauls at 5.28pm) and calls were made at Rochester Bridge at 6.23pm, Rochester at 6.27pm, Chatham at 6.33pm and Faversham at 6.57pm and, after detaching the boat portion, called at all stations to Ramsgate, reached at 8pm precisely.

In 1894 instead of following the procedure of the previous two summers the down *Kent Coast Express* was dropped entirely from July to September inclusive (the *Cliftonville Express* took over its role for this purpose) and resumed again in October. Thereafter the combined train arrangement continued winter and summer.

Further alterations were made to the schedule of the down train although the up service remained undisturbed. From 1 January 1896 the departure from Victoria became 5.33pm and timings were three minutes later throughout. This lasted until July when the train left Victoria at 5.45pm and with the same stops was timed into Faversham at 7.10pm and Ramsgate at 8.20pm. A reversion to the 5.33pm departure from Victoria was made at the beginning of 1897 and in December the Rochester call was exchanged for one at Sittingbourne at 6.50pm. The 5.33pm finally ran at the end of May, 1903.

Victoria, which had been served so long by the up train, suddenly found itself passed over in favour of Cannon Street (10.7am arrival) and Charing Cross (10.15am arrival) from the beginning of July 1904 following the opening of Nos 1 and 2 loops at Chislehurst the previous month which allowed running to and from the old LCDR Chatham route to Charing Cross and Cannon Street. Exactly a year later in July the title was removed from this train which had to be content with nothing more than a columnar note of Kent Coast Fast Train.

Despite the anomaly of *Kent Coast Express* titles being borne by trains by both companies in Kent for several years, further services were introduced in 1899 with the same or not dissimilar titles. For the summer a Mondays and Fridays – only *Kent Coast Express*, starting on 3 July and finishing on 29 September, left Victoria at 9.2am and called at Brixton and Herne Hill (for Holborn Viaduct and St Pauls traffic) and then ran fast to Margate West (10.53am), Broadstairs (11.3am) and Ramsgate (11.10am). This was repeated, with an additional call at Herne Bay at 10.35am, for July, August and September in 1900 and again in 1901 when it was extended to Saturdays only in June leaving Victoria at 9am. For 1902 it ran to the 9am schedule in June on

The D class 4-4-0s dealt with much of the Kentish traffic including the titled trains: in 1925 No A743 climbs from Beckenham Junction towards Shortlands with an unidentified Victoria-Ramsgate Harbour train. Again non-corridor coaches with a Pullman marshalled fourth. *Lens of Sutton*

Saturdays only and then daily (except Sundays) July to September inclusive. In 1903 the Saturdays-only June arrangement was repeated but for July, August and September the train ran on Mondays and Saturdays only with additional calls at Chatham (9.57am) and Faversham (10.21am).

To complicate matters an existing Sunday service was accelerated in June 1903 and took the title also! This train was booked to leave Victoria at 10.45am and Herne Hill at 10.55am and arrive at Herne Bay at 12.15pm, thereafter calling at Westgate-on-Sea, Margate West, Broadstairs and Ramsgate where it was due at 12.50pm. It continued in October in amended form calling at all stations between Faversham and Ramsgate Harbour (due 1.2pm) except for Margate East and had a portion for Canterbury East, Kearsney, Dover Harbour (arrive 1.4pm) and Deal (arrive 1.22pm), for which purpose the title became the *Kent Coast, Dover and Deal Express*. The Deal portion ran direct from Kearsney to Martin Mill calling there and at Walmer.

July 1904 saw the 9am from Victoria *Kent Coast Express* operating again on Mondays and Saturdays only until the end of September. To step up the pressure July also witnessed the introduction of *two* Sunday *Kent Coast Express* services: the first of these left Victoria at 10am, Herne Hill at 10.10am, Chatham at 10.56am and split at Faversham, the front part going fast to Dover Priory (11.58am) and Dover Harbour, the other part serving all stations, except Margate East, to Ramsgate Harbour (12.32pm). The other *KCE* left at 10.45am, called at Herne Hill ten minutes later and then paused at Herne Bay (12.15pm), Westgate-on-Sea, Margate West and Broadstairs to terminate at Ramsgate Harbour at 12.50pm. In October the 10am ceased and the 10.45am called at Faversham and had Dover and Deal portions all as the *Kent Coast, Dover and Deal Express* of October 1903 and virtually to the same times. From May 1905 this service became Fast Train to the Kent Coast with the lapse of title after the journey of 30 April.

Kent Coast and Canterbury Express
Kent Coast, Canterbury, Dover and Deal Express
Dover, Deal and Kent Coast Express
Herne Bay and Kent Coast Express
A whole crop of notes appeared in the June 1898 LCDR public timetables including such gems as 'Clacton, Ipswich, Harwich and Yarmouth Boat Train' (the 10.15am Victoria to Gravesend service) and 'Newspaper and Parcels Express'. Indeed at this time and for a few years after the formation of the SECR the train nomenclature tended to get completely out of hand, so much so that the public timetables would on occasion label the same train with differing versions of a name or Bradshaw's version would **n**ot coincide precisely with

SECR E1 class 4-4-0 No 504 ascending the bank to Bickley with the down *Thanet Pullman* a year or so before the 1923 Grouping. *Lens of Sutton*

that in the company tables. For the purposes of this chapter, in all its sections, the treading of this minefield has been done with the aid of Bradshaw on the assumption that the editor of that publication would only put in the name provided by the company and, as Bradshaw published monthly rather than irregularly, it should provide a surer guide.

Anyhow, among these notes appeared the *Kent Coast and Canterbury Express* which was applied to an existing slip coach portion from the Calais boat express which was dropped at Faversham. Departure from London (Victoria) was at 9am and Herne Hill at 9.10am and after the slip portion was detached at Faversham it was split, the front part leaving at 10.28am for Selling and Canterbury (due 10.50am) and the rear section at 10.30am for all

In Southern Railway days, wth the Pullmans in umber and cream livery, the down *Thanet Pullman* on the 1 in 100 incline from Beckenham Junction to Shortlands in the charge of E1 class 4-4-0 No A506. *Lens of Sutton*

stations – except Margate East – to Ramsgate, taking exactly one hour to get to its destination. From July to September it operated Tuesdays to Fridays inclusive with a ten minute later schedule from Faversham to Margate and the Canterbury part being extended to serve all stations to Dover Priory, where it was due at 11.35am. In October the same procedure obtained except that stations beyond Canterbury were not catered for. In November the service reverted to the June arrangements. The summer schedules for 1899 repeated those for the previous year but embraced Mondays and Saturdays as well.

For the months of March, April and May 1900 the title became the *Kent Coast, Canterbury, Dover and Deal Express* and to justify this the train left Victoria at 9.30am (combined with the Ostend boat service), called at Herne Hill at 9.42am, Chatham at 10.26am, Sittingbourne at 10.43am and at Faversham divided, one part going to Ramsgate Harbour (due 11.58am) as usual and the other calling at Canterbury East at 11.12am, Kearsney 11.33am (further division for all stations to Deal due 11.58am), Dover Priory 11.37am and Dover Harbour at 11.42am. It also ran on Sundays but did not call that day at Sittingbourne nor have a Ramsgate portion. June saw the *Kent Coast and Canterbury Express* basic arrangements restored followed by the same July to October scheduling that had held sway previously.

Another title variation was tried in November 1900; this time the *Dover, Deal and Kent Coast Express* ran in the 9.30am from Victoria path virtually all as for the spring of the year but without a Sittingbourne call. This then continued except for July, August and September 1901 also the same three months in 1902 and 1903 and then expired as a title at the end of June 1904.

However the *Kent Coast* title with appendages had not gone for good because in July 1904 the *Herne Bay and Kent Coast Express* suddenly popped up this being the 4.20pm departure from Victoria, 4.30pm from Herne Hill with city connections, running fast to Herne Bay, where it was due at 5.41pm, and then all stations except Margate East to Ramsgate Harbour where it terminated at 6.23pm. No more was heard of this title after the end of September 1904.

Cliftonville Express

The first use of the title *Cliftonville Express* was curiously isolated in that it was applied to a new summer weekday service in 1894 which lasted but three months – July, August and September. The 5.30pm *Kent Coast Express* from Victoria was dropped and as a replacement a 5.15pm departure (Holborn Viaduct 5.10pm, St Pauls 5.13pm) called at Herne Hill at 5.25pm and then ran non-stop to Herne Bay (6.41pm), after which it called at Westgate-on-Sea and stations to Ramsgate Harbour where it was due at 7.20pm. No corresponding up service was titled. Starting on 2 July it concluded operations on 29 September.

Re-introduction of the *Cliftonville Express* in October 1911 broke a barren period of over six years without a titled train on the South Eastern & Chatham. There was, in September 1911, a 'Kent Coast Cheap Fast Train' in the timetable which left London (Victoria) at 9.10am and, after picking-up at Brixton and Herne Hill, ran without a stop to Whitstable Town and served all stations thence, except Margate East, to Ramsgate Harbour where it was due at 11.42am. In the reverse direction there was a service indicated in the timetable as 'Fast Train to London' which departed from Ramsgate Harbour at 5pm on a two-hour schedule to Victoria and called at Broadstairs, Margate West, Westgate-on-Sea and Herne Hill en route. These two services were used as the basis for the *Cliftonville Express*.

Commencing on 2 October 1911 the new titled train left Victoria at 9.10am and ran non-stop to Margate West (due 10.47am) and then called at Broadstairs at 10.56am before terminating at Ramsgate Harbour at 11.2am. A portion was slipped at Faversham at 10.21am which gave a stopping service (all stations except Margate East) to Ramsgate Harbour, which was reached at 11.23am. In the up direction the timings were Ramsgate Harbour depart 5pm, Broadstairs 5.7pm, Margate West 5.20pm with arrival at Victoria at 6.55pm. It served admirably for travellers requiring a day return trip from London but did not run on Sundays.

Minor adjustments were made in the timings as from May 1912 when Margate West was reached at 10.40am, Broadstairs at 10.53am and Ramsgate Harbour at 11am with the slip portion arriving at Ramsgate Harbour at 11.20am. In the up direction the amended timings were Broadstairs 5.12pm, Margate West 5.22pm and Victoria 6.52pm. As from July the slip portion called at Margate East, while, from June 1913, it was given five minutes extra to its final destination to arrive at 11.25am.

Inevitably World War I took its toll and as from January 1915 the down service dropped the title and the slip portion, and made additional stops; the slip portion returned in February but finally vanished in December's timetable. The up train, however, continued as the *Cliftonville Express* making it a one-way titled service until the end of November 1915 when it too lost its name. Both services ran throughout the war in varying forms and reasserted themselves in the summer of 1919 much as pre-war except that they lacked the title.

After the coal strike of the spring of 1921 there came the revival of titled trains and once again, from 11 July, the *Cliftonville Express* name was allocated to the 9am down and 5pm up services; the down train now ran

The last of the *Belle* all-Pullman trains to be introduced was the *Thanet Belle* which the railway's advertising department used to advantage on various material – in this case on a leaflet promoting the *Belle* trains in general and the *Thanet Belle* in particular. *Author's collection*

non-stop to Margate West (arrive 10.35am), then Broadstairs (10.47am), terminating at Ramsgate Harbour at 10.55am and the portion slipped at Faversham gave a service thence all stations to Ramsgate Harbour where it was due at 11.21am. In the London bound direction calls were made at Broadstairs at 5.8pm and Margate West at 5.20pm with an arrival at Victoria booked for 6.58pm. These weekday services were also extended to Sundays – but only until October in the case of the down train – with the up one making a call at Herne Bay that day at 5.37pm and arriving at Victoria at 7.2pm. For the winter of 1921/2 the up Sunday service – complete with Herne Bay call – was combined with the *Thanet Pullman Limited* as fully described under that train's history elsewhere in this chapter.

A first class Pullman Tea Car was incorporated in the weekdays up service as from 12 February 1922 and from 11 June that year the Sunday services again appeared, the up train regaining its previous independent existence while the down train ran earlier. It left Victoria at 8.45am, called at Margate West at 10.17am, Broadstairs at 10.30am and arrived at Ramsgate Harbour at 10.36am with the Faversham slip portion calling at all stations to Ramsgate Harbour where it was due at one minute past eleven o'clock, such was the precision of the SECR timetable draftsmen.

The train formations of up and down services were entirely dissimilar: in this summer of 1922, for example, the down train consisted of a three coach set and a couple of ten compartment bogie thirds forming the front part, after which came the slip portion of slip brake composite and another three coach set. Coming up from Ramsgate there were two brake thirds, a lavatory third, an ordinary third, a couple of ten compartment thirds, three composites, all non-corridor plus the Pullman, a rather cosmopolitan collection of bogie coaches.

Pre-war the motive power had been a 4–4–0 of the D (or perhaps E) class but afterwards these served in rebuilt form as D1 and E1 classes.

For the winter of 1922/3 the Sunday trains ran on 1 October but thereafter the down service ceased and the up train again combined with the *Thanet Pullman Limited*. The first summer of the grouping saw the down Sunday service follow the weekday timing but without title and the up Sunday train, titled, run five minutes later throughout but without the Herne Bay stop or a Pullman car. The weekday timings remained almost unaltered as from 1 October 1923 and the up Sunday service ran tandem again as in previous winters.

From the summer of 1924 onwards there was hardly a timetable introduced that did not produce an amendment to the *Cliftonville Express*. From 14 July 1924 the train on Mondays to Fridays left Victoria at 9.6am, called at Faversham, Margate West, Broadstairs and Ramsgate Harbour (due 11.10am) while on Saturdays its London departure was advanced to 8.50am, the Faversham stop was omitted and Ramsgate Harbour was reached at 10.55am. The return service left Ramsgate at 5.5pm called at Broadstairs and Margate West to arrive at Victoria at 7pm; on Saturdays it was twelve minutes later into London and on Sundays seven minutes and that day did not have a Pullman car.

For the winter service commencing 22 September 1924 the summer service on Mondays to Fridays did duty for weekdays except that 9.5am was the London departure time. Tandem working up as previously operated was the order of the day on Sundays.

For the summer service of 1925, commencing 12 July, the down service was graced by a first class Pullman Mondays to Fridays, this being dispensed with on Saturdays when the train called at all stations from Faversham to Ramsgate Harbour arriving there at 11.30am. The up train was retimed at 5.15pm from Ramsgate Harbour and, with the same stops as previously, was due at Victoria at 7.14pm (Saturdays 7.25pm). On Sundays the down service operated without a title and the inward trip left at 5.5pm to arrive in London, complete with Pullman, at 7.11pm.

Yet more alterations were made for the winter timetable starting on 21 September 1925 when the train still left Victoria on weekdays at 9.5am and then called at Chatham at 9.56/8am, where a Dover portion was detached, Whitstable Town at 10.31am and all stations, except Margate East, to Ramsgate Harbour where it was due at 11.24am. The up service now left Ramsgate at 5.10pm and arrived at Victoria in two hours exactly. The first class Pullman car in the trains now became an established feature. The up train on Sundays was again run in tandem with the *Thanet Pullman*.

The summer of 1926 produced new arrangements for the down service which ran Mondays to Fridays only from Victoria at 8.55am fast to Margate (10.35am) and then called at Broadstairs and Dumpton Park before terminating at the new Ramsgate station at 10.57am. Coming up to London the departure time was set at 5.6pm and, with calls at Dumpton Park, Broadstairs and Margate, Victoria was reached at 7.10pm (7.15pm on Saturdays). For Sundays the name was dropped completely.

In the Winter of 1926/7 a reversion was made to the previous winter's timings for the down direction except, of course, that a call was made at Dumpton Park and the train concluded its run at the new station at Ramsgate at 11.30am. In the up direction the summer 1926 schedule obtained and the title was again not seen on Sundays. The coup de grace, insofar as the title was concerned, came on 9 July 1927, although the service did continue thereafter.

City Express

Stand during the weekday morning peak hour at the eastern end of London Bridge station's platform 3 and observe the unbroken procession of trains bringing in the commuters; without exception every train is composed of electric multiple-units, whether they come from Dartford or Dover or Hastings or Hayes. If it is a good day the traffic will be coming in with military-like precision aided by reversible line working and modern signalling, trackwork and traction. It needs nothing more than a points failure between London Bridge and New Cross to disrupt matters completely: marvel then, not at the delay, but that the disruption is kept to manageable proportions. But then this particular stretch of line might be termed the cradle of commuting.

Go back to 1852 – April say – and see what was on offer then. A 20-minute regular interval service to and from Greenwich throughout the day (Sir Herbert Walker is so often credited with instituting the regular interval service in the south of England but all he did was to revive it!); the North Kent line had some services from Woolwich, Blackheath and one from Strood and Gravesend; there was one train from Tunbridge (the present day Tonbridge) and a couple from Dorking all of which came via Reigate Junction. Eventually all this blossomed out so that within thirty years there was an identifiable long distance daily business traffic especially to places on the coast between Whitstable and Ramsgate. Just what was so attractive about this length of coastline of which all locations, except for Broadstairs and Ramsgate, faced north is not entirely clear although probably low land prices had an influence.

So firmly established was the habit by December 1911 that it was possible to form the Association of Regular Kent Coasters for season ticket holders. After a short while reserved compartments on one up and one down train daily was arranged for its members and eventually this became a saloon with RESERVED labels and by the time war was declared in August 1914 this association had arranged five reserved saloons and two trains with reserved compartments for its members' use each weekday, all of which makes the efforts of present day equivalent organisations look like small beer. That the railway company was alive to its responsibilities is demonstrated by a letter from the Superintendent of the Line to, among others, the stationmaster at Birchington on 15 November 1923 headed 'Working of Morning and Evening Business Trains' and relating to giving 'personal attention . . . to ensure quick and rapid handling of the trains when at your station.' And all had to be worked by mechanical means rather than electrical both in regard to motive power and signalling. But we run too far ahead.

1 July 1896 marked the inauguration of the *City Express to the Kent Coast*, a service confined to the City of London without any West End portion. This was timed to leave Holborn Viaduct at 5.10pm, pick up at St Pauls at 5.12pm and then run non-stop to Westgate-on-Sea (due 6.45pm), Margate (6.51pm), Broadstairs (7pm) and finish at Ramsgate at 7.5pm. A slip portion was dropped at Faversham at 6.19pm which then called intermediately to Ramsgate arriving there twenty minutes after the main train. These arrangements were amended in October: a stop was made at Faversham and the whole train proceeded to the timing of what had previously been the slip portion. This did not last long for at the beginning of 1897 the main train again went through to Ramsgate for the 7.5pm arrival and the slip made at Faversham for all stations to Dover. This lasted until December when the

Westgate-on-Sea call was omitted giving an arrival at Ramsgate at 7pm with the slip serving stations to Ramsgate.

An up *City Express* was introduced as a new Mondays-only service starting on 6 June 1898. This left Ramsgate at 7.45am, called at Broadstairs, Margate and Herne Bay (8.18am) and then proceeded non-stop to St Pauls in 90 minutes. The next month this became a daily (except Sundays) train until October when it reverted to a Mondays-only service which then lapsed at the end of that month.

For 1899 the up train was resurrected on a Mondays-only basis just for the month of June when it left Ramsgate at 7.40am, called at Broadstairs, Margate, Herne Bay and Whitstable (8.21am) and then ran without further interruption to St Pauls where it was due at 9.50am. The same month a new weekdays up *City Express* appeared taking exactly two hours between Ramsgate (depart 7.20am) and St Pauls serving Broadstairs, Margate and Herne Bay; it ceased at the end of September. Meanwhile the down service went on week in and week out without any major amendment.

Another variation was tried for the summer of 1903 when, for the months of July to September, a new *City Express* (to Herne Bay and Kent Coast) service was put on running Mondays to Fridays in the down direction leaving Victoria at 4pm, Holborn Viaduct at 4.15pm, St Pauls at 4.17pm and Herne Hill at 4.26pm and then serving Herne Bay at 5.41pm and all stations – with the customary omission of Margate (East) – to Ramsgate Harbour where it finished at 6.22pm.

Further introductions, following completion of the Chislehurst-St Mary Cray loops, came in July 1904 with the 9.50am from Ramsgate which called at Broadstairs, Margate West and Westgate-on-Sea and then ran non-stop to Cannon Street where it was due to put in an appearance at 11.47am. From October the train ran two minutes earlier throughout. In January 1905 a rather early homeward departure, so far as the city would be concerned, appeared under the *City Express* banner leaving Cannon Street at 3.20pm, London Bridge at 3.23pm and giving arrival times of 4.53pm at Westgate-on-Sea, 5pm at Margate West, 5.7pm at Broadstairs and 5.15pm at Ramsgate Harbour. Evidently these two trains were little patronised and probably were a misjudgment by the traffic department because they melted away at the end of February 1905.

Finally, at least for this period, in July 1905 the 5.10pm from Holborn Viaduct lost the title and had to be content with a note of City Fast Train.

Resurgence had to wait until 1921 when, from 11 July, a multiplicity of *City Express* titles surfaced in the timetables mostly on services already existing. Dealing with the down services in time order, the first was the Saturdays-only

1.15pm from Cannon Street which called at London Bridge at 1.18pm and next at Whitstable Town at 2.40pm after which it was all stations except the inevitable Margate East to Ramsgate Harbour, where it was due at 3.30pm. Next in the time scale was the 5.5pm (Saturdays excepted) from Holborn Viaduct which had no call before Margate West (6.40pm) and after that went round to Broadstairs (6.54pm) and Ramsgate Harbour (7pm). This was quickly followed by the 5.10pm (Saturdays excepted) from Holborn Viaduct which picked up at St Pauls at 5.12pm and then called all stations from Whitstable Town to Margate West where it terminated at 7.10pm. It slipped at Faversham at 6.29pm an all-stations to Ramsgate Harbour (except Margate East) portion which also allowed all stations to Dover being served. On Saturdays it ran in the same manner except that the first call for the main train was Margate West at 6.53pm after which it called at Broadstairs at 7.7pm and Ramsgate Harbour at 7.14pm. Last of the down *City Express* trains was the 6.10pm from Cannon Street, which operated Mondays to Fridays, calling at Chatham (6.59pm), Faversham (7.24pm), Margate West (7.53pm), Broadstairs (8.6pm) and, finally, Ramsgate Harbour at 8.12pm. All stations connections were given from Faversham to both Ramsgate Harbour and Dover Harbour. This train suffered an early alteration from the beginning of November 1921 when it was retimed to reach Ramsgate Harbour at 8.30pm having called all stations from Faversham with the customary exception of Margate East. A portion for Canterbury East, Kearsney, Dover Priory and Dover Harbour had an all-stations connection from Canterbury onwards.

Two trains carried the *City Express* title inwards and both ran daily except Sundays. The first was unusual in that it avoided the climb up Sole Street bank by taking the route via Gravesend and the North Kent line via Greenwich and in the process gave Gravesend a one-way titled train service. Due to leave Margate West at 7.23am it called at stations to Whitstable Town which was left at 7.56am, then Gravesend Central at 8.39am, London Bridge at 9.15am and finished in platform 8 at Cannon Street at 9.19am. It carried no luggage (this was indicated in the timetable) and on foggy mornings called at Strood as well (this was not indicated!). It was followed about 40 minutes later by the 8.5am from Margate West which called everywhere to Faversham (8.45am) and took on a Dover part of three coaches there and then ran without further halt to Cannon Street where it was due at 10.3am.

From 13 February 1922 sundry amendments were made to these trains. The 5.5pm from Holborn Viaduct had a first class Pullman tea car included in its formation. The Saturdays 5.10pm from Holborn Viaduct called at Faversham at 6.30pm and then proceeded to call at stations to Ramsgate Harbour where it terminated at 7.37pm. The up 7.23am had minor timing adjustments (7.20am from Margate West, three minutes earlier thence arriving at London Bridge at 9.16am and Cannon Street at 9.20am) and the up 8.5am called at London Bridge to arrive at Cannon Street at 10.8am.

With the summer timetable starting 11 June 1922 the Saturdays 1.15pm from Cannon Street sported a first class Pullman (the standard supplementary fee for these on the Kent Coast route was two shillings) making its formation ten coaches made up of the Pullman, two three-coach sets (one of which was detached at Margate West), a ten compartment bogie third, a bogie picnic saloon and a bogie lavatory first.

The 6.10pm from Cannon Street was retired to a 6.12pm departure and reverted to the original summer arrangement of coastal calls at Margate West, Broadstairs and Ramsgate Harbour (8.12pm) and an all stations portion from Faversham to Ramsgate Harbour. The whole, double-headed by D class 4–4–0s, consisted of two three-coach sets, two bogie picnic saloons (half of these formed the four coach slow portion from Faversham) and a six-wheel picnic saloon which did not run on Mondays. Six wheel vehicles in titled trains in 1922 could not have been too common!

Pullmans were drafted into two more of the *City Express* services from 2 October – the 5.10pm Mondays–Fridays train and the up 8.5am other than on Saturdays.

Starting in February 1923 the 7.20am up train was extended backwards to serve Ramsgate Harbour, leaving there at 7.5am, and Broadstairs. Another spate of alterations came with the summer timetable effective for 9 July 1923. The Saturdays-only 1.15pm from Cannon Street exchanged its *City Express* sobriquet for that of *Thanet Express* with slightly varied departure times and a new service bearing the *City Express* title appeared on Saturdays leaving Cannon Street at 12.50pm and London Bridge three minutes later running without call to Herne Bay (2.22pm), Margate West (2.38pm), Broadstairs (2.51pm) and Ramsgate Harbour (2.57pm). The 5.10pm service no longer operated on Saturdays and the 5.5pm also changed to *Thanet Express* while the 6.12pm slipped the all stations portion at Faversham and the through part made a call at Herne Bay at 7.37pm. In the up direction the 8.5am was brought forward to 8.3am, given a Pullman breakfast car (except Saturdays) and accelerated to get into London Bridge at 9.48am and Cannon Street at 9.52am and eventually had to be double-headed for the purpose.

At the end of September the 12.50pm from Cannon Street to Ramsgate Harbour was withdrawn and for the period 14 July – 21 September 1924 the 8.3am train from Margate West was revised to serve Ramsgate Harbour (7.45am) and Broadstairs on Saturdays. Holborn Viaduct lost its titled train service when, from 12 July 1925, the 5.10pm train to Margate was completely recast – although continuing with the title – to run weekdays (except Saturdays) from Cannon Street at 5.20pm, London Bridge at 5.23pm fast to Faversham (6.34pm) after which it called everywhere (except Margate East of course) to Ramsgate Harbour getting there at 7.35pm if events were favourable. The 6.12pm service forfeited its title and then ran to slightly amended times but the two up trains continued unaltered.

Dumpton Park station was opened on 19 July 1926 two weeks after the new Ramsgate station on 2 July (that at the harbour being abandoned) and these improvements occasioned some timetable amendments. The down *City Express*, still with first class Pullman, now left Cannon Street at 5.16pm and ran non-stop to Faversham (6.32pm) after which it got to Ramsgate at 7.30pm having called at all stations except Margate East. In the up direction the 7.5am left Ramsgate at the same time and included the Dumpton Park call running as usual via Gravesend Central (but altered to run via Sidcup and Hither Green instead of via Greenwich) and still made the London Bridge halt before arriving at Cannon Street at 9.20am. The other up titled service changed over to a revised time complete with a first class Pullman and a total prohibition on luggage thus:

		am
Ramsgate	dep	7.30
Dumpton Park	dep	7.32
Broadstairs	dep	7.35
Margate	dep	7.43
London Bridge	arr	9.20
Cannon Street	arr	9.24

This proved too tight a schedule and had to be eased out from 3 January 1927 to 7.26am, 7.29am and 7.34am for the first three departure points. As with most of the other titles on this route that of *City Express* was dropped finally after 9 July 1927 but the services lived on for many years and even in 1987 there was still a 17.14 from Cannon Street arriving at Ramsgate at 18.58 as well as departures from Ramsgate at 07.04 and 07.25 getting into Cannon Street at 08.50 and 09.10 respectively although the earlier morning train does not travel via Gravesend.

Thanet Express

The title *Thanet Express* was introduced on 1 October 1896 and applied to the 10.45am departure from London (Victoria) which called at Herne Hill, at 10.55am for the Holborn Viaduct (10.40am) and St Pauls (10.43am) connection and then ran without further stop to Faversham and then all stations, with the exception of East Margate, to Ramsgate Harbour where arrival was timed for five minutes after one o'clock. There had been a not dissimilar service previously and its timings had been amended for the new titled train which ran every weekday: as was not unusual at the time there was no move to bestow the title on an up service to balance matters. It pursued an undisturbed existence suffering nothing more than minor retimings, such as five minutes later from Faversham to Ramsgate Harbour for the months of July, August and September 1901, until the title was dropped on 30 June 1905. Even then the train went on unamended with the columnar note of Thanet Fast Train in the timetable.

After nearly seven years lying dormant the title was dusted off and used again, this time for an established high season down service. From 3 May 1912 it was applied to the Friday and Saturday service leaving Victoria at 10.15am booked non-stop to Westgate-on-Sea due at 11.50am, after which calls were made at Margate West at noon, Broadstairs at 12.9pm and the journey completed at Ramsgate Harbour at 12.15pm. In June the train ran each weekday and throughout July, August and September it operated on Sundays as well but then ceased entirely until the following May when the same pattern was followed except that the Sunday service was extended to the month of June and during October it operated as in May. This was repeated in 1914 but not thereafter because of the war.

Second revival of the title came with the 11 July 1921 timetable and was as complicated as the previous services had been simple. No less than four weekday services, each customarily in charge of a newly rebuilt 4 4 0, were designated as *Thanet Express*; the first of these was a late morning train from London to Ramsgate which left Victoria at 11.30am complete with first class Pullman Luncheon Car (two shillings supplement) and ran without call until it reached Whitstable Town at 12.52pm and, missing only Margate East, took until 1.49pm to arrive at Ramsgate Harbour. This was a comparatively short-lived service which operated for the last time on 31 October 1921. Another down service carried the title – the 7pm from Victoria – again with first class Pullman car, which also ran non-stop to Whitstable Town where it was due at 8.24pm and then called at Herne Bay, Westgate-on-Sea, Margate West, Broadstairs and Ramsgate Harbour where it was due at 9.14pm. From 2 October 1922 a call was also made at Birchington-on-Sea and times were two minutes later throughout from there. This was a nine coach train of non-gangwayed bogie stock made up of two lavatory brake thirds, three composites, two ten-compartment thirds, a picnic saloon and a Pullman. Apart from the addition of a call at Dumpton Park and an arrival at 9.20pm at Ramsgate when the new stations were opened this service continued virtually unaltered until the last titled run on 9 July 1927.

The *Thanet Belle* in the London suburbs taking the Catford Loop line at Brixton on its journey to North Kent on 7 August 1949 headed by light Pacific No 34062 *17 Squadron*. *Pamlin Prints*

Of the two up services given the title in 1921 one was the afternoon fast train leaving Ramsgate Harbour at 3pm, calling at Broadstairs at 3.8pm, Margate West at 3.20pm and Herne Bay at 3.39pm and then running without further stops to Victoria where it was due at 5.3pm. It started with a first class Pullman Tea Car, with the usual two shilling supplementary charge, but this was dropped as from March 1922 to be reinstated on a Mondays, Fridays and Saturdays only basis for that summer after which it again disappeared. It returned for the summer of 1923 again on a three day basis and so continued until mid-July 1924 when it made a daily appearance. The Herne Bay call was omitted on Saturdays from 14 July 1924. For the winter of 1924/5 the Pullman was confined to Saturdays plus Mondays and Fridays in September and October 1924 and from May 1925.

Composition of the train for the 1922 summer was eight bogie coaches – two lavatory brake thirds, two ten-compartment thirds, two composites, a picnic saloon and the Pullman. From 12 July 1925 departure from Ramsgate Harbour was made 3.5pm with arrival at Victoria at 5.10pm and on Saturdays the call at Herne Bay omitted: the Pullman ran every day. From 21 September 1925 the service ceased until the timetable of 19 July 1926 when it came back on Saturdays only – again without calling at Herne Bay but complete with Pullman – and had a 5.15pm arrival in London. The final run of this afternoon service was made on 18 September 1926.

The other up service was a morning one – the 7.42am from Ramsgate Harbour complete with first class Pullman breakfast car. This train picked up at Broadstairs at 7.49am and Margate West at 7.58am and then ran fast to London (Cannon Street) where it was due at 9.30am: it was very obviously a business service as was demonstrated by the timetable note, when a call was introduced at Herne Bay from 19 July 1926, that luggage would not be carried from that station. From 12 February 1922 a call was made at London Bridge at 9.28am, the departure times from the Thanet calls being two minutes earlier and the arrival at Cannon Street two minutes later. From 11 June 1922 a Mondays-only train was introduced – duly designated *Thanet Express* and with Pullman – which left Margate West at 7.43am, called at Herne Bay at 7.59am, London Bridge at 9.28am and arrived at Cannon Street at 9.32am. This affected the by now 7.40am which had four minutes more added to its London arrival times. The Monday-only working continued until the end of October and recommenced in May 1923 but, from 9 July 1923, the title was taken away from the 7.43am train from Margate West.

Bogie stock was allocated to the 7.40am from Ramsgate in the form of a three-coach set, a Pullman, a half saloon lavatory first, a picnic saloon and two composites except for Mondays and Saturdays. On Mondays an extra third class carriage was added while on Saturdays the two composites were omitted. Various alterations were made to the times of the 7.40am; from 21 September 1925 departure from Ramsgate Harbour became 7.35am and correspondingly earlier from Broadstairs and Margate West; when the new station at Ramsgate was commissioned the timing reverted to 7.40am, the Broadstairs call was exchanged for one at Herne Bay at 8.8am and the London Bridge and Cannon Street arrivals became 9.32am and 9.36am respectively and from May to October each year the *Thanet Express* was booked into London four minutes later on Mondays than other days. The final run with the title was made on 9 July 1927 but the service carried on long after that: even in

May 1987 there was a 07.42 from Ramsgate which was due at Cannon Street – without calling at London Bridge – at 09.30!

If matters were not complicated enough with *Thanet Express* departures from Victoria at 7pm and Ramsgate Harbour at 7.40am and 3pm on weekdays the Southern Railway decided that, with the timetable introduced on 9 July 1923, another one should join the trio to balance the up morning working. Accordingly, the 5.5pm from Holborn Viaduct, which ran Mondays to Fridays non stop to Margate West (6.40pm) and then called at Broadstairs at 6.54pm and terminated at Ramsgate at 7pm, was selected for the honour. This train ran with a first class Pullman Tea Car. For Saturdays the *City Express*, leaving Cannon Street at 1.20pm with calls at London Bridge and all stations (other than Margate East) from Whitstable Town (2.40pm) to Ramsgate Harbour (3.30pm) and having a first class Pullman Luncheon car, exchanged its title for that of *Thanet Express*.

From 12 July 1925 the 5.5pm from Holborn Viaduct was switched to Cannon Street with a departure time of 5.8pm but otherwise unaltered. Next summer, with the start of the timetable of 19 July, the Saturday service was amended to eight minutes earlier leaving Cannon Street at 1.12pm and completing its run at Ramsgate at 3.27pm after making a call at Dumpton Park. The 5.8pm also called there when the new arrangements came into force. With the blanket de-titling of the summer of 1927 these two trains ran under the *Thanet Express* banner for the last time on 8 July for the 5.8pm and 9 July for the 1.12pm although continuing to serve the commuters otherwise unchanged, so much so that even in July 1985 the 17.08 from Cannon Street was booked into Ramsgate at 18.52!

The title *Thanet Express* therefore has been carried by no fewer than nine distinct services between London and Thanet.

Thanet Pullman Limited
Desecration of the Sabbath had been going on for some years on the western side of the dividing wall at Victoria station in London in the running of excursion trains of an elite nature and, either out of desire for not letting the LBSCR directors stand alone in the matter on the Day of Judgement or – as was more likely – with a view to assisting the finances, their opposite numbers of the South Eastern & Chatham decided in 1921 that this monopoly should be broken. Thus on 10 July there set off from platform 6 at Victoria the Sundays-only *Thanet Pullman Limited* at 10.10am running non-stop in an hour and a half to Margate West, calling at Broadstairs at 11.51am and completing its journey a couple of minutes before noon at Ramsgate Harbour. The return was timed for 5.30pm, with departures from Broadstairs at 5.36pm

and Margate West at 5.45pm and an arrival in the metropolis at 7.15pm. First class passengers only were catered for at a single fare of twenty-four shillings (£1.20) or return for two guineas (£2.10) inclusive of Pullman supplements.

The limitation was to 124 passengers who were carried in the Pullman cars *Sorrento*, *Ruby*, *Topaz*, *Leghorn*, *Daphne* and *Corunna*, all eight-wheelers. Because the all-Pullman concept was a novelty at the time for the SECR, none of these vehicles was equipped with a guard's brake compartment and the six car Pullman ensemble had to be saddled with an undignified van in which the

For the Festival of Britain in 1951 part of the *Thanet Belle* was diverted to serve Canterbury and the train's title was altered to *Kentish Belle*. The three-coach portion is about to leave Canterbury East on 5 July on its return to London headed by Class D1 4-4-0 No 31145 as far as Faversham. No headboards were carried on the Canterbury portion. *Arthur G. Wells*

guard travelled together with any heavy luggage that might appear. This anomaly persisted into the era of the Southern Railway. The E1 class rebuilt 4–4–0s had become available in 1920 and proved very suitable for running this train of about 220 tons to a ninety minute schedule for the 74 miles to Margate.

Winter patronage could, understandably, be expected to be light (the prospect of spending about five hours on the storm lashed Margate promenade on a wet Sunday is less than inviting) and it was decided to combine the *Thanet Pullman Limited* with the 10.10am down service and the 5pm from Ramsgate Harbour. In an effort to maintain the illusion of a separate train the timetable showed the *Thanet Pullman Limited* leaving at 10.10am, running without a stop to Margate West, calling at Broadstairs and terminating at Ramsgate Harbour at 12.5pm. In the adjoining column was the 10.10am departure from Victoria slipping a portion at Faversham and running non-stop to Westgate-on-Sea, then calling all stations to Ramsgate Harbour where it arrived at 12.5pm. So, in effect, the Pullmans were part of a combined train. In a similar manner the up service coalesced with the 5pm *Cliftonville Express* from Ramsgate Harbour due at Victoria at 7.2pm. The *Cliftonville Express* was indicated as serving Herne Bay at 5.37pm but otherwise the calls were identical. In theory a passenger wanting to travel in the Pullman part of the train from Herne Bay could be denied his choice because the *Cliftonville Express* did not advertise such accommodation.

This modus operandi set the pattern for succeeding years so that the train in its own right operated for about a dozen Sundays annually. The summer schedules varied from year to year with a major amendment under the Southern aegis when the return was put back about an hour and a half and the return day fare was dropped to what had been the single fare in 1921 (the fares, including supplement, became 17 shillings single, 24 shillings return from 15 July 1923). The timing of 90 minutes each way between London and Margate and about 1¾ hours to and from Ramsgate remained constant for the summer services but the departure times were altered almost yearly as the following summary makes clear:

Year	From Victoria	From Ramsgate
1921	10.10am	5.30pm
1922	10am	5.30pm
1923	10.15am	7.5pm
1924	10.15am	7.5pm
1925	10.10am	7.0pm
1926	10.10am	6.50pm
1927	10.5am	6.50pm
1928	10.5am	6.50pm

The departures of the combined winter service did not change as much as those of the summer. The time from Victoria was always 10.10am, except for the winters of 1923/4 and 1924/5 when it was 10.20am, while for the first three seasons it was 5pm from Ramsgate but then became 5.5pm.

From 2 July 1926 the new station at Ramsgate rather than that at the harbour was used and from 19 July a call was also made at Dumpton Park in the down direction only. The *Cliftonville Express* lost its title for the winter of 1926/7 and thereafter but gained a first class Pullman in 1925/6 although whether this was a Pullman in its own part of the combination or the vicarious use of a Thanet Pullman is not entirely clear.

In its own right the *Thanet Pullman Limited* ran for the last time on 30 September 1928; carrying the title but combined with the 10.10am and 5.5pm services it made its final trip on 30 June 1929. From 7 July 1929 until 28 June 1931 the combined train procedure applied summer and winter to the former overall timings with the note that Thanet Limited Cars (First Class) operated in the services. From 5 July 1931 even this reference was dropped and the train which had played host was simply indicated as having first class Pullmans as part of its facilities. The name as such had just managed to last for a decade, the depression finally sounding its death knell.

Thanet Belle
Kentish Belle
Although not brought to fruition until British Railways' days the reintroduction of an all-Pullman service to the Kent coast resorts was undoubtedly the result of planning by the Southern Railway. Inauguration of the *Thanet Belle* took place on 31 May 1948 when Battle of Britain class Pacific No s21C170 *Manston* headed the ten Pullman cars out of London (Victoria) at 11.30am. This was a daily train operating only in the summer the timings being:

		am	pm		pm	pm
Victoria	dep	11.30	3.5	arr	7.10	8.20
Whitstable	dep	12.52	4.30	arr	5.44	6.57
Herne Bay	dep	1.1	4.39	arr	5.35	6.48
Margate	dep	1.17	4.56	arr	5.18	6.29
Broadstairs	dep	1.28	5.7	arr	5.10	6.20
Ramsgate	dep	1.34	5.15	arr	5.5	6.15

Grubby D class 4-4-0 No 31591 shortly after leaving Canterbury East with the *Kentish Belle* on 16 August 1951. *Arthur G. Wells*

In complete contrast to No 31591 on the *Kentish Belle* is LMR type class 4 2-6-4 tank No 42068 approaching Chartham Crossing with the up service on 26 July 1951. *Arthur G. Wells*

Surprising motive power for the down *Kentish Belle* on 30 August 1958 pictured in the heart of the Garden of England near Newington. Ashford shed's duty 265 (which the engine carries) should have been the 3.26pm Victoria-Margate rather than the *Belle* so some disorganisation at Sewarts Lane shed had caused Class L 4-4-0 No 31766 to be promoted. *S. C. Nash*

The 11.30am down did not run on Saturdays, which day the 3.5pm took its place; in the up direction the 5.5pm from Ramsgate did not run on Saturdays and Sundays because the 6.15pm service operated those days. In 1949 the Monday to Friday departure from Ramsgate was speeded up to give a two hour timing to Victoria (due 7.5pm) and, in 1950, from 1 July to 2 September an additional Saturday service was provided each way leaving Victoria at 7.55am calling at the same intermediate places and arriving at Ramsgate at 10.13am and returning from there at 11.15am on a two hours and thirteen minutes booking to Victoria with the same stops en route.

Ten Pullman cars usually comprised the train of which two were first class.

The inaugural train, which may be taken as typical, was made up of first class cars *Coral* and *Formosa* and third class cars 11, 15, 16, 96, 132, 133, 135 and 137 giving a seating capacity of 44 first and 225 third class. After a time *Formosa* was appropriately replaced by *Maid of Kent*. The late-morning departure from London, doubtless made in the interest of serving luncheon, made little more than a half-day excursion by the train possible and consequently business traffic from London must have been slight although in this respect the 5.5pm return would have been more helpful; the Saturday services were obviously orientated towards holiday traffic.

Customary engine power for the train was a light 4–6–2, usually a Stewarts Lane duty out and back, although Ramsgate shed did later provide a similar type for some of the up trips. On Saturdays the 3.5pm train did not always secure this degree of power owing to demands of boat and other traffic and perhaps would be hauled by a Schools class 4–4–0 locomotive.

Probably few passengers on the 6.15pm from Ramsgate on Sunday 24 September 1950 had any inkling that they were travelling on the final run of the *Thanet Belle* for, in the 1951 summer timetable, the train was recast, as part of the Festival of Britain activities, to serve Canterbury on Mondays to Fridays.

Another surprising class of engine on the down *Kentish Belle* – U1 class 2-6-0 No 31895. The date was 10 August 1957 and the location Shortlands. *Author*

For this purpose the 11.30am called at Faversham at 12.43pm to detach three cars (two brake thirds – 16 and 95 – and first class car *Maid of Kent*, about 68 seats in all) for Canterbury East which was reached at 1.6pm; the times of arrival of the main train along the coast were later by about five minutes than hitherto. For the return the departure time of the main train was advanced by ten minutes with the Canterbury portion leaving the city at 5.30pm and being shunted, after arrival at Faversham, on to the rear of the coastal section of the train ready for a 5.53pm departure. In view of this extension to Canterbury the term Thanet was not geographically accurate and so that of *Kentish Belle* came into being. The previous summer's schedules, with the odd minute difference in one or two cases, obtained for the Saturday and Sunday workings, including the high season 7.55am and 11.15am trains.

At this time the American tourist invasion was in the future and the Canterbury portion was not well patronised, some journeys being made without any passengers at all. It was all the more strange, therefore, that the rake was strengthened with another car for the late July/early August Cricket Week but presumably this followed an edict made by somebody at headquarters and remote from the scene of operations. The portion did not stay over at Canterbury but was worked empty to and from Faversham, a variety of locomotive types being utilised. During that summer 4–4–0s of Classes D, D1 and L1 as well as the LMR series of 2–6–4 tank engines, all usually from Dover shed (duty 440) were noted filling in between turns on other trains they had brought to Faversham and were not specially maintained for the train. No locomotive headboard was carried for this short length. The first service to Canterbury ran on 2 July and the last one on 7 September which gave a total of 50 round trips.

With the Festival year past, the 1952 services reverted to arrangements closely paralleling those for 1950 without any amendment to the train's title. Departures from Victoria were at 7.55am (Saturdays high season), 11.35am (Mondays to Fridays) and 3.6pm (Saturdays) with corresponding arrivals at Ramsgate at 10.13am, 1.38pm and 5.15pm. Return bookings were 11.15am (Saturdays high season), 5.5pm (Mondays to Fridays) and 6.15pm (Saturdays and Sundays) with arrivals at Victoria at 1.29pm, 7.5pm and 8.20pm respectively. These timings were maintained until 1957 when small adjustments were made for that year and, it transpired, for 1958 also to allow for delays due to electrification works.

Initially ten Pullman cars were rostered daily but in later years this loading was confined to Saturday and Sunday workings with eight cars sufficing for traffic on the other days of the week. It was the locomotive rosters that probably afforded as much interest as any aspect of the train from 1952

The last of the season's Saturday 3.6pm ex Victoria service of the *Kentish Belle* passing Clapham on 13 September 1958 with Schools class 4-4-0 No 30937 *Epsom* in charge instead of the booked Pacific. *S. C. Nash*

onwards. Whereas in 1954 every working was booked for a Battle of Britain class 4–6–2 (Stewarts Lane duty 11 with the 11.35am down Mondays to Fridays and 6.15pm up on Saturdays; the same shed's duty 15 both ways on Sundays while on Saturdays the 7.55am was duty 18 with Ramsgate duty 470 on the 5.5pm up, duty 473 on the 3.6pm down and duty 476 for the 11.15am up) in some later summers Ashford based class N 2–6–0s were reported working one or more of the Saturday trains nominally diagramed for a King Arthur from that shed (duty 343).

In the event, as already mentioned for the *Thanet Belle*, demands on Saturdays were such that the 3.6pm got whatever engine was available – often a Schools 4–4–0 but sometimes a 2–6–0 or even, on one occasion, an L class 4–4–0. Standard Class 4 4–6–0s were noted at times on the eight coach formation in the middle of the week but eventually, with the influx of modified light 4–6–2s, it became distinctly unusual to find anything but a Pacific at the head other than at weekends.

It would have been possible to have worked the train upon electrification with electric locomotives but the over-riding demands of a regular interval uniform service hardly made such prospects very bright. And so it proved: when the new electric service schedules for 1959 were published, it was confirmed that the final run of the *Kentish Belle* had been made with the 6.15pm from Ramsgate on 14 September 1958 and that Pullman cars in non-continental services were to be no more. So, after a decade, ended the second attempt to serve Thanet with an all-Pullman train.

CHAPTER EIGHT

To Dover for Paris

Club Train

Towards the end of May 1889 a series of announcements appeared in *The Times*. First of these was one by the South Eastern Railway, under the heading of Club Train Services, stating that commencing 4 June a special train would leave Charing Cross daily, Sundays excepted, at 4.15pm arriving in Paris at 11.53pm and that a similar train would return from Paris daily (Saturdays excepted) at 4pm and arrive at Charing Cross at 11.30pm. This was followed by an insertion from the London, Chatham & Dover Railway informing the public that commencing 4 June a special new limited Saloon and Dining Car Express (first class only) would leave Victoria at 4.15pm (except Sundays and days as advertised) and be due in Paris at 11.55pm with customs examination in the cars, table d'hôte 7 francs, and the company's ships, the new *Calais-Douvres*, *Empress* or *Victoria* would run in connection. Finally, the International Sleeping Car Company announced that the first train of a new Club Train (Paris Limited Express) service would leave London (Charing Cross, Holborn and Victoria) on 4 June and following days at 4.15pm reaching Paris at 11.55pm and, furthermore, from the end of June the train would be entirely composed of new luxurious saloon cars of the International Sleeping Car Company and from then onwards custom house examination would take place in the train. The company asked for applications for seats and private deck cabins on the new steamer *Calais-Douvres* to be directed to them.

The scene vis-à-vis England and France at about the time that these slightly conflicting announcements were made is of interest. The Entente was, to put no finer point on it, rather less than Cordiale but there was much activity in France. The Northern Railway of France was making improvements at Boulogne by putting in a chord line which would overcome the drawback of Calais-Paris trains having to reverse there; harbour improvements were being made as well at Boulogne and also at Calais, where a maritime station was to be built; and to crown it all there was to be the Great Exhibition in Paris opening in May 1889 complete with the Eiffel Tower. In England the Channel Tunnel Company had been formed, various large engineering works – the Severn

163

The South Eastern's *Club Train* passing Dunton Green en route from Charing Cross to Dover in the charge of F class 4-4-0 No 241. The angle of the camera allows no more than the guard's ducket on the side of the brake van at the rear to be recorded. *L & GRP/David & Charles*

Tunnel, the second Tay Bridge and the Forth Bridge – were either recently completed or about to be and there had been the railway Race to the North, all of which were to have a stimulating effect on schedules; and the SER and LCDR were still managing to avoid entering into a working union.

Against this background the South Eastern's general manager received a letter from M. Mathias, his opposite number of the Northern Railway of France (Nord) dated 2 January 1888 indicating it was proposed to run a new service of trains between London and Paris via Calais starting from each capital at about 4 or 4.30pm and arriving at the destination by midnight (a 7½ to 8 hour service) and that details were still being worked out with the International Sleeping Car Company (Wagons-Lits). This was reported to the South Eastern Railway board at its meeting on 12 January and duly noted; commercial interests had presented petitions for a first class service at about these hours to both SER and LCDR so a demand for such a pair of trains did exist but the degree was perhaps the uncertain factor.

By the time of the board meeting on 3 May a draft of the agreement with Wagons-Lits (W-L) was available with the suggestion that the starting date be 1 January 1889. All the SER had to do was to provide motive power between Charing Cross and Dover, because the LCDR was to be responsible for the provision of the steamer and W-L would supply special rolling stock and staff on both sides of the Channel. As this probably appeared a none-too-onerous agreement, the board gave approval and at the 23 August meeting it was noted that the seal was affixed on the Agreement as to running of the *Club Train* between London and Dover.

Meanwhile procrastination was the order of the day in the LCDR's boardroom. At the meeting of 28 June 1888 – nearly two months after the SER had approved the proposal – the subject of a special rapid train service between London and Paris was discussed and the only decision arrived at was to await a further report. A new cross-channel vessel was suggested as being required but not necessarily in connection with the proposed rapid service. The LCDR directors eventually, at their meeting of 23 January 1889, had the agreement with W-L to consider with a suggested commencement of 1 May 1889. Already there had been a four-month slippage but even so time was very short for an introduction on the revised date. So it proved but the four parties – Nord, W-L, LCDR and SER – sheltered behind the explanation of the doubt of the Paris Exhibition being completed in time for the 6 May opening: in the

This view of the pier at Dover from the landward end gives some idea of the spartan facilities which patrons of the *Club Train* would have found there during its period of operation. A train is on the LCDR line, the South Eastern company's metals being to the right.

event it wasn't completed but it was opened even if it was June before the lifts in the Eiffel Tower were being tested!

At that period it was usual for timetable alterations to be made as from the first of the month irrespective of the day of the week. The LCDR was making general accelerations on its continental services from 1 June and wanted to include the train but it was then appreciated that the French President would be inaugurating the new works at Calais harbour on 3 June and consequently it was decided that, so far as the *Club Train* was concerned, its debut would be on 4 June 1889. The new LCDR paddle steamer *Calais-Douvres* would be delivered just in time to make its maiden channel crossing on 3 June.

The *Club Train* consisted of one train for the Paris (Nord) – Calais Pier section and two trains in England, one each between Dover Pier and London (Victoria) and Dover Pier – London (Charing Cross), all stock being provided by W-L powered by local company locomotives and the LCDR steamer link between the ports. The timings were:

		pm	pm		pm	pm
London (Charing Cross)	dep	4.15	–	arr	11.30	–
London (Victoria)	dep	–	4.15	arr	–	11.30
London (Holborn Viaduct)	dep	–	4.15	arr	–	11.30
Herne Hill	arr	–	4.23	dep	–	11.22
	dep	–	4.25	arr	–	11.20
Dover Pier	arr	5.55	6.0	dep	9.45	9.45
	dep		6.5	arr		9.32
Calais Pier	arr		7.20	dep		8.22
	dep		7.40	arr		8.13
Amiens	arr		9.58	dep		5.55
	dep		10.3	arr		5.50
Paris (Nord)	arr		11.53	dep		4.0

Outwards Sundays excepted: inwards Saturdays excepted: first class only: French time was ten minutes in advance of English so the elapsed journey time was 7 hours 28 minutes outwards and 7 hours 40 minutes inwards.

The South Eastern announced in its timetable a 3 June start (which has misled authors ever since) but corrected this in its newspaper announcement; the time of arrival in Paris of 11.53pm, although seemingly at odds with LCDR and W-L times of 11.55pm, appears correct because, in the LCDR timetable, that was the arrival time given. The SER and W-L referred to the service as the *Club Train* from the start but the LCDR, straining to obtain some cachet, tried to call it anything but that (Paris Limited; 1st Limited; Limited Saloon and

Plan of Dover Harbour. The arrows show the manoeuvres necessary for *Night Ferry* sleeping cars and vans to be embarked and disembarked from the ship described on page 202 (adapted from Wagon Lits brochures).

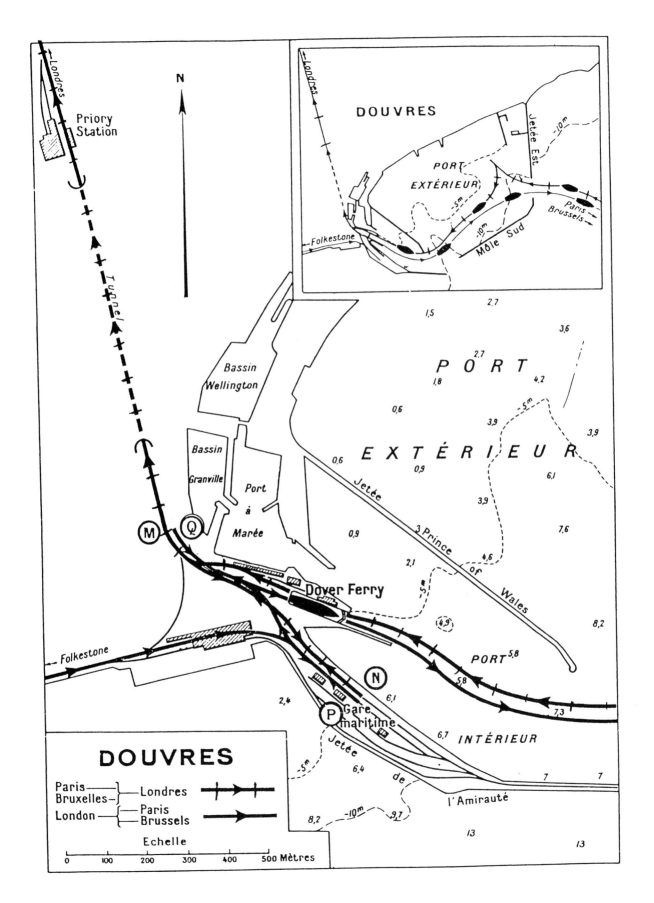

N

Priory
Station

Tunnel

Londres

DOUVRES

Jetée Est

-10ᵐ

PORT
EXTÉRIEUR

-5ᵐ

Folkestone

-10ᵐ

Môle Sud

Paris
Brussels

Londres

Bassin
Wellington

Bassin

Granville

Port
à
Marée

M Q

Folkestone

Dover Ferry

1,5

2,7

3,6

P O R T

1,8

2,7

4,2

0,6

-5ᵐ

3,9

3,9

E X T É R I E U R

0,6

0,9

6,1

3,9

7,6

0,9

Jetée

2,1

4,6

-5ᵐ

(4,9)

8,2

Prince

of

Wales

PORT *5,8*

N

6,1

5,8

7,3

2,4

P Gare
maritime

6,7

INTÉRIEUR

-5ᵐ

Jetée

6,4

de

7

7

l'Amirauté

8,2

-10ᵐ

9,7

13

13

DOUVRES

Paris
Bruxelles——— Londres
London ——— Paris
Brussels

Echelle

0   100   200   300   400   500 Mètres

Dining Car Express; and Paris Limited Mail although one thing the *Club Train* did not carry was mail). Doubtless reminded by W-L of the agreement, the LCDR gave the title in its July 1889 timetable and onwards, for it was the international company which wanted to reproduce a club atmosphere for first class businessmen and others and underline it by so titling this de-luxe service.

If there had been a Trades Description Act in 1889 it could have been invoked in respect of the suggestion that the PS *Calais-Douvres* would operate the sea link because its first appearance in this connection was not until 12 December 1889! Understandably W-L had not had time to build the special rolling stock and each railway had to provide a make-shift set for the train they hauled for a month or so from the start.

Interest was sufficient to draw a crowd to Victoria to witness the start of the train's maiden trip on Tuesday 4 June 1889. The stock consisted of two first class saloons and two first class compartment coaches, it being rumoured that the first of the special cars being built in Belgium would appear at the end of that week. A stop was made at Herne Hill to take aboard the City passengers from Holborn Viaduct and those from Manchester, Liverpool and elsewhere who had come down by expresses from those cities and changed into a London & North Western Railway local connecting service at Willesden Junction. The LNWR train on this important occasion unfortunately brought no passengers! The *Club Train* then proceeded via Chatham to Dover, where tickets were collected (this happened at Herne Hill inwards), and then on to the Pier where it arrived punctually at 6pm. The South Eastern Railway's *Club Train* due at 5.55pm had arrived and its four passengers were already embarked. The 21 persons from the LCDR train quickly joined the steamer and at 6.6pm it cast off. It was not the new PS *Calais-Douvres* – that was not yet ready for service only having made its first voyage across the channel the previous day – but the three year old PS *Victoria* which conveyed the Duke of Hamilton and the other 24 passengers across in a time of seventy minutes to arrive at Calais a shade before schedule. There the new Gare Maritime was not yet ready but the train of temporary stock, a dining car, two drawing-room cars, a compartment car and a baggage wagon (all with uncovered through communication) was waiting complete with attendants having *Club Train* on their caps. This was booked as the fastest train in France at a little over 43mph and the *mecanicien* demonstrated this with some very lively running down towards Boulogne which scattered the wine bottles in the dining car in the process. Paris was reached a few minutes before midnight. Earlier, on the inaugural train to London 30 people had booked for the journey. So far so good!

Next day another thirty passengers came from England but they did not fare

The Wagon Lits saloons and fourgons from the SER and LCDR Club trains of 1889. *Courtesy Robin Barnard*

so well. The LCDR locomotive was reputed to have broken a spring a few miles from the start and so there was a late departure from Dover. Not to be outdone by the LCDR the French locomotive lost time from Paris and the London arrival was reported 15 minutes late. Worse was to come: the arrival due at Charing Cross on 10 June at 11.30pm turned up next day at 1am in the pouring rain and to rub salt into the wound all the cabs had been allowed to go home! This was not an isolated instance because a day or two later the arrival was noted as 12.45am. As one gentleman wrote – 'Advice to people about to travel by the club train – Don't'. Despite this the first Friday and Saturday of the service saw the outward LCDR train fully booked, due possibly partly to curiosity and partly because it was the Whitsun weekend.

In addition to the punctuality failings there were also grumblings about the fares. These were first class express plus supplement (16s – 80p) and booking charge (2s 6d) for the International Sleeping Car Company which, seeing it was ordinary stock anyway, was an obvious irritant to travellers. Passengers in Britain have never taken kindly to additional charges on trains and this instance caused queries to be raised as to the legality of the fares demanded.

At first the timetable was of an erratic nature for on certain days the train did not run at all; these were (outwards) 14, 15 and 29 June and 1, 2, 3, 15, 16, 29, 30 and 31 July with not dis-similar omissions inwards. Then the schedules for some days were altered to a 2pm departure from both Victoria and Charing Cross giving an arrival in Paris at 10.5pm and, in the opposite direction, a 2.40pm departure from Paris with an arrival in London timed exactly eight hours later. This arrangement was advertised for 1, 2, 12, 13, 14, 15, 27, 28, 29 and 30 August, 10, 11, 12, 13, 14, 26, 27, 28 and 30 September, 9, 10, 11, 12, 14, 25, 26, 28 and 29 October and 1, 2, 4 to 9, 11 to 16 November. The reason for these departures from the standard timetable is not entirely clear but it is thought to be connected with either tidal problems at Calais or with lower class special excursion traffic for the Paris Exhibition – trains de plaisir as the French termed them – and it is known that there was an intention to use the smaller vessels on some of these amended services. From 1 September the basic inward service left Paris at 3.45pm and was due in London at 11.15pm.

Last day of the exhibition was 31 October and from 18 November 1889 the schedule settled down to a period of stability with a departure from London at 3.15pm (Sundays excepted) and an arrival in Paris at 11.12pm and a departure from the French capital at 3.30pm (Saturdays excepted) giving arrivals in London at 11.15pm.

Meanwhile the specially-constructed stock had put in an appearance, probably at the end of July or beginning of August. The two trains for use in England were similar and consisted of bogie saloon cars (two for the SER, three – reduced to two by 1890 – for the LCDR) and bogie *fourgon* or van to which each company added a small brake van at the opposite end to the *fourgon*. The saloons were divided into two sections each seating 16 passengers and were vestibuled to one another and the *fourgon*, which was equipped for preparing teas and refreshments. The green livery coupled with polished brass fittings gave an attractive ensemble although the *fourgon* did have an oddly truncated clerestory roof arrangement. In France the train ran to four saloons, a dining car and a *fourgon*, part of which had a coupe for passengers. To power these trains the SER used their F class 4–4–0s (one of which, No 240, was awarded a gold medal at the Paris Exhibition) while the LCDR at first relied on the 2–4–0s of the *Europa* class and then, from late 1891, on the newly-constructed M3 class 4–4–0s.

The paddle steamers usually used were *Empress* or *Victoria* with the older, smaller boats assisting from time to time. As previously mentioned, the much lauded *Calais-Douvres* did not put in an appearance until December all its voyages on the service in 1889 being made on consecutive days. The 335 sailings from inception to the end of 1889 were distributed among the fleet thus:

Empress	127	*Samphire*	21	*Petrel*	11
Victoria	104	*Breeze*	19	*Calais-Douvres*	9
Maid of Kent	25	*Foam*	16	*Invicta*	3

Timetable alterations during 1890 were not extensive. The South Eastern advertised a departure from Cannon Street at 2.45pm in January (which was apparently a suitable connecting service rather than the inward empty stock picking up there), small boats were regularly advertised for certain days and the LCDR, from 1 April inserted a call at St Pauls at 11.15pm for the inwards connection and from 1 July outwards at 3.12pm. The LCDR directors' report for the half year ending 30 June bemoaned '. . . heavy expenditure incurred in running the additional train and boat service to and from the continent known as the 'Club Train'.' Note the 'known as'!

15 May 1891 saw the service become daily, the Saturdays (from Paris) and Sundays (from London) exceptions being dropped, followed by a first class coach without supplement being made available in France and a small reduction in the supplementary fares. Then, from 1 June, the departure from London became 3pm (arriving Paris 10.57pm) and from Paris 3.15pm (due London 11pm) and from 1 July a 15 minute earlier departure from Dover Pier to London was reflected in an arrival at Victoria or Charing Cross at 10.45pm. The schedule between Victoria and Dover and vice versa had always remained at 105 minutes. Thereafter there were a few changes to the Paris arrival time: to 10.47pm from 1 November 1891, to 11.7pm from 1 June 1893 and finally, from 1 August 1893 to 11.10pm. From the winter of 1891/2 the pretence that a passenger might get a large, modern steamer was abandoned. With paddle steamers *Petrel* and *Foam* being advertised as running the service such names must have been less than reassuring to the traveller who was prone to turn as green as the tempestous Channel he was crossing. Additionally there were reports that the French customs examination had been altered from en route to on arrival at Paris.

The early 'nineties were not very prosperous because trade and agriculture was generally depressed and this in turn affected business intercourse between Britain and France, so the LCDR decided to rid itself of the service and gave notice to W-L it would cease operating it after the end of November 1892. However, as the company was a party to the Continental Traffic Committee it could not be done as simply as that. A special meeting was called for 19 October to review the position. There the train passenger statistics for the period 28 August to 27 September (inclusive) were tabled. These gave the interesting figures of:

	817 passengers outwards	966 passengers inwards	Total
By SER	493	613	1106
By LCDR	324	353	677

The steamer records give 832 passengers outwards and 1011 inwards for the period so there was some local traffic to and from Dover other than by the *Club Train*. The lowest number on any train was two (outwards SER 12 September and inwards LCDR 22 September) although there were several instances of three for the LCDR. Comparing this month with the similar period in 1889 covering the same number of 62 sailings the earlier figures were 1336 outwards and 1146 inwards so clearly there had been a decline, as might be expected without the attraction of the Paris exhibition. The traffic had not built up sufficiently in the years that followed. It was little wonder the LCDR wanted to terminate the agreement with 62 per cent of the rail traffic now being handled by the SER.

Much to the chagrin of the LCDR the meeting decided that matters would remain unaltered because the Nord explained there was pressure by the French government for the service to continue. The French saw no reason why the English should not continue to foot the bill, especially if they were stupid enough to run *two* trains to and from their capital while, with commendable Gallic logic, only one was necessary to connect Paris with Calais!

Not content with this decision the LCDR next tried to make a new agreement with W-L. This came to the knowledge of the SER who wrote to W-L with injured surprise that their friends (1890's euphemism!) the LCDR were attempting to make a unilateral agreement with W-L and requested details. M Nagelmackers took it upon himself to reply that this was for a five year period for W-L to charter train and vessel at its own expense plus other payments but that W-L wanted to ensure that large steamers were used instead of the small ones as had happened during the whole of 1892. At one time it is stated that Nord and W-L had even agreed to share with the LCDR the extra cost of running large steamers but to no avail. Eventually, however, the Continental Traffic Committee agreed to discontinue the de-luxe service and announced it would operate for the last time on 30 September 1893. It fell to the paddle steamer *Petrel* to make the sailings on the final day with 70 passengers outwards and 34 on the return. At six minutes past nine in the evening she tied up at Dover leaving the two trains to London to ring down the curtain.

Failure of the service was basically because it could not attract sufficient passengers due, in some measure but by no means entirely, to the supplementary fares and the use of 30 year old small steamers on what was presented as a de-luxe service. Without exception regular travellers were full of praise for W-L as '. . . with its attendants, its teas and soda-waters on this side and its excellent dinners on the other. The service was simply perfect . . .' but one searches in vain for any excuse for the LCDR for its myopic attitude to the service let alone commendation. Despite the reputation of being the most expensive journey in Europe there were those who sought improvement rather than cessation of the amenity and the Calais Chamber of Trade in asking for reinstatement of the facility were told if this were to happen the Nord would have to bear the continuing monetary loss. So the train passed into history but not before it found itself immortalised in *Lady Windermere's Fan* (first produced on 20 February 1892 at St James's Theatre) wherein Mrs Erlynne announces 'I'm leaving this afternoon by the *Club Train*.'

The Lord Nelson class hauled the *Golden Arrow* from the start: No 864 *Sir Martin Frobisher* passes Bromley on 31 October 1931. *H. C. Casserley*

Golden Arrow

A second attempt to establish a de-luxe service between London and Paris had some curious parallels with the original effort in that the title again came from the continent, a new steamer was constructed for the start of the service, supplementary charges were levied and the de-luxe character could not be sustained by itself.

Grouping had seen the absorption of the South Eastern & Chatham into the Southern Railway and, in the summer of 1923, the re-organization of the continental services. These became based on Victoria as the London terminus with a total of seven services between the British and French capitals on weekdays. The main flagship service was the 11am from London with a corresponding noon departure from Paris; on the French side the train was almost exclusively first class having but a modicum of second class accommodation and was a fully reservable limited train although for the English section there was a first and second class brake coach with the Pullman cars. On 20 October 1925 a letter appeared in *The Times* from Sir Davison Dalziel of the Wagons-Lits and Pullman Car Companies indicating the introduction shortly of new all-Pullman car services throughout Europe. While Wagons-Lits were having Pullman cars built in England for a Pullman boat train between Calais and Paris the Southern Railway, in its July 1926 timetable, advertised a Pullman car train running ten minutes in advance of the 11am service to Dover and a 5.40pm return but it appears that one or two ordinary coaches were included in the formation. This was in anticipation of the new first class all-Pullman *La Flèche d'Or* which was inaugurated on 13 September 1926, the only alteration to the schedule being the change in departure time to 10.45am of the Pullman train from Victoria. Wagons-Lits adapted the Pullman slogan of the 'Golden Way' for the train title but, despite operating a Pullman train in connection, the Southern Railway refrained from adopting the title preferring to bide time until plans could be fully implemented.

At its meeting on 25 January 1928 the SR Docks and Marine Committee were first apprised, by the general manager, of a proposal to introduce an additional service between London and Paris via Dover and Calais with a special steamer, for which a supplement would be payable on board, to be known as the *Golden*

Post-war re-introduction of the *Golden Arrow* came in April 1946 and for the first few days of the service the Southern Railway appropriately used Merchant Navy Pacific No 21C1 *Channel Packet*. Here the train approaches Bickley Junction on 19 April. *LCGB Ken Nunn Collection*

Light Pacifics took over the *Golden Arrow* duty on a regular basis as evidenced by un-named No 21C157 east of Tonbridge on 10 June 1947. *Author*

Arrow service. It was agreed to ask William Denny & Brothers Limited of Dumbarton to submit a quotation. The shipbuilders quickly did so – in just over two weeks – and eventually the contract was placed at £220,225. Launching, at which the ship was christened *Canterbury*, was on 13 December 1928 and trials took place early in the following March during the course of which the maximum speed over the measured mile was 22.67 knots attained on run 3 down on 11 March. The principal dimensions of this twin-screw oil-burning turbine steamer were: 329ft in length; 47ft beam; 17ft 9in to main deck; gross registered tonnage 2912; accommodation for 1754 passengers. It was Denny's ship number 1218 (with engine No 970) and was in effect a de-luxe version of the TSS *Isle of Thanet* but having a boat deck unobstructed by lifeboats by reason of the use of Welin over-frame type davits, a Palm Court or garden lounge as well as screened alcoves on the Awning Deck, a good number of private deck cabins and a 100-seat dining saloon on the main deck. The decor was described as a 'warm cream', a late alteration in the specification from white. TSS *Canterbury*, the pride of the SR fleet, steamed into Southampton Docks at noon on 15 March 1929 exactly two weeks late on contract date although, possibly because of design amendments during construction, no penalty was exacted of the builders. Port of registration was London.

Two months later, on 15 May, the SR *Golden Arrow* was inaugurated to the following timetable:

		am		pm
London (Victoria)	dep	11.0	arr	6.35
		pm		
Dover Marine	arr	12.35	dep	4.57
	dep	12.55	arr	4.40
Calais Maritime	arr	2.10	dep	3.25
	dep	2.25	arr	3.10
Paris (Nord)	arr	5.35	dep	12 noon

This was a first class de-luxe service with the ship carrying passengers solely from these trains and not, as previously, other classes as well. Consequently the 1700 passenger capacity was particularly generous for the 250 to 300 travellers for each crossing. A special £5 inclusive tariff was introduced which embraced fare, supplements and reserved seats on the trains but not supplements for alcoves or cabins on the steamer. The French customs carried out examination on the train en route but the best their British counterparts could offer was a rapid examination at Dover for hand luggage. However the SR managed to arrange a facility whereby passengers signed a form en route

Dover to London and handed their heavy luggage keys to the SR representatives who then had the luggage examined by customs at Victoria after which it was delivered to its destination the same evening in the London delivery area or on the next day elsewhere – all for a small fee, of course! Haulage of the train on Southern metals was placed in the hands of Battersea (later to be known as Stewarts Lane) shed which used its Lord Nelson class locomotives by now numbering eleven members allocated between Battersea and Nine Elms depots.

Just over three weeks had elapsed when, on the outward crossing from Dover on 7 June, TSS *Canterbury* suffered a lubricating pump failure to the port engine before the spare pump could be actuated and consequently had to be taken out of service for repairs until 24 June. On the railway side a curious accident happened on 23 January 1930 when locomotive No E853 *Sir Richard Grenville* became partly derailed while hauling the up train through Kent House station and managed to re-rail itself into the bargain while the enginemen were completely oblivious to the mishap. Driver Chapman was more than surprised to be told of this on arrival at Victoria and although track damage extended for quarter-a-mile that to rolling stock was minimal and staff, bystanders and passengers escaped unscathed.

Renovated Pullman cars *Adrian, Diamond, Ibis, Lady Dalziel, Lydia, Onyx, Pearl* and *Princess Elizabeth* all with the new style of painting the fascia umber instead of cream were allocated to the service in July 1930 and all should have been set for success. Outside forces, however, intervened and one of the seemingly cyclic trade depressions (somewhat similar to the early 1890s) gripped the country. Two years after inauguration the SR announced that from 15 May 1931, because of the continued industrial depression and consequent loss of traffic by the *Golden Arrow* services, the 11am and 11.15am services would be combined for the sea crossing and because of loss of exclusiveness the all-in tariff was reduced to £4 12s 6d. The 11.15am train was advanced to 10.45am and the *Golden Arrow* schedules became:

		am		pm
London (Victoria)	dep	11.0	arr	7.0
		pm		
Dover Marine	arr	12.35	dep	5.25
	dep	12.55	arr	5.0
Calais Maritime	arr	2.10	dep	3.45
	dep	2.50	arr	3.30
Paris (Nord)	arr	5.40	dep	12.20

Further plebeianisation followed in the following May when the 10.45am and balancing return train were withdrawn, the *Golden Arrow* in England losing its all-Pullman attraction to accommodate first and second class and first class Pullman passengers. In France the all-Pullman formation was diluted with the introduction of second class Pullmans and Wagons-Lits sleepers for destinations beyond Paris. The year 1932 was a particularly poor one for cross-channel traffic with the total passenger journeys plunging dramatically thus:

Period	Passengers	
1925–1930	1,500,000	(per annum)
1931	1,440,000	
1932	975,000	
1933–1935	1,125,000	(per annum)

Even though the depression was lessening a further economy was introduced from 6 October 1935 when the inward service was routed via Boulogne and Folkestone so that the same Pullman cars could be used both ways in France. The departure from Paris was advanced to allow time for the empty Pullmans to be worked from Boulogne to Calais and the schedule now read:

		am
London (Victoria)	dep	11.0
Dover Marine	dep	12.55
Calais Maritime	arr	2.10
Paris (Nord)	arr	5.43
		am
Paris (Nord)	dep	10.30
		pm
Boulogne	dep	1.50
Folkestone	arr	3.20
London (Victoria)	arr	5.20

This was not really a new timing because it simply exchanged an existing one for another and it was still possible to leave Paris just after noon and arrive in London by 7pm. One effect of the alteration was that the *Canterbury* could cover only one leg of the *Golden Arrow* service any one day.

The train now settled down to a routine existence and could be seen plying to and fro daily with three or four first class Pullman cars in the centre of the formation which at the London end sported one or more baggage trucks and general utility vans. Headed by a Stewarts Lane Lord Nelson class locomotive the train's normal route was via Herne Hill and Tonbridge, although if delayed by the inwards steamer it might find itself diverted via Maidstone East. From 14 November 1938 the ordinary stock appeared in refurbished form; internally the alterations were similar to those for the *Bournemouth Limited* renovated at about the same time with the upholstery in the first class compartments based on suggestions made by H M Queen Mary. The wheel treads were made flatter but the most noticeable amendment was the new shade of olive – or Dover, as it was termed (after the route) – green in which the coaches were decked out externally. Four Lord Nelson locomotives were repainted to match and completed the unity of eight ordinary and four Pullman vehicles.

Declaration of war on 3 September 1939, when the port of Dover became closed the next day, however abruptly stopped the service a few months after the *Golden Arrow* in England had celebrated the completion of its first decade.

Restoration of the service had to wait until 15 April 1946 when the Southern Railway demonstrated that it was prepared to make another endeavour to run a de-luxe service even though – or perhaps because – the journey times were rather long due to the state of the track, especially in France. The daily timetable was:

		am		pm
London (Victoria)	dep	10.0	arr	8.30
Dover Marine	arr	11.40	dep	6.50
		pm		
	dep	12.30	arr	5.50
Calais Maritime	arr	1.50	dep	4.30
	dep	2.47	arr	3.30
Paris (Nord)	arr	6.45	dep	11.35am

The French train had first class Pullmans and first and second class ordinary coaches. The SR made its *Golden Arrow* all-Pullman (first and second class) so had to run a separate train each way to carry non-Pullman first and second class travellers. Second class Pullman ticketholders travelled ordinary second class in France.

SS *Canterbury*, which had been refitted after release from government service including being equipped with radar navigational devices (the first in the SR fleet), restarted the Dover-Calais service, her daily each way sailing being the only one at this period.

Second class Pullmans for the service were provided by converting three vehicles, the new and old numberings being:

Merchant Navy class No 35027 *Port Line* makes vast smoke effects on the climb to Bickley in May 1951 with the outward *Golden Arrow* service. *Author's collection*

	New number	Old number/name
Parlour car	193	35
Parlour car	194	36
Brake parlour car	154	*Flora*

The other, first class, vehicles were kitchen cars *Adrian*, *Cecilia* and *Sappho*, parlour cars *Niobe* and *Onyx* and brake parlour car *Lady Dalziel* plus an innovation in the *Trianon Bar*. These ten cars formed the *Golden Arrow* Pullman allocation to be drawn upon as necessary and were fitted with two arrows each side springing from the name or number panel with 'Golden Arrow' or 'Flèche d'Or' painted on beyond the arrow heads. The bar car finish was far removed from the traditional Pullman panelling being plastics laminate sheeting in pink and grey with the bar top in cream. Unfortunately the bar car disgraced itself on the press run of 13 April by developing a hot axle box and so missed the first fortnight of the public service, its place being taken by another bar Pullman.

Pre-war the train had left Victoria from platform 2 and arrived at platform 8 but now the latter was used for both departure and arrival and had a suitably embellished entrance barrier. For the re-inaugural run the doyen Merchant Navy class 4–6–2, *Channel Packet*, was fittingly used and continued in the service for two weeks after which Stewarts Lane based light Pacifics (then un-named) took over the duty. The locomotives were embellished with an arrow in the direction of travel each side on the upper part of the sheeting, a round headboard with the train title bisected diagonally by an arrow pointing downwards fixed to the smokebox door and the Union and Tricolor flags in V-form on the buffer beam. As the route each way was via Tonbridge the route code discs of one over each buffer fortunately presented a balanced effect. To cement the entente locomotive crews from each side of the Channel visited their opposite numbers and in Paris La Chapelle locomotive depot was on the itinerary with Nine Elms (rather than Stewarts Lane) being inspected by the Frenchmen.

The winter saw various alterations. SS *Invicta*, which was launched in 1939 but went direct into government service, came on station in mid-October and took over the crossing from SS *Canterbury*; the French dropped the second class accommodation and, like the British, ran a separate train for that traffic; and the schedules were altered to give departures from London and Paris at 9am and noon with arrivals at 7pm and 5.50pm respectively.

From 4 May 1947 the second class Pullmans were removed making the train all first class again, the lower class cars being replaced by kitchen cars *Chloria* and *Zenobia* and brake parlour *Montana*. The French responded by making their train all first class Pullmans. From 31 October 1948 the London departure became 9.30am with an arrival in Paris at 5.30pm, the inward times being 12.15pm from Paris and 6.30pm in London.

Second class Pullman cars were reintroduced on the English side from 2 October 1949 and in the summer of 1950 the French had both classes in Pullmans and ordinary stock in their train, all to the following timetable:

		am		pm
London (Victoria)	dep	11.0	arr	7.30
		pm		
Dover Marine	arr	12.35	dep	5.55
	dep	1.0	arr	5.20
Calais Maritime	arr	2.20	dep	4.0
	dep	2.38	arr	3.40
Paris (Nord)	arr	5.52	dep	12.30

After the Festival of Britain in 1951 two BR Standard Britannia class Pacifics were allocated to Stewarts Lane shed and No 70004 *William Shakespeare*, which had been on exhibition at the Festival, took over the *Golden Arrow* duty. It is pictured here, with two non-Pullman open seconds (marshalled second and third) near Shepherds Lane with the outward service on 20 April 1957. *S. C. Nash*

As the *Golden Arrow* headed by light Pacific No 34084 was approaching Victoria on the evening of 9 December 1949 locomotive No 34085 running light side-swiped the train, damaging No 34084, a baggage van and some of the Pullmans, before tilting over to be hit by a local electric train. The 95 passengers of the *Golden Arrow* fortunately were uninjured and were able to detrain without a lot of difficulty.

Festival of Britain year saw a new set of Pullmans for the service; seven cars were built new, being a suspended pre-war order, and three were rebuilds. The new vehicles were first class cars, *Aquila*, *Orion*, *Carina* (all kitchens, using Calor gas for the first time), *Cygnus*, *Hercules*, *Perseus* (parlours) and the parlour bar *Pegasus*: the rebuilds were parlour brake first *Minerva*, parlour second 35 and parlour brake second 208, giving a total capacity of 262 passengers (184 first and 78 second class). This train was introduced on 11 June 1951 and as soon as the Festival had closed the new British Railways Standard 4–6–2 Britannia class No 70004 *William Shakespeare*, which had

Diesel-electric locomotive No 10203, of Southern Railway parentage, traversing the Bickley Junction – Petts Wood Junction connection with the down *Golden Arrow* during its spell on the service in March 1955. *S. C. Nash*

been on exhibition at the South Bank site, was sent to Stewarts Lane shed to work the train, making its debut, complete with arrows on the smoke deflectors, on 11 October. Unfortunately, ten days later it fractured a side rod at Headcorn and the whole class had to be withdrawn for examination, and not until 10 December did No 70004 make its return to the duty.

For the summer of 1952 the *Golden Arrow* allocation of Pullmans became, and remained for many years, first class kitchen cars *Aquila, Aries, Carina* and *Orion*, parlour firsts *Cygnus, Hercules, Phoenix* and *Zena*, parlour brake firsts *Isle of Thanet* and *Minerva*, parlour bar car *Pegasus*, parlour seconds 34 and 35 and parlour brake seconds 36 and 208 all of which had detachable train titles and arrows so that their use was not necessarily restricted to the service. *Zena* dropped out after the winter of 1952/3 and car 35 after the 1954/5 winter, all the remainder staying on until 1960 at least.

Echoes of the pre-war use of Folkestone Harbour for the *Golden Arrow* were heard when it was announced that to enable businessmen to spend a full morning in London the service would leave in the afternoon and be routed that way as from 15 September 1952. This time the French port was Calais, rather than Boulogne, but it did allow the use of only one train set in France. In turn this necessitated the use of two different ships so for the outward service the French SS *Cote d'Azur* was employed with the SS *Invicta* covering the inward crossing. The schedules now became:

		pm
London (Victoria)	dep	1.0
Folkestone Harbour	arr	2.38
	dep	3.15
Calais Maritime	arr	5.45
	dep	6.17
Paris (Nord)	arr	9.34
		pm
Paris (Nord)	dep	12.30
Calais Maritime	arr	3.44
	dep	4.5
Dover Marine	arr	4.23
	dep	4.58
London (Victoria)	arr	6.30

As a by-product some interesting locomotive workings resulted on the English side for the service. Stewarts Lane duty 3 for a Class 7 Pacific covered both the down and up service; on arrival at Folkestone Junction sidings an R1 class 0–6–0 tank from the local shed came on to the rear of the train and reversing direction headed it – bunker first – down the 1 in 31 incline to the

On 28 February 1959 R1 class 0-6-0 tank descends to the harbour at Folkestone from the junction with the outward service of the *Golden Arrow*. *Author*

harbour thus releasing the Pacific, which went on to the shed, turned, and took coal and water. Shortly after, three or four of the R1s struggled up from the harbour with the empty stock, and the Pacific worked the train tender-first to Dover Marine ready for the late afternoon up service.

Diesel-electric traction had two trial spells on the train, each of one week working the train both ways, No 10202 for the week commencing 8 February 1954 and No 10203 starting on 20 March 1955. A small curiosity in this connection was that a special locomotive headboard was made for each occasion; in the first the arrow went diagonally upwards left to right and the second had it going down diagonally right to left! The steam one, of course, went down diagonally left to right. At this period an odd second class ordinary coach would creep into the formation presumably as an overflow for the preceding ordinary service and thus rather spoil the uniform effect of the train. The two Britannias (Nos 70004 and 70014) which had appeared on the train were transferred away in June 1958 and eventually rebuilt Bulleid Pacifics arrived to add variety to the scene and, later still, Western Region 0–6–0 pannier tanks monopolised the Folkestone Harbour branch workings.

From 29 May 1960, following a loss of patronage with the afternoon service, came a reversion to a morning departure via Dover the times being:

		am		pm
London (Victoria)	dep	11.0	arr	7.50
		pm		
Dover Marine	arr	12.37	dep	6.13
	dep	1.5	arr	5.40
Calais Maritime	arr	2.25	dep	4.20
	dep	2.52	arr	3.55
Paris (Nord)	arr	6.10	dep	12.45

This once again enabled one steamer to work the service both ways. The French made the train solely first class Pullman despite which BR maintained both classes of Pullmans in the British train. At this same time the SNCF *Flèche d'Or* was turned over to electric traction between Paris and Amiens. Engineering works in connection with the Southern Region's electrification of the main line via Tonbridge from time to time blocked the route when, if diverted via Chatham, diesel-electric traction would deputise for steam. The final steam hauled run took place on 11 June 1961 with No 34100 *Appledore* in charge. Electric traction with the E5000 class locomotives started the next day. Acceleration of the service came in the following summer timetable thus:

		am		pm
London (Victoria)	dep	11.0	arr	7.35
		pm		
Dover Marine	arr	12.22	dep	6.10
	dep	12.50	arr	5.30
Calais Maritime	arr	2.10	dep	4.10
	dep	2.40	arr	3.45
Paris (Nord)	arr	5.50	dep	12.39

Apart from the departure time from Paris being advanced to 12.21pm each winter and the inevitable out-of-step summer time dates between England and France which had always plagued the service with an hour's difference for certain dates these times went unamended until 30 May 1965 when 12.30pm became the departure time from Paris throughout the year. Concurrently the second class Pullmans were withdrawn between London and Dover the *Golden Arrow* now becoming first class Pullman and ordinary second class in its accommodation. Previously, at the end of 1963, the parlour bar car had been withdrawn which, with hindsight can be seen as the first straw in the wind of the decline of the service, the Pullman Car Company having been absorbed by British Rail at the beginning of 1963.

From 22 May 1966 the London departure was brought forward to 10.30am giving an arrival in Paris at 5.25pm. In France the last steam-hauled run was on 11 January 1969, diesel-electric power taking over from steam the next day, and the Pullman cars bowed out on 31 May that year. In England the Pullman cars, under the new management, were being given a facelift, the old livery giving way in 1968/9 to blue and grey with the train title appearing in place of the car name or number with the class designation and vehicle numbers at each end of the blue panel. This livery change failed to make a clear enough distinction between first class and first class Pullman, there being no indication by way of external lettering that these were Pullman cars. In 1969 the customary formation of the *Golden Arrow* could be described as four first

Last of the line of steam locomotive classes which were responsible for the *Golden Arrow* were the rebuilt light Pacifics of which No 34088 *213 Squadron* is pictured in Folkestone Warren with the down train on 27 May 1961. *Author*

Electrification works in the early 1960s caused diversions and unaccustomed motive power for the *Golden Arrow*. The combination of diesel-electrics Nos D6513 (leading) and D5017 was recorded on the down service on 11 March 1961 as the train neared Canterbury East having been diverted via Chatham. *Author*

BR class 2 2-6-2 tank No 84022 brings into Victoria the empty stock for the penultimate steam working of the *Golden Arrow* with the train engine attached at the rear. *Author*

Re-liveried Pullman car S308S and electric locomotive No E5013 typified the final years of the *Golden Arrow* as they waited at Dover Marine to work the up service on 30 September 1972. *S. C. Nash*

class Pullmans, three ordinary second class coaches, a second class buffet car and a couple of bogie luggage vans augmented as necessary to suit traffic demands. Since the requirement for Pullmans was four, a total of six cars was retained to give cover for repairs and failures these being parlour S301S (*Perseus*) , S302S (*Phoenix*), S306S (*Orion*), kitchen cars S307S (*Carina*), S308S (*Cygnus*) and parlour brake car S208S.

Pullman cars tending to be viewed by BR as an anachronism and not in keeping with the projected image, the end came in September 1972. The last week the train made a brave sight with Class 71 No E5013 – adorned with the arrows on its sides and the headboard with fluttering flags – heading the resplendent ensemble to and fro and for the final journey on 30 September. Will the arrow ever be regilded for another de-luxe *Train à Grand Vitesse* service linking London and Paris on completion of the Channel Tunnel?

CHAPTER NINE

Train Across the Channel

Night Ferry

Unique has become an overworked and devalued term in recent years but if ever a train merited such description it must surely be the *Night Ferry* with its through sleeping cars between, initially, London (Victoria) and Paris (Nord), for it boasted the only Wagons-Lits sleeping cars to operate in the United Kingdom and, at its height, had as its destinations three capitals – London, Paris and Brussels – and a major city – Basle – in a fourth country. Add to this several other singular features, such as the dock works and vessels specially built for its operation and, for certain periods, the sole operation of British Railways staff on a train in a foreign country and the heaviest timetabled passenger working on BR and the claim becomes unrivalled.

Restoration of the umbilical cord which was broken as the Ice Age retreated northwards and gave the British Isles isolation from the European mainland had been a recurring theme in the nineteenth and twentieth centuries. A tunnel was first mooted in 1802 to connect Britain and France and every so often came into prominence in public debate only to suffer the inevitable objection of invasion by unfriendly armies – as though nobody could possibly devise a way to stop such unwelcome visitors! Eventually, in 1872, a Channel Tunnel Company was formed and on at least two occasions (1880 and 1973) work was commenced and then ceased.

Another method of through communication which would wax when the tunnel project waned and vice versa was a train ferry. The first train ferry in Britain was built in 1849 and, in 1872 and again in 1905, there were proposals for a train ferry from Dover to France but these came to naught.

It was after one of the perennial rejections of the tunnel proposal in 1930 that the Southern Railway general manager (Sir Herbert Walker) determined to promote a through London-Paris train using a ferry. At a board meeting on 27 November 1930 he explained the proposal to establish a train ferry between Dover and Boulogne. At the following meeting in December Sir Herbert stated that the Northern Railway of France was investigating a goods ferry across the channel and suggested that the Southern should not stand aside and see the

191

In pre-war days double-heading of the *Night Ferry* by a pair of 4-4-0s was customary. The up train nears Bromley South with Class L1 No 1754 leading Class D1 No 1246 on 12 September 1937. *H. C. Casserley*

loss of a potentially lucrative part of the continental business. The Nord had suggested Calais-Richborough but the Southern wanted Boulogne and somewhere other than Richborough. Then followed the first intimation that the SR proposed to operate a night passenger service.

On 25 June 1931 the general manager wrung authority from the board to announce that the Southern would supply ferry boats and a terminal at Dover. This disposed of the problem of an isolated terminal at the wartime port of Richborough (which had seen train ferry operation) and the consequent problems for running a passenger service through there. During the summer co-operation for a Dover-Boulogne route had been secured although works at Boulogne were not likely to be ready until April 1935 and at Dover rather sooner.

A special SR board meeting was called for 19 October 1932 solely to consider the train ferry proposal and, in the face of the French threatening to support a Calais-Harwich service unless they obtained an assurance about the SR plans, the board agreed a train ferry operation between England and France should be established by the Southern.

A month later Dunkerque was first mentioned and authority was given for a public announcement to be made and tenders to be invited for the boats (the SR habitually referred to boat rather than the nautical term of ship!). During 1933 the technical matters were put in hand with three coalfired ships ordered from Swan, Hunter & Wigham Richardson Ltd for £436,900. The first of these, *Twickenham Ferry*, was launched at the Neptune Yard, Walker-on-Tyne on 15 March 1934 to be followed by *Hampton Ferry* and *Shepperton Ferry*.

The three ships, whose names had been chosen by Gilbert Szlumper, the SR's docks and marine manager and assistant general manager, were almost identical. The length was common at 359ft although the beam varied from 62ft 10in to 63ft 9in and the tonnage from 2839 to 2996, all having a maximum speed of 16½ knots. In each case the train deck was approached by two tracks at the stern which then branched out into two sidings once within the superstructure, giving maximum accommodation for twelve sleeping cars

Twickenham Ferry in Southern Railway ownership, as the port of registraton indicates, at Dover in 1934 before entering regular service. *National Maritime Museum*

which, it is believed, was only once required – on the inward inauguration trip. Cabin and saloon accommodation was over the train deck. Delivery was made between July 1934 and March 1935 and at first the ferries were moored at Southampton New Docks and then later at Dover. So far as is known, the vessels remained laid up (except that the *Twickenham Ferry* on 2 January 1935 took a detachment of the 12th Lancers comprising 6 officers, 74 other ranks, 8 armoured cars, 8 motor cycles, 8 motor lorries, 5 motor cars, 2 trailers, 2 pedal cycles and 500 gallons of fuel from Dover to Calais in connection with the Saar policing and brought them back again two months later) until required for service in October 1936. The registered port in each case was London.

Trouble – never far away in *Night Ferry* operations throughout its life – had meantime loomed up in problems in the construction of the dock in Dover Harbour. A fissure in the chalk allowed the sea water to flood the excavation and prevent pouring of the reinforced concrete base of the dock and a lot of time had to be spent overcoming this contingency. Overcome it was – at a price – not only monetary (the company had to appoint a quantity surveyor to deal with that aspect) but also in that precious commodity of time, a whole year virtually. Neither was all well with the ships because on trial runs they showed a tendency to roll and to lessen this the floors of the motor garage decks had to have additional ballast in the form of 200 tons of discarded railway metals concreted over.

Twelve Wagons-Lits sleeping cars were designed in 1933 and constructed by Ateliers de Construction du Nord de la France Blanc-Misseron, between November 1935 and May 1936, carrying numbers 3788 to 3799 and known as type F (for Ferry). They were, of course, specially built for the British loading gauge, smaller in width and height than normal continental stock although not prohibited from working elsewhere on the continent: there were nine compartments in each car, each having upper and lower berths, of which four pairs were capable of conversion by communicating doors to make four-berth compartments. Each vehicle had two inward opening doors, one each side at one end, and were fitted along the frames with securing rings so that the cars could be chained to the ship's deck to avoid movement on the sea crossing. The Southern Railway built three four-wheel baggage vans (numbered 1 to 3) at Ashford in 1935 of distinctive appearance, with a guard's central roof look-out higher than the general roof line, and painted in blue to match the sleeping cars. The Nord had built a dozen or so four-wheel vans, some with and some without guard's accommodation, in 1928-9 and these were adapted for British loading gauge in 1936. These were the vehicles which would run through on the ships in the *Night Ferry* service; 100 vans and 50 wagons were built by the SR for freight use as well as two bogie loading wagons (numbered 61324/5) adapted from existing frames and bogies which served as shunters' trucks coupled to the front end of the steam shunting engines which were not, at first, allowed in ordinary circumstances onto the ships.

Eventually the day drew near for the inauguration of the new service. The existing night boat service from Folkestone Harbour to Dunkerque run by the French company Société Anonyme de Navigation Angleterre-Lorraine (ALA) was to sail from Folkestone for the last time early on Monday 5 October 1936. As this would have displaced the crew the French Minister of Marine required one of the new ferries to be under the French flag and manned by its nationals. Consequently, the *Twickenham Ferry* was transferred to ALA on 22 September and the port of registration changed from London to Dunkerque.

On Tuesday 6 October 1936 the ferry dock was used for the first time commerically for passenger traffic. The 11pm service from London (Victoria) on 5 October was diverted from Folkestone Harbour to Dover Marine and the coaches were shunted onto *Hampton Ferry* to allow the 25 passengers to detrain and go to their cabins on board. The coaches were then shunted off and *Hampton Ferry*, with 26 loaded wagons on the rail deck, left at 2am for Dunkerque. Presumably this modus operandi obtained until the through sleeping cars had to be accommodated. Inward that morning the *Twickenham Ferry* brought over 37 passengers and four unoccupied Wagons-Lits sleeping cars, three of which were destined for display at Victoria, Waterloo and Cannon Street (one report gives Charing Cross) respectively, the other it is assumed being retained at Dover for training personnel in the securing of cars on the train deck.

The inauguration ceremony took place on Monday 12 October 1936. The French Ambassador, M Corbin, arrived in a special train from London at Dover Marine at 10.23am. There followed a demonstration of loading a sleeping car and a large number of the assembled company then went on board *Hampton Ferry* after which M Corbin performed the first of the two-part inauguration — the waving of a green flag to signal the sleeping cars (doubtless the four brought over the previous week) to be shunted onto the ferry. He then proceeded to the dock pump-house and at 11.50am pressed a bell-push for lowering of the dock gate; at 11.55am *Hampton Ferry*, under the command of Captain H. L. Payne, steamed away to Calais. There the official party split, part returning to Dover in the afternoon with the majority proceeding to Paris for a celebratory dinner. The *Hampton Ferry* meanwhile had gone on to Dunkerque with the sleeping cars.

Sir Herbert Walker, the SR general manager, was that evening invested as a Commander of the Order of the Legion d'Honneur and doubtless all was conviviality, although the day did have its doubters and disappointed guests. The President of the Calais Chamber of Commerce spoke of his regret that Calais had not been chosen as the French port while the Mayor of Dover lamented the advent of the ferry because it would displace a lot of labour (fifty years on the same argument was resurrected for the Channel Tunnel!) although admittedly they were a bit old fashioned in Dover and they had to keep up with times and go forward.

The guest list for the Paris party numbered 187. All twelve sleeping cars were pressed into service to convey the party back that night to Dunkerque, Dover and London so clearly single occupancy could not have been offered to more than 29 persons. Two trains were formed up and in due course were shunted on board the French *Twickenham Ferry* which then set forth for Dover. On arrival on the morning of the 13th the French boat struck the dock head with her stern setting up deck plating on her link span step. Worse was to

Typical of double-heading prevalent in the post-war era on the *Night Ferry*, Class L1 4-4-0 No 31789 and light Pacific No 34070 *Manston* bring the up train through Herne Hill on 27 June 1956. *Author*

follow: the rear sleeping car was derailed by an obstruction – whether or not it had anything to do with the collision of the vessel is not clear – as it left the ship, and its passengers, which as luck would have it included Sir John Simon and Sir Herbert Walker, had to be transferred to another part of the train. Very fortunately it was the last rather than the first coach which was derailed and at least it could be abandoned to its fate rather than the whole procession being blocked if it had been the first.

To round off this less than propitious inauguration two trains ran to London (Victoria) with the party, the first, leaving just before 9.30am, consisted of six sleeping cars, a Pullman and a couple of corridor coaches and was headed by Schools 4–4–0 No 939 *Leatherhead* and an L1 class 4–4–0 and arrived at Victoria at 11 o'clock, while the second was headed by Lord Nelson 4–6–0 No 855 *Robert Blake*, and consisted of six vehicles, the remaining five underailed Wagons-Lits sleepers and probably a corridor brake for the guard. The guests presumably breakfasted at Dover either in the Pullman or the Lord Warden hotel.

After these junketings day-to-day operation commenced with the outward service on the evening of 14 October and the first departure from Paris on the following day. The timings advertised were:

London Victoria	dep	22.00	arr	08.30
Dover Marine	arr	23.36	dep	06.50
	dep	23.40	arr	06.47
Dover Ferry Berth	arr	.23.48	dep	06.39
	dep	00.35	arr	06.15
Dunkerque Ferry Berth	arr	04.30	dep	02.00
	dep	05.10	arr	01.30
Paris Nord	arr	08.55	dep	21.50

On Southern metals the usual route was via Herne Hill and Tonbridge in both directions. In addition to first and second class sleeping car accommodation there was ordinary first, second and third class available. An all-in sleeping car tariff (fare; sleeping car supplement; reservation fee and sleeping car conductor's gratuity) of £4.19s 6d single, £9.4s 0d return for first class and £3.16s 6d and £7.2s 0d respectively for second class was quoted. The customary motive power was a pair of 4–4–0s usually of Classes D1 and L1, with occasional interlopers of Class L, because the Lord Nelson class – the most powerful locomotives the company had – was not up to the task. A couple of trial runs in May 1938 with No 853 gave confirmation of the correctness of this decision.

Before the inauguration ceremonies had faded it was found that *Hampton Ferry* had a damaged bow rudder and so the spare ship *Shepperton Ferry* was prepared to take over, only for it to be discovered that she, too, had a similar defect. Not surprisingly the third sister of the trio suffered in the same way! It was then decided that the ferries would have to be placed in the dock at Dover by a tug until a satisfactory remedy was found for the defect. Then, in November, the elements began to show their teeth with gales and these added to the difficulties in docking at Dover. There were reports of the sleeping cars shuttling to and fro on board the ships (or not at all) with ordinary stock being used each side on terra firma. So bad was it that after a month's working there still had to be recorded a right time arrival at Victoria; the nearest approach to this was 20 minutes in arrears, due not to poor locomotive performance but to difficulties with the sea crossing. This was to be the Achilles heel of the *Night Ferry* throughout its existence.

Realism prevailed and the arrival time at Victoria was retarded from 1 December 35 minutes to 09.05. Some solace was given passengers because, from the previous day, a Pullman car (one of either Nos 17 or 19, both 12-wheelers) was included in the train formation so that sleeping car clients could take supper from 21.15 onwards or breakfast and not have to rely on the spartan refreshments available from the car conductors. A typical English train formation would be five sleeping cars, the Pullman, two corridor coaches and a couple of vans. Later a third class Pullman was introduced so that the non-sleeping car passengers could take nourishment. The wasteful use of two Pullmans was the result of the British authorities refusing to carry out customs inspection on the train and also requiring strict segregation of sleeping and walking passengers, the former undergoing customs examination at Victoria.

The inward service was plagued by this customs inspection which was a bane to be endured on the English side (the French, of course, did their perfunctory examination en route) and this, when compounded by reason of late running as so often was the case, made onward connections for the north, such as the 10 o'clock trains from Euston or Kings Cross, a hazardous business.

From 4 July 1937 the Paris arrival was made 09.00 and for the summers of 1938 and 1939 the London arrival became 09.10 but otherwise there was little alteration. Punctuality improved after the ships' bow rudders had been modified and during favourable weather conditions.

No 35028 *Clan Line* at Petts Wood Junction with the up *Night Ferry* in the late 1950s. The two baggage vans behind the locomotive came over with the sleepers on the ferry. *Robin Russell*

In its last months of steam traction, on 29 March 1959, the inward *Night Ferry* passes Bickley Junction headed by L1 class No 31754 and No 34070 *Manston*. Note the headboard with Brussels incorporated and that seven sleeping cars were required for the service. *Derek Cross*

It was not until June 1937 that the motor car service could start with the completion of the inclined carriageway at Dover Ferry Berth, but, nonetheless, it was an encouraging year with the highest number of passengers (1,468,116) ever crossing the Channel by railway owned ships of which the *Night Ferry* operation contributed 73,288 to the total, 37,488 of whom were sleeping car travellers. The ships averaged about 450 sailings and 18,000 nautical miles each. However, just short of the third anniversary of its advent, the war came and cut off the service, the last passenger departures from the capitals being made on 25 August 1939.

With the war in Europe over and Hitler's alleged plan to enter London in triumph on the *Night Ferry* thwarted, the Southern Railway was keen to restart the service. Unfortunately the ferries were vital to the support of the British army in Germany and were not released until over two years after the end of the conflict and then had to be renovated and converted from coal to oil burning. So far as the Wagons-Lits sleeping cars were concerned nine were available for work which was just about adequate for requirements; five (Nos 3788/93/95/96/99) had been lost completely, three (Nos 3789/90/97) were serviceable, two (Nos 3791/2) were under repair, two (Nos 3794/8) were missing but were later found and repaired and six (Nos 3800–5) were new construction uncompleted in 1939 but made operational after the war.

It was intended to recommence the service simultaneously from each capital on 1 December 1947 but, as there was a railway strike in progress in France, it was delayed two weeks. Indications are that the train left Paris for London on 14 December but the arrival at Victoria on the morning of 15 December appears to have escaped notice. However that evening your author was on Tonbridge station and was rewarded by seeing the electric headlights of the leading engine rounding the curve from London and witnessing the colourful procession of Battle of Britain class 4–6–2 No 21C156 (then unnamed) with a circular smokebox headboard (having a blue ground with NIGHT FERRY on a black band across the centre with LONDON and PARIS respectively above and below the train name and quarter moon bisected by the band) – an innovation for the train – followed by L1 class 4–4–0 No 1757 and twelve vehicles of which one was a Pullman and four were the blue sleeping cars. The train accelerated away into the night and towards Dover with the 55 ton sleepers making their characteristic rumbling passage. True to tradition trouble was met with. The outward ferry arrived off Dunkerque to find a sister ship trapped behind the lock gates which would not open owing to a heavy swell whipped up by a gale and had to heave-to until the elements abated and the lock could be operated. Consequently arrival in Paris was several hours late.

Double heading was required if the train's load included more than three

Wagons-Lits cars. A typical formation, noted on the inward service on 27 December 1947 was two vans, three sleepers, a restaurant car, a buffet car, two compartment coaches and a Pullman, a total of ten vehicles, which was in the sole charge of the still unnamed No 21C156.

The reopening schedules were:

London Victoria	dep	20.30	arr	09.10
Dover Ferry Berth	arr	22.10	dep	07.20
	dep	23.10	arr	06.00
Dunkerque Ferry Berth	arr	04.00	dep	01.50
	dep	04.30	arr	01.20
Paris Nord	arr	09.30	dep	20.30

The down train was booked via Nunhead and the Catford Loop line although the up service held to travelling via Herne Hill, both trains using the Orpington and Tonbridge route. By 1949, however, the down train was again booked via Herne Hill.

For the traveller the *Night Ferry* was certainly an unusual train. At Victoria there would be a view of a small, possibly tank, engine and some vans and away beyond the barrier the blué sleeping cars. After proceeding through passport control and customs and separation from the walking passengers one would find oneself on platform 2 and being conducted to a sleeping car berth. Consequently, unless one elected to have supper, little was seen of one's fellow passengers. There was no opportunity to have a look at the locomotive about to haul the train to Dover and if the number of the engine was required almost the only way to obtain it was to ask the policeman to request the guard to come to the barrier to pass over the information! The walking (as opposed to sleeping) passengers meantime would have made their way down platform 1 and, once beyond the sleeping-car portion of the train, would proceed through one of the sliding folding gateways in the wall dividing platforms 1 and 2 to their section of the train. For them obtaining the engine number would be less of a problem!

Once away from Victoria there was little to attract attention outside the train because the journey, even in high summer, would be in darkness and so one could retire for the night safe in the knowledge that should a sudden flood be encountered through the Weald of Kent a life jacket was at hand for use! Probably the train's manoeuvres at Dover would go undetected: from London it would approach Dover Marine Station from the Folkestone direction and there the ordinary carriages and restaurant cars would be uncoupled so that a shunting locomotive coming onto the rear of the train could draw out the vans and sleeping cars to point Q – Hawkesbury Street Junction – as indicated on

A nightime picture as befits the *Night Ferry*: an E5000 class electric locomotive waits with the train at London Victoria ready for the journey to Dover Marine. *Brian Stephenson*

the plan on page 167. This locomotive would then propel the train forward onto the ferry and, depending on the soundness of the sleeping passengers, the securing of the sleeping cars and vans to the ferry's deck would be executed in varying degrees of stealth. The ferry would then sail for Dunkerque and there some not dissimilar shunting operations would take place to allow the train to proceed to Paris.

In the inward direction the ship would enter the outer harbour and go astern (as indicated by the inset sketch) into the dock. The reverse procedure of the outward shunt operation would take place and, when ready for departure, the train could leave either via Folkestone or via Chatham (as indicated).

It was at Paris Nord that the train really became an entity because the French executed the customs formalities en route and there was no segregation – just an open welcoming platform. That also was the way it was on returning en route for England.

The reinstated *Night Ferry* had just over a fortnight under the Southern Railway banner before it became part of British Railways on 1 January 1948. That apart there were but minor adjustments in timings to break into a period of consolidation. The scheduled arrival at Victoria remained at 09.10 for decades – somewhat to the annoyance of operating staff who could have done without this train towards the end of the morning peak period. There was the complication of the time difference of one hour for certain periods of each year between England and France and this was adjusted by varying the departure times from the capitals and keeping the arrival times constant.

From 9 May 1948 the departure from Victoria became 21.30 and then, from 31 October that year, 21.00 and this was maintained, along with its 22.00 variation, for very many years. For Paris the departures times grew progressively later: 21.30 from 31 October 1948; 21.45 from 20 May 1951; 21.50 from 22 May 1955 until 5 October 1958 when it became 22.00. The arrival times at Paris Nord also improved: 09.20 from 14 May 1950; 09.15 from 8 October 1950 and 09.00 from 20 May 1951. Third class accommodation for walking passengers was dropped by May 1949.

Provision of another ferry vessel was the first major event. This was the newly Danish-built 3094 ton *Saint-Germain* – naturally a stern loader – registered at Dunkerque and operated by the French Railways (SNCF) and of more modern appearance with single, instead of twin, funnel. It went into regular service at the end of July 1951 when the *Hampton Ferry* became relief vessel. Next seven more sleeping cars (nos 3983–9) were built and delivered during the first six months of 1952 which made a total of twenty now available and so placed the service in a good position for expansion.

A purely domestic amendment came into effect from 20 September 1954 when the up train from Dover was routed every day via Chatham and Herne Hill and the departure time from Dover Marine had to be advanced by ten minutes to 07.10. This was occasioned by the introduction of a Mondays to Fridays Tunbridge Wells–Charing Cross commuter train taking the *Night Ferry* path between Tonbridge and Petts Wood Junction, and on Saturdays the 07.38 from Ashford to London blocking the ferry service. The time honoured arrival of 09.10 at Victoria remained sacrosanct. As from 10 April 1955 there was a reversion to the Tonbridge route on Sundays.

From 3 June 1956 the train became first class only and this cut down the potential number of passengers at a stroke but the following summer (from 2

June) came the breakthrough that had been sought for several years – a through sleeping car to Brussels. As with the Paris service the sleeping car was confined to first class although a concession was made for Brussels in allowing both first and second class walking passengers. The Brussels sleeping car – usually one but at times of pressure a couple – was due to leave Dunkerque before the Paris train and serve Lille Sud (06.22), Tournai (07.13) and arrive at Brussels Midi at 08.43. Except on Saturdays and Sundays it also served the Central and Nord stations in Brussels and terminated at Schaerbeck at 09.05. In the opposite direction the daily departure from Schaerbeck was at 20.53 with balancing calls, that at Lille being made at the main station rather than Sud. In the autumn of 1958 the stop at Lille Sud was transferred to the main station. The BR locomotive headboard was replaced by one including BRUSSELS in the lower panel with three stars also, one each side of London and one between Paris Brussels.

Electrification made its mark in 1959. First of all, SNCF introduced electric traction between Paris and Arras from 11 January and a stop was made at Arras to change the electric locomotive for the Chapelon 4–6–2 (and vice versa), which had previously taken the train to and from Paris. As a result of this it was possible to pare five and ten minutes off the Paris arrival and departure times respectively. Secondly – perhaps rather more importantly in British eyes – Stage 1 of the Southern Region's Kent electrification scheme was inaugurated and from Monday 15 June the train was hauled by an E5000 class electric locomotive each way via Chatham, the arrival and departure times at Victoria remaining unaltered. In fact the first electric hauled *Night Ferry* was on 8 June with No E5003 on the down service which started a week in advance of the full electric service on the route. However, at the weekend steam re-asserted itself in the shape of Nos 31753 and 34068 (Friday/Saturday) and rebuilt Merchant Navy No 35015 (Saturday/Sunday). For some time before this the three Southern four-wheel baggage vans had not been at work in the train and with electrification they were not seen again. The old smokebox headboard was superseded by the standard BR rectangular type carried on the front of the electric locomotive.

During steam traction days, with odd exceptions, the locomotive duty had always been the preserve of Dover shed and men. Rather unusually the duty number – 430 – remained with the working for the whole period save for a short time at the end. Upon reinstatement of the train in 1947 light Pacifics Nos 21C156 and 21C157 had been transferred from Stewarts Lane to Dover, which shed had to provide an L1 class 4–4–0 to work with the 4–6–2 when necessary. In April 1948 Dover received newly-constructed Nos 34071 and 34072 and gave up the earlier pair and later received No 34073 as well as other members of the class down the years. Double-heading, occasioned when there were more than three sleeping cars in the train, was deemed necessary because of fears of water shortage if the 4–6–2 had to work the train single-handed.

To overcome this difficulty three of the last batch of Merchant Navy 4–6–2s, which had 6000 gallon tenders, Nos 35028–30 were transferred in October 1949 to Dover shed to work the service unassisted. In the summer of 1954 duty 430, worked by one of the Merchant Navy engines, comprised the up *Night Ferry* from Dover Marine to Victoria and the propelling of the empty stock into the carriage shed outside the station, a down and up Calais boat train (to Folkestone Junction and from Dover Marine) and then the down *Night Ferry*. Dover had one other duty – 458 – involved with the train: this was the 20-hour stint of a C class 0–6–0 (in pre-war days the E2 0–6–0 tanks had sometimes served) which shunted the Ferry Dock sidings and included pulling out from and propelling onto the ferry the sleeping cars and vans. Stewarts Lane shed was responsible for steam heating the sleepers at night, drawing them with the vans into platform 2 at Victoria and then giving banking assistance as the train left. Here some variety entered into the duties for Mondays to Fridays an H class 0–4–4 tank on duty 52 performed, while on Saturdays it fell to an E1 4–4–0 on duty 21 and on Sundays duty 55 encompassed the turn with a 2–6–0 of Class N.

This was shortly to be changed. It will be recalled that the up train was diverted via Chatham from 20 September 1954 to allow the Tunbridge Wells commuters to have an extra train. The Merchant Navy engines thus had to tackle the Chatham road with its formidable Sole Street bank. On the fourth day the *Night Ferry* gremlin struck! No. 35027, in climbing the bank, lost adhesion and slipped so badly that it failed with fractured side rods. The train had to be drawn back to Rochester to dispose of the disabled locomotive and eventually it arrived in London 145 minutes late. With autumn at hand and its attendant falling leaves and slippery rails on the incline (and probably with some encouragement from the Dover drivers) the decision was taken to revive the 4–4–0 and light 4–6–2 combination which had last served five years previously.

With a reversion to the Tonbridge route on Sunday mornings in 1955 the opportunity was taken to dispense with double-heading that day. It was arranged that a Merchant Navy engine would work three *Night Ferry* trips

From time to time titled trains would be diverted away from their normal paths, usually because of engineering works, to alternative routes. Nowhere were these alternative routes so numerous as on the approaches to London from Kent and here the *Night Ferry*, headed by No E5010, has been diverted via Crystal Palace and Streatham Hill (which station it is just clearing) on the inward run to Victoria. *Stanley Creer*

each weekend unassisted. It went down Saturday evening (duty 2) and then did the round trip on Sunday as part of duty 9. This came into force for the weekend of 16/17 July and Dover men still did the work albeit with a Stewarts Lane engine.

In the autumn of 1956 there were some amendments to the up assisting engine on Mondays, when it was booked for a Stewarts Lane E1 4–4–0 (duty 18), and on Saturdays, when another light Pacific from Dover had the job (duty 434). This latter was one of the rare bookings for double heading with Pacifics on the Southern Region. There was always an enormous variety in the types of locomotives diagramed for the empty stock and banking turn at Victoria among which were E1 4–4–0s; N 2–6–0s; H 0–4–4 tanks; E2 0–6–0 tanks; LMR class 2 2–6–2 tanks; C 0–6–0s and BR Class 5 4–6–0s.

In the last months of regular steam traction of the train duty 430 gave way to duty 426 for the up service and 427 for the down, both Battle of Britain class duties for different engines, and diesel locomotives ousted the time-honoured C class on the shunting turn at Dover Ferry sidings.

From time to time strangers put in an appearance on the train. Two Britannia 4–6–2s, Nos 70004 and 70014, were stationed at Stewarts Lane shed for a long period and in June and July 1952 more than once powered the train and this was repeated in May the following year when No 70030 was loaned to Dover to cover for temporary withdrawal of the Merchant Navy engines. Trials with the Southern's main line diesel-electric locomotives took place in 1954 and 1955: No 10202 was booked to work the train in both directions from 8 to 14 February 1954 (in the event the up journey on the first day does not appear to have run) and No 10203 headed the train in the down direction for a week starting on 13 March 1955 and both ways during the following week. For the diesels a new BR standard oblong train headboard was provided. At odd times Schools class 4–4–0s have appeared as assisting engines, more often than not on a Saturday when Dover substituted one for the light Pacific diagramed for the work. On one occasion the train was powered by a blue locomotive: if not of precisely the same tint as the Wagons-Lits livery No 35026 was at least the same colour when it found itself, in the spring of 1950, after recently being transferred to Stewarts Lane shed, working the train, doubtless as a stand-in for a Dover-based engine.

Even after the summer of 1959, when electric traction took over, steam sometimes had to come to the rescue as, for example, on 3 and 4 November 1961 when a landslip between Selling and Canterbury caused the train to be diverted via Tonbridge not then electrified and to be powered by a pair of light Pacifics. The most famous occasion was probably the last time it happened. On New Year's Day 1962 the electric locomotive due to work the duty was so late coming down from London that N class 2–6–0 No 31412 assisting rebuilt West Country No 34100 *Appledore* (oddly a Kentish name also) were turned out to work the train, about 1½ hours late, amidst the snow up through Chatham to Victoria. This, as a matter of interest, appears to have been the sole recorded instance of a rebuilt light Pacific appearing on the *Night Ferry*. Steam held sway, so far as England was concerned, for 15 of the train's 33 years existence.

From the autumn of 1960 the arrival time at Brussels drifted back to around 9 o'clock and from the spring of 1961 second class seating was re-introduced to and from Paris. With the electrification via Tonbridge completed in 1961 the *Night Ferry* reverted to that route in the down direction from 12 June 1961 as well as for the up service on Saturdays and Sundays. Over in France Arras to Dunkerque was brought into the electrification orbit from 30 September 1962 and this allowed a twenty minute earlier arrival in Paris at 08.40 and diesel traction took over from steam in Belgium at about the same date. So steam traction was completely eliminated on the *Night Ferry*.

Summer 1963 saw the introduction of one class only on the ships and first class walking passengers could claim a refund for the sea voyage. The train was now proving to be very popular. From 2 December 1963 the loading was increased to 19 vehicles, of which ten were sleeping cars (550 tons), three were vans (54½ tons), two buffet cars (78 tons – being two of S1755/56/72), one restaurant car (36 tons – either S1006 or S1018), two seconds (66 tons – from S4031/3/5) and a composite brake (37 tons) thus giving a tare weight of 851½ tons, the heaviest regular passenger train on British Railways. The *Night Ferry* star was at its apogee!

When the Hazebrouck–Lille section of SNCF became electrified the *Night Ferry* to and from Paris was re-routed, from 25 September 1966, via Lille in both directions so saving two separate trains between Dunkerque and Lille.

At the end of 1967 there came the fourth terminal destination – Basle, or Bâle as the board on the side of the sleeping car had it. This started on 16 December from Victoria and back from Basle the next day: it served a variety of towns and cities en route, including Strasbourg, and arrived in Basle at 14.12 returning at 15.50. It was purely a seasonal winter sports venture lasting until 16 (London)/17 (Basle) March 1968 and was resurrected for the period 20 December 1968 – 1 March 1969. The popularity of the train was now in decline as Queen's messengers, politicians, diplomats and businessmen abandoned it in favour of air transport which became more dependable and was in the ascendancy. To counter the fall in traffic, tariffs were reduced in 1967 and again in 1968.

In its time the *Night Ferry* carried royalty – HRH Princess Elizabeth on 13

The *Night Ferry* in steep decline. Seen here approaching London Victoria on 16 July 1979, by which time one van, four sleeping cars and the brake composite for the guard was sufficient for high-season operation. Electro-diesel No 73 119 is the locomotive. *Brian Morrison*

February 1948 and the Duke of Windsor on the various occasions when he visited the country in a private capacity – as well as Prime Ministers. Sir Winston Churchill caused a panic in Customs circles when he decided he would motor over from Chartwell to Sevenoaks (Tubs Hill) and join the train there at a special stop. 'C'est moi, Churchill!' caused the Customs to have the whole station closed and patrolled before and during the time the Premier entrained.

Meanwhile the train operation went on as usual, or much as usual. The elements regularly upset advertised arrival times, strikes – by the French in particular despite this usually being considered the preserve of the English – stopped the working entirely on occasions and there were sundry domestic upsets, such as when the incoming train over-ran its stopping place at platform 2 at Victoria or when the author was surprised to be confronted by a

Wagons-Lits conductor mounting the steps at Bromley South at 8 o'clock one morning to inspect Bromley High Street because his defective sleeping car was in a siding, having been extracted from the outward service the previous evening.

After well over thirty year's service *Hampton Ferry* was taken off the service in the spring of 1969 remaining on freight work until the autumn when it was replaced by a multi-purpose ship *Vortigern* registered at London by BR taking vehicular and train traffic as occasion demanded. *Shepperton Ferry* followed her sister in the summer of 1972 and in February 1974 the SNCF introduced the new multi-purpose ship *Chartres* of Calais shortly after which the last of the original trio, *Twickenham Ferry*, had her final sailing in May. Last of the ferry ships was the *Saint Eloi*, owned by ALA and registered at Dunkerque, which was commissioned in March 1975 and remained the principal ship for the rest of the time.

From here on it was all downhill. Perfidious Albion, in the shape of Harold Wilson, unilaterally stopped work on the Channel Tunnel early in 1975 but this was not to be the saviour of the *Night Ferry*. From 1 June that year BR separated the sheep (sleepers) from the goats (walkers) reserving the *Night Ferry* for the sheep and putting the goats into an electric multiple-unit which, of course, made complete economic nonsense, whatever sense it might have done in other directions. By this time one conductor was staffing two adjacent cars (to the same destination) instead of one and this had meant remarshalling the stock so that the doors of adjoining sleepers were buffer-to-buffer. On 4 July 1976 the new dock at Dunkerque Ouest was first used for the *Night Ferry* and with the Wagons-Lits staffing contract due to end in October steps were taken by BR to recruit attendants from their own staff to take over these duties, which transition took place on New Year's Day 1977. SNCF purchased seven of the sleeping cars and hired those others they required and eventually painted some of the former in their own livery.

A timetable amendment came into force from 22 May 1977 when the arrival time at Victoria was brought forward to 07.45 (except Saturdays and Sundays when it was 07.35). This in turn meant reduced breakfast patronage and so the restaurant car was taken off in the autumn and this allowed the *Night Ferry* to be all sleeping cars plus an ordinary brake composite for the guard to travel in and any vans required (much diminished because most mail to the Continent was going by air). With the train formation so drastically reduced there was no need to retain the E5000 (by now Class 71) electric locomotives for the duty which could be dealt with adequately by the Class 73 electro-diesels or the Class 33 diesel-electrics and so the Class 71 disappeared from the scene at the end of 1977.

In the spring of 1978 a snack vendor replaced the dining car between Dunkerque and Paris but that was too much! By the autumn it had been reinstated and thereafter ran in the winter. Departure from Victoria was advanced to 21.25 from 1 October 1978 so that the ship could take the sleepers over and bring the others back as one round trip, instead of two vessels being employed, and this allowed an extra 1½ hours sleep at Dunkerque without the train moving, to maintain the same arrival time in Paris. With one sleeper for Paris and one for Brussels plus a van and a coach for the guard it was a feeble ensemble that could be seen, when there were few patrons about, leaving and entering Victoria's platform 1. Mercifully it was to end in 1980. It was announced in the spring that it would cease on 31 October because, with an average complement of 37 passengers each way nightly, the outlay for overdue replacement stock could not be justified.

So it strangely fell to two well established services to bow out together: the London Evening News published for the last time on Friday 31 October 1980 and at 21.25 that night No 33043 left from Victoria, complete with a replica old style headboard made by Stewarts Lane staff, with seven sleeping cars, two vans and one ordinary coach as the final outward *Night Ferry*. Inwards next morning on the very last public working came, without headboard, No 73142 *Broadlands* with two vans, five sleepers and the ordinary coach. BR had finished with its sole international through train and could devote its energy to the commuter traffic – it was all over!

Or was it? As this is penned there is talk of a private Orient Express type revival. However, if it materialises it would be for a nostalgic touristic clientele rather than for the business fraternity. Sleeping cars take up a disproportionate amount of ship space per passenger and this economic fact coupled with weather uncertainties rules out a revival of the tradition. With automatic landing available at Heathrow the fog menace of air travel has been tamed and the seemingly always full first morning flight from Charles de Gaulle airport bears testimony to how the customers travel now. Through rail travel –by tunnel (fixed link) rather than ferry (flexible link) – may return but that will be the *Night Chunnel* rather than the *Ferry de Nuit*.

Penultimate departure from London, Diesel-electric locomotive No 33043, complete with replica headboard, ready to head the outward service on 30 October 1980. *Barry Edwards*

Appendix

A note on SR coaching stock marshalling

Unlike the other three grouped companies the Southern was meticulous in the marshalling of much of its carriage stock in fixed formation numbered sets and allocating the sets to specific workings day in day out. In this it was following practices of its three main constituents but the SR brought the discipline of carriage marshalling to a fine art which even today has never been matched to quite the same extent elsewhere on BR. For each section of the SR there were two main working documents, the carriage working notice which listed the train formation for each service including the actual set number for the more specialised formations or the type of set where similar formations were used on a number of services, together with individual loose coaches added to the sets to provide a given capacity with day to day variations. The second document was the carriage working appendix which listed the individual coach numbers formed into the numbered sets.

The shorter sets were fairly predictable in the make up. A two corridor set for example was normally composed of a brake third and a brake composite, while a three corridor set would be a brake third, composite, and brake third. For much of the Southern Railway's life these would have been side door corridor coaches but in its last years and on into BR days the Bulleid stock mostly had end doors linked to compartments by side corridor and also introduced much more open saloon accommodation including some saloon brake thirds which included part open saloon and part side corridor seating. The 'six dining sets' on the Bournemouth line in their later years were formed of a saloon brake third at each end, a composite, dining first, kitchen third and an open third.

At the grouping in 1923 the LBSCR and SECR had very little corridor stock, most coaches being of the compartment type and those for main line use sometimes equipped with between-compartment toilets. This was why the Brighton line Pullmans for example were such a contrast with the ordinary stock on other services. On the South Eastern & Chatham there was nothing other than non-corridor lavatory stock except for a few corridor coaches built

214

Two-set No 28 allocated to the Waterloo–West of England service working on the Bodmin North branch. The carriage next to the engine – No 6569 composite brake – is typical of the composite brakes which were included in the *Atlantic Coast Express*. From the engine comes the guard's brake, a first class compartment, a non-smoking first, a non-smoking second and then three second class compartments giving a total capacity of 48 passenger seats. *Author's collection*

mostly for boat train services in the early 1920s or a handful for through workings to the north until the SR gradually introduced corridor stock later in that decade. Much of the SECR's main line stock was formed into three-coach sets – the Trio sets of various types – usually with birdcage roof lookouts on top of the guards' compartments and as built with first, second and third class accommodation. Second class was abolished by the Southern except on boat train services soon after the grouping, but in 1956 the wheel turned full circle when in common with most mainland European railways third class was renamed as second and what had been second class was abolished or merged with the old third class. The SECR 10-compartment thirds, which seated 100 passengers, were mostly loose coaches added to the three sets as required on specific services. They were fairly spartan and were built as suburban coaches with the aim of later conversion for electric use on suburban electrification projects, but were never in fact converted. As described in the text they appeared on certain named trains and on which even when new must have been the most austere coaches of any named train this century anywhere in the country. In their last years they could be found on branch services still worked by steam and in excursion sets.

Southern electric stock was also carefully marshalled in sets but was classified by the number of coaches and the type of stock by a figure and three letters. The five-car *Brighton Belle* sets were naturally 5BEL, while the usual Brighton line corridor sets were known as 6PUL being six car formations including a single Pullman car. The special sets for the electrified version of the *City Limited* 6CIT (or sometimes 6CITY) had a higher proportion of first class with three first class trailers replacing the two composites and one third of the 6PUL sets. The three letter electric stock classifications have survived until the present day although with more modern stock some of the equipment of the unit is reflected in the code, the 4CEP units used on the *Conquerer* being four-coach formations equipped with electro-pneumatic brakes, a distinction needed when they were originally built in the late 1950s when much of the SR electric stock was then equipped only with Westinghouse automatic air brakes but not so necessary today when nearly all SR electric stock has ep brakes.

Sources, Further Reading and Acknowledgements

Foundation of the whole volume rests upon the public timetables published by the pre-grouping companies, the Southern Railway, British Railways Southern Region and, by no means least of all, Bradshaw's Railway Guide. The last of these, by virtue of being published monthly, is sometimes to be preferred to the company publications which would be qualified by the issue of amendment slips or supplements which have not always survived. Examples – indeed long, if not complete, runs – of all these are held by the Public Record Office at Kew although those for the LCDR and South Eastern Railway tend to be patchy.

Other sources common to all chapters include the periodicals *Railway Gazette* (good on technical descriptions of rolling stock and events pre-nationalisation), *Railway Magazine*, *Railway Observer* (under D. E. White's editorship excellent for traffic reports) and *Railway World*. Details of Pullman trains may be found in *Pullman* by Julian Morel (strongest on post–1946 matters, particularly good on the organizational side and has a list of Pullman cars not entirely without blemish) and *Pullman in Europe* by George Behrend (a comprehensive list of cars but the text has its pitfalls). The official carriage working notices and appendixes thereto together with engine workings (from the author's own collection) have been used but, apart from a few scattered items at PRO, Kew, these are not readily accessible to researchers.

Items peculiar to each chapter are:

Chapter 1 Perspective
The early days of the *Lancing Belle* are culled from the LBSCR working timetables (PRO, Kew).

Chapter 2 Westward Ho!
The *Southern Railway Magazine* of the period has been drawn on for details of the competition which resulted in the *Atlantic Coast Express* title. For the daily flagging episode at Sidmouth Junction the author is indebted to Mr E. S.

Youldon and this gentleman also read and commented upon the draft for this chapter. Pre-war engine workings west of Exeter were kindly provided by Mr J. Bamsey and Mr G. Jacobs did likewise for carriage and engine workings for 1939.

Rather surprisingly there has not been published a book devoted to the *Atlantic Coast Express* other than those describing points of interest to be observed en route. Of these *A.C.E.* by S. P. B. Mais with illustrations by Anna Zinkeisen published by the Southern Railway (1937) is the most notable.

Chapter 3   Into Wessex

Dates of cessation of the services in 1939 were provided by Mr J. A. Young. The stopping of the *Royal Wessex* at Hinton Admiral reached high places and is recorded in Hansard.

Chapter 4   Outward Bound

Reliable sources for the titled trains included in this chapter are scarce and although most of the developments may be placed in broad date bands it is not easy to arrive at specific start and finish points. In some cases it is because the operational periods for the continental traffic did not coincide with those for the domestic winter and summer timetables. For the irregular ocean liner traffic special traffic notices used to detail requirements; no complete record of these would have appeared to have survived to enable the commencing and finishing dates to be pinpointed. Mr S. Rocksborough Smith went to pains to extract from his collection of such notices certain dates relevant to the operation of the titled trains and Mr B. I. Fletcher made available his records of headboards and carriage roofboards for the services concerned. Mr J. N. Faulkner kindly examined the first draft of this chapter and in consequence it has benefited from his knowledge and suggestions and some misconceptions have been avoided as a result.

Chapter 5   To Sussex-By-The-Sea

The *Southern Belle* coming-of-age brochure was examined through the good offices of Mr A. M. Fisher. Details of the engine workings of the *Eastbourne Sunday Limited* for its last dozen years have been provided by Mr S. C. Nash.

A booklet entitled *The Brighton Belle* by Nicholas Owen is strong on the electric traction aspect of the train while the various editions of *Southern Electric* from the pen of G. T. Moody give much information on that type of traction, its stock and operation.

Chapter 6   Through The Garden of England

In addition to the newspapers referred to in the text useful information on the Granville Hotel was extracted from the Hotel Portfolio held at Ramsgate Library. Much of the detail of the Canterbury portion of the *Kentish Belle* has been made available through the kindness of Mr Arthur G. Wells who was resident there at the time.

Chapter 7   To Dover for Paris

For the whole period of the *Club Train The Times* proves most useful for reports, letters and advertisements: the Board Minute Books of both LCDR and SER (PRO, Kew) record the various decisions made – even if only to defer making one! – without giving clues to the arguments which prevailed. Unfortunately the agreement between W-L and SER which is listed at PRO, Kew has been missing for some years but the LCDR Dover Sailings Journal, which is available, lists every sailing made in connection with the service including times at the ports and numbers of passengers carried. The hackneyed tale of the two train conductors fighting for the custom of the sole passenger has not been repeated because there could be more than a trace of hyperbole about it.

Correspondence in several issues of the *Southern Railway Magazine* has been useful for rolling stock and motive power details of the *Club Train*.

The specification together with modification, building and trial notes of TSS *Canterbury* (all at PRO, Kew) have been drawn upon as have various board minutes as to the contract and payments for the ship.

A. Hasenson's book *The Golden Arrow* by no means confines itself to the subject train but ranges over the wider aspect of the short sea routes and is particularly strong on maps and timetable extracts. Rixon Bucknall's *Boat Trains and Channel Packets* is best on historical matters backed with some good illustrations, the maps and diagrams being its weak point.

Chapter 8   Train Across the Channel

Apart from the Board Minute books there is some scattered information held at PRO, Kew on the *Night Ferry* to be found under various heads. However, a prolific source is the *Dover Express* which, in the late 1930s, chronicled life in the town assiduously even to publishing a weekly summary of train ferry events. Mr A. G. S. Davies and Mr George Behrend kindly answered one or two queries relating to train operation.

The attractive volume *Night Ferry* by George Behrend and Gary Buchanan is strong on atmosphere and workings on the continent and has useful appendixes on the ships and sleeping cars.

Appendix

This has been prepared by Mr G. M. Kichenside.

The librarians and staff of Bournemouth, Croydon, Dover, Eastbourne, City of London, Margate, Ramsgate, Southampton, Westminster and Weymouth Central libraries and the Public Record Office, Kew gave valuable assistance for viewing local newspaper records and archival material and to them, coupled with all those persons mentioned in the course of the foregoing resume, I am indebted for providing information incorporated in the text and, by no means least of all, to Mr S. C. Nash who readily examined the complete draft and made valuable suggestions thereupon. This acknowledgement is but a token of my thanks. Any shortcomings are mine alone.

Index

Air raid damage, 102
Albion, perfidious, 211
Albion Hotel (Ramsgate), 129
Ambulatory refreshment service, 128
Amiens, 166,187
Andes RMS, 83
Andover Junction, 21
Arosa Line, 11,12,82
Arras, 204,209
Arundel Castle RMMV, 83
Ashford, 119,122,123,124,125,194,
   203
Ashford Junction, 118,120,121,123
Ashford shed, 161
Association of Regular Kent Coasters,
   145
Ateliers de Construction du Nord de
   la France Blanc-Messeron, 194
Atlantic Coast Express, 8,11,12,
   21–49,51,217,218
Axminster, 39,42,54

Baggage trucks, 178
Baggage vans, 184,194,204
Baked beans upon toast, 102
Bale—see Basle
Ballast, additional, 194
Banana boats, 86
Barnstaple Junction, 23,26,34,35,39,
   40,44,45,47,50
Barnstaple Junction shed, 38
Barnstaple Town, 23,26,31,50
Basingstoke, 14,21,83,87,88
Basle, 191,209
Bath, 14
Battersea shed, 110,112,113,177
Battle, 128
Beaulieu Road, 66
Beeswing, 7
Belgium, 168,209
Bere Alston, 27,41
Bicycle Belle, 20
Birchington, 134,135
Birchington-on-Sea, 150
Birmingham, 16
Blackheath, 145
Blue Riband, 82
Boulogne, 163,168,178,185,191,192
Bournemouth, 14,56,61,62,68,69,70,
   72,83,87
Bournemouth Belle, 11,12,69–79
Bournemouth Central, 56,57,60,61
   62,64, 65,66,68,70,72,74,77,78,79
   87
Bournemouth Limited, 11,12,
   56–62,64,69,179
Bournemouth shed, 60,61,65,66,79,86
Bournemouth West, 14,57,60,61,62,
   64,65,66,68,70,72,74,78
Bow, 31,41
Bow rudders, 198
Brake vans, 77,78
Braunton, 29,50
Bread rationing, 74
Breeze PS, 171
Brentor, 39,41
Bridestowe, 39,41

Brighton, 9,12,13,14,15,16,17,26,27,
   29,36,39,90,91,92,93,97,98,99,101,
   102,103,105,106,108,109,110
Brighton Belle, 11,12,17,101–105,114,
   216,219
Brighton Limited, 9,11,90–92
British Railways, 62,128,156,184,188,
   190,191,203,211,212,214,217
Brittany, 80,89
Brittany Express, 11,82,86,87
Brixton, 133,135,141
Broadstairs, 129,130,131,132,133,
   135,136,141,142,143,144,145,146,
   147,148,149,150,151,152,153,155,
   156
Broadstone, 14
Brockenhurst, 64,65,68
Bromley South, 211
Brussels, 191,204,209,212
Brussels Central, 204
Brussels Midi, 204
Brussels Nord, 204
Bude, 21,22,23,26,27,29,30,31,34,35,36,
   38,39,41,42,44,45,46,47,48,49
Budmouth, 62
Buffet cars, 44,45,87,126,127,190,201,
   209
Bulleid type stock, 65,66,124,214

Cable & Wireless, 17
Calais, 163,164,166,168,170,172,174,
   178,185,192,194,195,196,205,211
Calais boat express, 137
Calais Chamber of Commerce, 196
Calais Chamber of Trade, 173
Calais-Douvres PS, 163,166,168,171
Calais Maritime, 168,176,177,178,
   179,183,185,187
Calais Pier, 166
Caledonian Railway, 115
Camelford, 23,27
Canberra TES, 82
Cannon Street, 106,116,118,119,120,
   122,123,134,146,147,148,149,152,
   153,171,195
Canterbury, 116,119,120,121,123,
   137,140,159,160,208,219
Canterbury TSS, 176,177,178,179,
   182,219
Canterbury East, 136,140,147,160
Canterbury West, 118,122,123
Carriage roofboards, 16,29,60,82,89,
   102,108,114,121,124
Casterbridge, 62
Catford Loop line, 201
Central European time, 87
Channel Islands, 80,87
Channel Tunnel, 190,191,196,211
Channel Tunnel Company, 163,191
Charing Cross, 116,118,119,120,121,
   122,123,124,125,126,127,128,134,
   163,164,166,169,170,171,195,203
Charles de Gaulle airport, 212
'Chartex' train, 20
Chartres MV, 211
Chartwell, 210
Chatham, 132,134,136,140,144,147,

   168,187,202,203,204,205,209
Chichester, 17
Chilham, 123
Chislehurst, 134,146
Chislehurst tunnel, 122
Churchill, Sir Winston, 210
City Express, 11,144–149,153
City Express to the Kent Coast, 145
City Limited, 9,11,105–109,216
'Clacton, Ipswich, Harwich and
   Yarmouth Boat Train', 136
Clapham Junction, 38,90,91
Clapham Yard, 52
Cliftonville Express, 11,134,
   140–144,155,156
Cliftonville Hotel, 129
Club Train, 11,163–173,219
Coal strike, 9,23,97,141
Coleford Junction, 46
Columbia TSS, 83
Conqueror, 11,128,216
Continental Traffic Committee, 172
Corbin, M, 195
Corfe Castle, 57,61,64,65,66
Cote d'Azur SS, 185
Cravens, 97
Crediton, 36,41
Cunarder, 11,82,83,84,86
Cunard Line, 12,82
Customs examination, 163,171,176,
   177,198,203

Dalziel, Sir Davison, 174
Dartford, 144
Davis, Edmund F., 115
Day Mail, 115
Deal, 118,119,120,122,123,124,136,
   140
Delabole, 27
Denny & Bros Ltd, William, 176
Devon Belle, 11,12,49–55
Devonian Express, 21
Devonport, 22,23,27,39,41,50
Diesel multiple units, 128
Dorchester, 56,57,61,64,70,72
Dorchester shed, 86
Dorchester South, 65
Dorking, 145
Dover, 118,119,120,121,122,123,124,
   136,144,145,147,164,165,168,169,
   171,172,173,174,176,177,179,187,
   191,192,194,195,196,198,200,201,
   203,208
Dover, Deal and Kent Coast Express,
   136–140
Dover Express, 219
Dover Ferry Berth, 194,195,197,200,
   201
Dover Harbour, 136,140,147,194
Dover Marine, 176,177,178,179,183,
   185,186,187,195,197,201,203,205
Dover, Mayor of, 196
Dover Pier, 166,168,171
Dover Priory, 124,127,136,140,147
Dover shed, 127,160,204,205,208
Dover Town, 121,122,123
Dumbarton, 176

Dumpton Park, 132,144,149,150,153, 156
Dunkerque, 193,195,196,200,202,203, 204,209,211,212
Dunkerque Ferry Berth, 197,201
Dunkerque Ouest, 211

Eastbourne, 14,109,110,111,113,114
Eastbourne shed, 114
Eastbourne Belle, 114
Eastbourne Pullman Limited, 11, 109–110
Eastbourne Sunday Limited, 11, 110–114,218
Eastbourne Sunday Pullman, 112
East Croydon, 16,90,91,110,111
East Devon Express, 21,33
Eastleigh, 66,72,83,87
Eastleigh shed, 68,86
Eastleigh works, 82
Eggesford, 39,40
Eiffel Tower, 163,166
Electric multiple units, 100,103,104, 105,108,128,144,211
Electrification, 61,68,89,98,99,103, 114,126,128,162,187,204,209,215
Electrification works, 68,74,126,160
Elizabeth, HRH Princess, 209
Elliott, J. B., 21
Empress PS, 163,171
Eridge, 20
Erlynne, Mrs, 173
Euston, 198
Exeter, 21,23,26,29,34,35,39,42,43, 46,50,51,86,218
Exeter Central, 31,34,35,36,38,39,40, 41,42,43,44,45,46,47,50,52,54
Exeter Queen Street, 22,23,26,27,29, 30,31,34,35
Exeter St Davids, 23,26,27,39,40,41, 46,47,50
Exmouth, 21,26,29,30,36,39,42,46,47
Exmouth Junction shed, 38,43,51

Fairsea SS, 82
Falaise SS, 81,88
Faversham, 132,134,136,137,140, 141,142,143,144,145,147,148, 149,150,155,160
Feniton, 42
Ferry de Nuit, 212
Festival of Britain, 62,159,184
1st Limited, 166
Flèche d'Or, La, 174,187
Foam PS, 171
Folkestone, 123,124,126,178,195, 201,202
Folkestone Central, 124,125,126,127
Folkestone Flyer, 7,124
Folkestone Harbour, 17,185,187,195
Folkestone Junction, 125,185,205
Forth Bridge, 164
Fourgon, 170
France, 87,163,168,170,171,178,179, 187,188,191,192,200,203,209
Fratton shed, 61
Fremington, 23,26,31
French flag, 195
French Railways (SNCF), 187,203, 204,209,211
French time, 166,187,203
Freshwater, 16

Gatwick Airport, 16
General strike, 23
Germany, 200
Golden Arrow, 11,12,174–190,219
'Golden Way', 174
Granville, 9,123
Granville and Cliftonville Special Express, 131
Granville and Deal and Walmer Express, 119–122
Granville and Dover, Folkestone, Shorncliffe and Sandgate Express, 119–122
Granville and Dover, Folkestone, Shorncliffe, Sandgate and Hythe Express, 119–122
Granville and Walmer and Deal Express, 119–122
Granville and Walmer and Deal, Sandgate, Shorncliffe, Folkestone and Dover Express, 119–122
Granville and Walmer and Deal, Shorncliffe, Folkestone and Dover Express, 119–122
Granville and Westgate-on-Sea Special Express, 11,129–132
Granville, Cliftonville and Westgate-on-Sea Special Express, 129–132
Granville Express (via Ashford), 11,119–122
Granville Express (via Faversham), 129–132
Granville Limited Express, 129–132
Granville Special Express, 11, 115–18
Granville Hotel, 115,129,219
Gravesend, 136,145,147,149
Gravesend Central, 147,149
Great Exhibition (Paris), 163,165,170, 172
Great Western Railway, 23,54
Greek Line, 11,82,83,85
Greenwich, 145,147,149
Grieve, John, 129
Grosvenor Bridge, 130
Grosvenor Road, 90
Grove Park, 123

Halwill Junction, 23,26,27,30,38,48
Hamilton, Duke of, 168
Hampton Ferry SS, 193,195,197,203, 211
Harwich, 192
Hastings, 128,144
Hawkesbury Street Junction, 201
Hayes, 144
Haywards Heath, 103,110,112
Hazebrouck, 209
Headborns (locomotive), 40,51,74, 82,84,85,88,89,98,102,160,182,186, 190,200,204,208,212
Headcorn, 185
Heathrow, 212
Herne Bay, 132,134,135,136,140,142, 143,146,148,150,151,152,155,156
Herne Bay and Kent Coast Express, 136–140
Herne Hill, 129,130,132,133,134,135, 136,137,140,141,146,149,166,168, 178,197,201,203
Hinton Admiral, 68,218
Hither Green, 149

Hitler, 200
Holborn Viaduct, 129,130,132,134, 135,140,145,146,147,148,149,153, 163,166,168
Holland American, 11,82,85
Hollingbourne, 17
Holsworthy, 22
Honiton, 41,51
Hove, 13
Hythe, 122

Ilfracombe, 22,23,26,27,29,30,31,34, 35,36,38,39,40,41,44,45,46,47,49, 50,51,52,53,54
Inspection saloon, 68
Interchange trails, 39
International Sleeping Car Company, 163,164,170
Invicta PS, 171
Invicta SS, 182,185
Irish Mail, 115
Isle of Thanet TSS, 176
Isle of Wight, 16
Isle of Wight Central Railway, 16

Kearsney, 136,140,147
Keble's Gazette, 129
Kensington (Addison Road), 14
Kent Coast and Canterbury Express, 136–140
Kent Coast, Canterbury, Dover and Deal Express, 136–140
'Kent Coast Cheap Fast Train', 141
Kent Coast, Dover and Deal Express, 136
Kent Coast Express (via Ashford), 11, 120,122–123
Kent Coast Express (via Faversham), 3,11,132–136,140
Kent House, 177
Kentish Belle, 11,12,160–162,219
Kent, Weald of, 201
Kings Cross, 198
Kippers, 105

La Chapelle locomotive depot, 182
Lady Windermere's Fan, 173
Lancaster, 93
Lancing, 14
Lancing Belle, 7,13,14,217
Lancing Carriage Works, 12,13,14,16, 66,106
Launceston, 22,23,27
Laycock, W. S. Ltd, 93,97
Le Havre, 80,83,86
Lewes, 114
Life jacket, 201
Lille, 204,219
Lille Sud, 204
Limited Mail, 115
Limited Saloon and Dining Car Express, 166
Liverpool, 14,168
Livery,
    BR Blue, 208
    BR Blue and grey, 104
    BR Blue and grey Pullman, 188
    BR Cream and crimson lake, 65
    BR Green, 66
    BR 'Jaffa Cake', 128
    BR Network South East, 128
    Pullman, 77,100,103,177,188
    SR Blue, 194

SR Dover green, 179
SR Malachite green, 62,79
Loading wagons, 195
Locomotive headboards—see
  Headboards (locomotive)
London, 9,17,26,29,38,39,43,46,50,
  56,61,62,68,69,70,72,74,82,86,90,
  91,98,103,105,109,110,111,113,
  114,116,117,118,119,120,121,122,
  123,124,128,131,132,141,142,143,
  144,150,152,153,155,159,164,165,
  168,169,170,171,173,174,177,178,
  182,183,185,188,190,191,194,195,
  196,198,200,203,204,205,209,211
London, City of, 106,145
London & North Western Railway, 14,
  15,115,168
London & South Western Railway, 9,
  14,21,22,68,70,80,115
London Bridge, 9,20,106,108,118,
  119,120,121,122,144,146,147,148,
  149,152,153
London, Brighton & South Coast
  Railway, 9,12,14,15,90,106,110,
  112,153,214,217
London, Chatham & Dover Railway,
  9,117,129,132,134,136,163,164,
  165,166,168,169,170,171,172,173,
  217,219
London Evening News, 212
London Midland & Scottish Railway,
  15,16,124
Lord Warden Hotel, 197
Ludgate Hill, 129,130,132
Luggage labels, 15
Lydford, 31,36,39,41
Lyme Regis, 29,41,42
Lynton, 23,26

Maddaford Moor Halt, 41
Maid of Kent PS, 171
Maidstone, 123
Maidstone East, 179
Manchester, 14,16,168
Man of Kent, 11,12,124–127
Marchwood Volunteer, 8
Margate, 117,118,119,120,121,122,
  124,125,129,130,132,133,140,144,
  145,146,148,149,155,156
Margate East, 132,136,140,141,144,
  146,147,149,150,153
Margate Sands, 122,123
Margate West, 130,131,135,136,141,
  142,143,146,147,148,150,151,152,
  153,154,155
Marsh Mills, 22
Martin Mill, 136
Mathias, M., 164
Medlanc, 7
Meldon Junction, 46
Metropolitan Amalgamated Railway
  Carriage & Wagon Co. Ltd, 93
Metropolitan-Cammell Carriage and
  Wagon Co., 100
Meyrick, Sir George, 68
Micheldever, 83,88
Midland Railway, 14,115
Millhouses, 93
Minature buffet car, 45
Minster Junction, 118,119,120,121,
  122
Mortehoe, 38,46,50
Mutley, 23,27,31

Nagelmackers, M., 172
Nationalisation, 12,14,39,62,79,
  80,114
Network South East, 43,128
New Cross, 118,144
New Cross Gate shed, 113
Newport (IOW), 16
Newton Poppleford, 26
Newton St Cyres, 39
Night Chunnel, 212
Night Ferry, 11,12,81,191–212,219
Nine Elms shed, 38,43,50,54,65,78,83,
  86,177,182
Nord—see *Northern Railway of
  France*
Normandy, 80,89
Normandy Express, 11,80,81,87
Normannia SS, 80,88
Northam, 87
North British Railway, 115
North Cornwall Express, 21,23
North Eastern Railway, 115
Northern Railway of France, 163,164,
  165,172,173,191,192,194
North Tawton, 39,41
Nunhead, 201

Ocean Terminal Old Docks
  Southampton, 80,83,89
Okehampton, 23,26,27,29,30,39,41,
  45,47,50
Olivier, Sir Laurence, 105
Order of the Legion d'Honneur, 195
Oriana SS, 82
Orient Express, 212
Orpington, 128,201
Ostend boat train, 134,140
Otterham, 23,27
Oxford, 14

Paddock Wood, 123
Padstow, 21,22,23,26,27,29,30,31,34,
  35,36,38,39,40,41,44,45,46,47,48,
  49
Paris, 17,81,163,164,165,166,168,
  169,170,171,172,174,178,182,183,
  187,188,190,191,195,196,197,198,
  200,202,203,204,209,212
Paris (Nord), 166,176,177,178,179,
  183,187,191,197,201,203
Paris Limited, 166
Paris Limited Mail, 168
Payne, Capt. H. L., 195
P & O Orient Lines, 82
Petrel PS, 171,173
Petts Wood Junction, 203
Pines Express, 8,14,16
Plymouth, 23,26,27,29,30,31,36,38,
  39,41,42,44,45,46,47,51,53,86
Plymouth Friary, 22,23,27,29,31,34,
  35,39,41,44,45,50
Plymouth North Road, 23,27,39,41,
  44,45,50
Poole, 14,56,57,61,64,65,70,72,87
Port Isaac Road, 27
Portslade, 13
Portsmouth Arms, 23,26,31,36
Pre-electrification works, 74,77
Premium fares, 88
Pressure ventilation, 100
Preston Park, 90
Preston Park works, 50
Proficiency tests, 15

Pullman cars, 9,17,20,49,50,51,54,69,
  70,74,75,77,78,80,82,83,86,87,88,
  90,91,92,93,97,98,99,100,101,102,
  103,104,105,106,109,110,111,112,
  113,114,131,132,143,144,147,148,
  149,150,151,152,153,154,155,156,
  158,159,160,162,174,177,178,179,
  182,183,184,185,187,188,190,197,
  198,200,201,214,216,217
Pullman Car Company, 49,98,102,
  174,188
Pyrotechnic display, 116

Queen Elizabeth (Queen Mother) HM,
  105
Queen Elizabeth RMS, 82,83
Queen Elizabeth 2 SS, 12
Queen Mary HM, 179
Queen Mary RMS, 82

Race to the North, 164
Radnor Park, 123
Railway strike (France), 200,210
Ramsgate, 9,115,116,117,118,119,
  120,121,122,124,125,129,132,133,
  134,135,136,140,144,145,146,149,
  150,152,153,155,156,158,159,160,
  162
Ramsgate Harbour, 129,130,131,132,
  136,140,141,142,143,144,146,147,
  148,149,150,151,152,153,155
Ramsgate shed, 127,159,161
Ramsgate Town, 122,123
Refreshment cars, 87,124,126
Regency Belle, 8,17
Reigate Junction, 145
Reservation fee, 197
Restaurant cars, 8,16,23,26,27,28,29,
  30,34,35,36,38,39,40,44,45,60,61,
  62,66,70,201,209,211
Richborough, 192
Rochester, 134,205
Rochester Bridge, 134
Rouen, 81
Royal Mail Lines, 12,82
Royal Wessex, 11,62–69,78,218
Rugby, 15
Ryde works, 16

Saar, 194
Safmarine, 12
Saint Eloi VM, 211
Saint-Germain SS, 203
St Budeaux, 41
St James's Theatre, 173
St Kew Highway, 23
St Lawrence, 115
St Lawrence Junction, 120,121
St Lawrence-on-Sea, 115
St Leonards, 128
St Leonards (Warrior Square), 128
St Malo, 80,81
St Mary Cray, 146
St Pauls, 134,135,140,145,146,147,
  149,171
Salisbury, 21,23,26,27,29,30,31,34,
  35,36,38,39,41,42,43,44,45,46,50,
  54,86
Salisbury shed, 38,51,52,79
Samphire PS, 171
Sandbourne, 62
Sandling Junction, 123
Sandown, 16

Sandwich, 118,119,120,123,124
Schaerbeck, 204
Scotch Express, 115
Seaco, 17
Sea Containers, 17
Seaton, 21,29,36,39,41,46
Seaton Junction, 46
Seat reservations, 30,50,52,54,74,103
Selling, 137,208
Sevenoaks (Tubs Hill), 210
Severn Tunnel, 163
Shanklin, 16
Shawford, 83,88
Shepperton Ferry SS, 193,197,211
Sherborne, 39
Shoreham-by-Sea, 13
Shorncliffe, 125
Shorncliffe Camp, 123
Sidcup, 149
Sidmouth, 21,26,29,36,39,42,46
Sidmouth Junction, 23,26,29,30,31,
34,35,39,41,42,44,45,46,50,51,217
Simon, Sir John, 197
Sitmar Line, 11,82
Sittingbourne, 131,132,134,140
Sleeping cars, 178,191,193,194,195,
196,197,198,200,201,202,203,204,
205,209,211,212,219
Slip portions, 110,137,141,142,143,
145,146,147,148,155
Snack vendor, 212
Societe Anonyme de Navigation
Angleterre-Lorraine (ALA), 195,211
SNCF—see French Railways
Sole Street, 147,205
Somerset & Dorset Joint Railway, 14
South Africa, 82,88
South American, 11,82,83,85
Southampton, 12,14,56,62,70,80,82,
86,87
Southampton Airport, 68
Southampton Central, 64,65,70,72,
74,83,87
Southampton Docks, 80,83,87,89,176
Southampton New Docks, 83,194
Southampton Old Docks, 86,87
Southampton West, 70,72
South Bank, 185
South Eastern Railway, 8,115,116,
119,129,163,164,165,166,168,170,
171,172,174,217,219
South Eastern & Chatham Railway,
9,121,136,141,143,153,154,214,215
Southerham bridge, 114
Southern Belle, 9,11,13,
92–101,109,110,113,218
Southern Railway, 7,8,9,12,14,15,16,
21,26,46,49,56,70,74,80,98,99,101,
108,153,155,156,174,179,191,192,
193,194,200,203,214,215,217,218
Southern Railway Docks and Marine
Committee, 174
Southern Railway Magazine,
21,217,219
Southwick, 13
Special Express Train, 129
Special Scottish Mail, 115
Springbok, 11,12,82,89
Statesman, 11,82,84
Stewarts Lane shed, 159,161,177,178,
182,185,204,205,208,212

Steyning, 17
Strasbourg, 209
Strikes (French), 200,210
Strood, 145,147
Sunny South Express, 8,15,16
Sunny South Special, 14
Supplements (charges, fees, Pullman),
50,70,102,103,104,114,131,148,
150,151,154,155,170,171,173,174,
176,197
Surbiton, 21,23,26,27,31
Swanage, 57,60,61,62,64,65,66,67,70
Swan, Hunter & Wigham Richardson,
193
Szlumper, Gilbert, 193

Tavern cars, 40,47,48,66
Tavistock, 22,23,27,29,39,41,52
Tay Bridge, 164
Templecombe, 39
Templecombe Junction, 22
1066 Route, 128
Thanet, 132,152,153,160,162
Thanet Advertiser, 116
Thanet Belle, 11,156–159,162
Thanet Express, 11,148,149–153
Thanet Fast Train, 150
Thanet Limited cars, 156
Thanet Pullman, 144
Thanet Pullman Limited, 11,142,143,
153–156
Times, 115,129,163,174,219
Tipton St Johns, 46,47
Toilets, separate for sexes, 93
Tonbridge, 122,128,145,178,182,187,
197,200,201,203,205,208,209
Torquay Pullman, 54
Torrington, 22,23,26,27,29,30,31,34,
35,36,38,39,40,41,42,44,45,46,47,
49
Tourist, 8,16
Tournai, 204
Train ferry, 191,192,194,219
Train formations, 13,14,16,17,20,28,
29,36,38,46,47,48,49,51,52,60,62,
65,66,67,70,74,75,78,83,90,91,92,
98,99,100,101,106,110,112,126,
127,128,130,132,143,148,150,152,
154,158,159,160,168,170,174,177,
178,179,182,184,185,186,188,197,
198,201,209,211,212,214–16
Trains de plaisir, 170
Trans-Atlantic traffic, 86
Tresmeer, 22
Trial runs, 194,197
Tunbridge, 145
Tunbridge Wells, 128,203,205
12th Lancers, 194
Twickenham Ferry SS, 193,194,195,
196,211

Umberleigh, 31,36
Union-Castle Express, 11,82,83,85
Union-Castle Line, 12,82,83
Union-Castle Safmarine, 11,82,88
United States Lines, 82
United States SS, 82

Venice, 17
Venice Simplon-Orient Express,
8,17,20

Ventnor, 16
Verini, G. F., 115
Victoria, 17,86,90,92,93,97,98,99,100,
102,109,110,111,114,122,129,130,
131,132,133,134,135,136,137,140,
141,142,143,144,146,149,150,151,
152,153,155,156,158,160,163,166,
168,170,171,174,176,177,178,179,
182,183,184,185,187,191,195,197,
198,200,201,203,204,205,208,209,
210,211,212
Victoria PS, 163,168,171
Vortigern MV, 211

Wadebridge, 27
Wagons-Lits (WL), 164,165,166,168,
172,173,174,178,191,194,195,197,
200,201,208,211,219
Walker, Sir Herbert, 145,191,195,197
Walker-on-Tyne, 193
Walmer, 119,120,121,122,123,136
Wareham, 57,60,61,64,65,67,70,72
Waterloo, 16,21,23,26,27,29,30,31,34,
35,36,38,39,40,41,42,43,44,45,46,
49,50,52,54,56,57,60,61,62,64,65,
66,68,70,72,74,80,81,82,83,86,87,
88,124,125,195
Waterloo East, 128
Waterloo Junction, 118,119,120,122,123
Western Region (BR), 42,43
Westgate, 130
Westgate-on-Sea, 130,131,132,133,
136,140,141,145,146,150,155
*Westgate-on-Sea and Granville
Special Express*, 129–132
*Westgate-on-Sea, Cliftonville and
Granville Special Express*, 129–132
West Worthing, 110
Weymouth, 56,57,60,61,62,64,65,66,
68,70,72,87
Weymouth Quay, 87
Whimple, 43
Whitstable, 134,145,146,156
Whitstable Town, 141,144,147,150,
153
Willesden Junction, 15,168
William, Duke of Normandy, 128
Wilson, Harold, 211
Wilton, 50,51,52,54
Winchester, 62,65
Winchester City, 64,65,83
Windsor, Duke of, 210
Wing plates, 51
Wintoncester, 62
Woking, 88
Wool, 64,65,66,67
Woolwich, 145
World War 1, 9,15,23,70,97,105,109,
141,145,150
World War 2, 12,17,38,56,62,73,102,
179,200
Worting Junction, 72
Wrafton, 30,31
Wroxall, 16
Wye, 123

Yarmouth (IOW), 16
Yeoford, 26,27,41
Yeoford Junction, 40
Yeovil Junction, 23,26,30,31,39
Yeovil Town, 41,42